PRAISE FOR
WHAT WE REMEMBER WILL BE SAVED

"Stephanie Saldaña long ago proved herself a poetic and perceptive essayist. In this book, she also proves herself a courageous one. Following refugees into the darkest and most dangerous spaces of recent history, she documents journeys that are about much more than bare survival, at once wrenching and radiant."

—**Geraldine Brooks**, *New York Times*–bestselling author and winner of the Pulitzer Prize for Fiction

"Amid the ashes of war and unimaginable losses in Iraq and Syria there is beauty, to which Stephanie Saldaña bears witness in *What We Remember Will Be Saved*, an indelible work that should be read widely and deeply. In powerful yet loving prose, Saldaña recounts the stories told to her by refugees and victims of war. Like Hana, who sews her city into a dress in remembrance, Saldaña weaves together the lives of these brave people. As we hear their stories, we learn there is one common thread: hope is to be found in what we keep and what we remember. It is a lesson we should all embrace."

—**Rubén Degollado**, author of *The Family Izquierdo*

"Stephanie Saldaña writes, 'I found myself among the listeners,' and surely she is one of the greatest listeners and writers among us. This compassionate, fiercely humane collection of stories is exquisitely composed, an act of deepest grace. It is a compendium of precious preservation. Every leader of every country would benefit from reading these treasured tender details, along with every humble wanderer."

—**Naomi Shihab Nye**, poet and the Poetry Foundation's Young People's Poet Laureate of the United States, 2019–2021

"A powerful read that delves into the lives of refugees and the stories they carry as they navigate the complexities of displacement and loss. The book explores themes of hope, resilience, kindness, new beginnings, and the importance of home while shedding light on the injustices, anguish, and hurdles they live through. An emotional and thought-provoking book that provides an insightful, moving, and nuanced portrayal of the refugee experience. I felt each and every word. I was there!"

—**Tareq Hadhad**, founder and CEO of Peace by Chocolate

"The story of refugees is often reduced, in even the best media coverage, to the tales of a large, faceless mass of people, anonymous and even homogenous. Stephanie Saldaña's gorgeous new book reminds us of the breathtaking individuality of the men, women, and children seeking refuge around the world. I found these stories deeply moving and a reminder of why we are called to welcome not just the 'stranger' or the 'alien' or the 'refugee' but the person."

—**James Martin, SJ**, bestselling author of *Jesus: a Pilgrimage*

"Beautiful, heartbreaking, and full of lush detail of creation and recreation. In her humane, years-long odyssey across Europe and the Arab world, Stephanie Saldaña asks the profound questions of our time: When you've lost everything, is it possible for memory to bring it back? When you can never go home, when your village is no more, can you somehow recreate it in the things you've carried? Can you resurrect your history with earrings and shoes, seeds, Damascus rose petals, a piece of soap, a lit candle, or the threads of an embroidered dress? *What We Remember Will Be Saved* is a profound journey of listening, of honest witness."

—**Sandy Tolan**, author of the international bestseller *The Lemon Tree: An Arab, a Jew, and the Heart of the Middle East*

What We Remember
Will Be Saved

WHAT WE REMEMBER
WILL BE SAVED

A Story of Refugees and the Things They Carry

STEPHANIE SALDAÑA

Broadleaf Books
Minneapolis

WHAT WE REMEMBER WILL BE SAVED
A Story of Refugees and the Things They Carry

Library of Congress Control Number 2022056982

Cover design: Olga Grlic

Print ISBN: 978-1-5064-8421-1
eBook ISBN: 978-1-5064-8422-8

In memory of all those who lost their lives searching for sanctuary

seeds   languages

           phones awash with voices

maps

                              estimated arrival times

      kanuns   lullabies

           daughters and sons and grandparents

                 whispered instructions from their mothers

      nightmares   the names of trees

           a prayer pressed against the heart

                       shrapnel lodged in the forearm

the name of a man to meet in a forest

                       a violin wrapped in plastic

      diplomas

           sumac   the imprint of orange blossoms

   beneath fences

           over mountains

                              across waters

CONTENTS

CONTENTS

CONTENTS

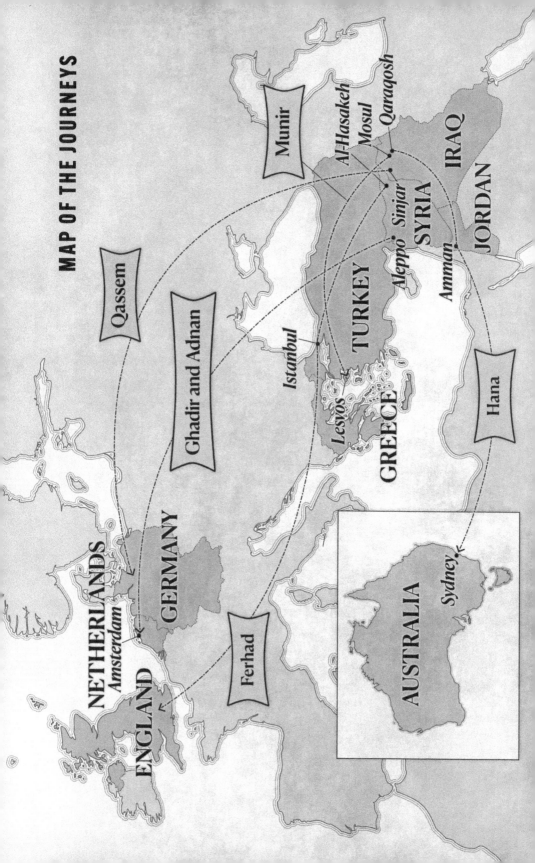

MAP OF THE JOURNEYS

Munir

Qassem

Ghadir and Adnan

Ferhad

Hana

NETHERLANDS
Amsterdam

GERMANY

ENGLAND

Al-Hasakeh
Mosul
Qaraqosh

IRAQ

JORDAN

Sinjar
Aleppo
SYRIA

Amman

TURKEY

Istanbul

Lesvos

GREECE

AUSTRALIA

Sydney

AUTHOR'S NOTE

This book tells the story of six women and men from Iraq and Syria and what they carried with them when they were forced to escape their countries because of war. In the process of writing it, I traveled to nine countries and interviewed dozens of people. The stories I focus on here concern individuals originally from five cities or towns roughly in the stretch between Qaraqosh, a town near Mosul in Iraq, and Aleppo in Syria—a region of incredible diversity and with a rich storytelling tradition that has now been devastated by conflict. After my initial meetings as described in this book, I traveled to meet them again for follow-up interviews in the subsequent years.

I have changed the names and identifying details of some characters in this book to protect their privacy and safety. This is particularly true of those who are still in the process of seeking asylum and those who have family members left behind. On rare occasions, I have removed characters from scenes at my own discretion to protect their safety and that of their families.

Other people I wrote about requested that I use their real first names, in part because they see the story of what they lived as a legacy for their children. As a result, readers will note that sometimes during the explanation of political events in this book, I refrain when I might have said more as many of the conflicts described remain ongoing.

I lived in Syria before the war and have lived in the Middle East for many years. To me, this has never been a work about strangers.

It was in Syria that I learned Arabic and fell in love with the region: its people, its food, its faith traditions, its landscapes, languages, music, attention to beauty, and craftsmanship. It was also in Syria, in 2004, that I first met Iraqis who were there as refugees escaping the war in the aftermath of the US invasion of their country. I hope this book in some way pays homage to those who are saving their cultural heritage, kindness, and hospitality in the face of unspeakable loss.

I have always known that I was able to write this book only because of the fact that I carry both an American and a European passport and am able to cross borders easily even as those I write about risked their own lives seeking safety, often being turned back at borders along the way. This is an uncomfortable truth that lies beneath every page.

Furthermore, I have found it necessary to use the term *refugee* in this book, and yet it is a word I use with great reluctance. To be forced to seek refuge because of war is something that happens to a person. It should never define them. I hope this book makes clear that the people we call "refugees" are artists, historians, musicians, chefs, mothers and fathers, children and siblings, and those on the front lines of heritage preservation. It could one day be any of us.

Finally, this book is an imperfect act of translation. I conducted my interviews largely in Arabic and later translated them, sometimes with the help of native speakers, into English. As a writer, I know that I cannot capture the totality of events as they happened. I know also that the memory of events—both theirs and mine—can have blank holes, especially in stories as difficult as these. There were many questions I chose not to ask. For me, these silences and gaps are also part of the story. If this book is of any genre, I hope it is simply seen as an act of remembering.

A portion of the proceeds from this book will go to organizations that support refugees.

PROLOGUE

There are always hidden historians among the survivors of war. These are the people who carry the stories of what happened with them when they escape, so that the past can be remembered. More often than not, they carry these stories not in books but through little things. A sapling, a spoon, a scarf, a recipe for eggplants stuffed with walnuts, a prayer in a dying language. I have come to believe that a lost neighborhood can be salvaged in a song and that an entire city can be carried in a dress. I have met those who save the past simply by speaking it aloud, who write the dead into living by planting a tree. This book is about these historians and the stories they rescue. It is also a chronicle of war and migration told to me by those who managed to stay alive.

In 2016, I set out on a series of journeys across the Middle East and Europe to try to understand what Syrian and Iraqi refugees were carrying with them as they escaped war, to listen to the stories these ordinary objects might have to tell us. I had lived in Syria as a student years before the war broke out, and I knew Syrians to be artisans: a people who love beauty, cooks who care about the way food is displayed on a plate, musicians and poets, makers of soap. By the time I began my journey, so many thousands of people had died in the war in Syria that the United Nations had stopped counting. More than half of Syria's population had been displaced, just as millions of Iraqis were also being uprooted as ISIS occupied their cities and towns. We were witnessing the largest refugee crisis in modern history. So much was being lost. The war introduced me to the terrible goneness of things.

Yet I trusted that those escaping were also finding ways of saving the stories of the cities they left behind. Where were the famous pastry chefs of Homs, still carrying their recipes? The traditional storytellers of Sinjar, carrying their epic poems? Who would remember the stories of the friendships that vanished in Mosul? Where were the oud musicians? The last speakers of Aramaic?

In time, I began to hear stories: of a young musician from Homs, Syria, who crossed the sea with his violin wrapped in cellophane. Of Syrian mothers teaching their children recipes for eggplant jam in the refugee camps of Lebanon. Of an entire orchestra created from Syrian classical musicians in exile in Germany. By their very being, these individuals were articulating a version of history in which they were not victims but agents, the small things they salvaged not mere fragments but windows into the histories they were now entrusted with remembering and transmitting to future generations. I felt that if I spent more time listening to stories like these, I might begin to understand not only what was being lost in war but also what was being rescued.

I knew I would need to meet these historians where they now were. I would travel to Jordan, Iraq, the Netherlands, Turkey, Switzerland, England, France, Greece, and Germany, speaking to Syrian and Iraqi chefs and gardeners in exile, painters and curators, a political cartoonist, photographers. I decided to narrow the focus of my writing on stories told to me by those who had escaped the swath of geography between Qaraqosh in Iraq and Aleppo in Syria, a borderlands region of extraordinary diversity that had been devastated by war, with entire populations now displaced. The people whose stories I tell in this book naturally reflect just some of the many voices of that region: religious and secular; Muslim, Christian, and Yazidi; Arabic-, Kurdish-, and Aramaic-speaking neighbors now scattered all over the world, many of whose very identities are bound up in living in conversation with one another.

I would meet a woman who saved her city in a dress. A musician who saved his city through his songs. A couple who saved not one pharmacy but two. A young man who saved stories of Muslim-Christian friendships as his city fell apart. A son who saved his family on a mountain and then saved the story of what happened so that it could be remembered.

In time, these individuals became my teachers. It is because of their stories I now know that, even in front of immense violence, there is always something small to be carried, some act to be done, and that these little things transform history in ways we only later understand.

"Awal al-shajara bithra," goes the saying in Arabic. A tree begins with a seed.

PART I

HANA'S DRESS

Qaraqosh, Iraq → Erbil, Iraq → Amman, Jordan → Australia

The town was like this—joyful and full of brides.

—Talal Acam

1 | A TOWN NAMED BLACKBIRD

The first time I saw Hana, she was standing at the back of a room, holding a dress in her hands. The dress resembled a quilt she could wrap around her body, and into that dress she had sewn a city. Inside that city she had sewn a world: with its own language, with fruit-bearing trees, and with friends interlocking their arms and dancing. I had no way of knowing how immense that world had been or even that it was now both gone and saved. I had no idea that I would follow that dress as it would follow me.

That late October seemed unusually cold, and I had not packed well. Even after more than a decade of living in the Middle East, I still forgot until it was much too late how frigid the autumn air becomes, especially in the barren areas along the desert. From my home in Jerusalem, I had traveled north and crossed the Sheikh Hussein bridge into Jordan. Now, as my taxi headed south toward Amman, I watched out the window as green fields slowly gave way to the sprawl of the city. I studied the name scribbled in my notebook: *Abouna Eliyan*. I had seen his name written in three different places in my notebook in three different ways—*Eliyan, Elian,* and *Alyan*—together with three different phone numbers. On a subsequent page, I had written the name of a city, *Qaraqosh*, which comes from the word "blackbird" in Turkish.

I was traveling in search of a man I had never met and a city I had never seen. In some ways, I felt as though I was also trying to

7

locate myself in a moment in history. The city of Qaraqosh itself is located in northern Iraq, some twenty miles southeast of Mosul, and I had decided that my journey would begin with those who had escaped from there. If I knew of Qaraqosh, it was because the town had now become synonymous with a tragedy. On August 6, 2014, ISIS had invaded Qaraqosh, and essentially the entire population, some forty-four thousand Christians, fled for their lives. Overnight, tens of thousands crossed the border to Iraqi Kurdistan to seek what they thought would be temporary shelter.

But ISIS remained in Qaraqosh. Months passed. Then a year. Much of Qaraqosh's population—either out of the exhaustion of waiting or because they could not ever imagine feeling safe in Iraq again—began to scatter across the world, crossing international borders and becoming refugees. Thousands traveled by plane to Amman, where the government welcomed them while they applied for visas at the embassies there in hopes of being resettled, largely in Australia. Almost all of them belonged to the Syriac Catholic Church, which was also the church to which I belonged in Jerusalem, where I lived with my husband and three children. The sudden emptying out of Qaraqosh had shaken the rest of the global Syriac community, especially those still living in the Middle East.

And so it had been the bishop of my own community in Jerusalem who had first scrawled that name into my notebook as he flipped through his address book—Abouna Elian, or Alyan, or Eliyan—referring to the priest in Amman responsible for pastoring the refugees of Qaraqosh. He asked that when I met him, I send his greetings.

It was with that small sliver of information and a note that said "Syriac Catholic Church—past the Tche Tche café, Sweifieh" that I arrived in Father Elian's office in Amman that October morning. I found him sitting behind a desk littered with papers, wearing a light-blue clerical shirt with the pocket weighed down by a cell phone, his white hair visibly thinning and blue eyes shot red from lack of sleep. He offered me espresso, which he had learned to make as a seminarian in Milan, and as we sipped, we took a moment to accustom ourselves to our different dialects of Arabic.

"Are you from here?" I asked.

"No, I'm from Qaraqosh in Iraq," he answered. "I was born there, lived there for twenty-seven years, became a priest, and then left to complete my studies in Italy. When I returned, I went to work in the seminary. And I was working there still when ISIS came. I lived at the seminary with another priest, and on the sixth of August 2014, on the Feast of the Transfiguration, we heard explosions. They landed near two children, who died. The rest of the town became frightened, and that is when they began to flee."

He was speaking in a rush, and I struggled to follow, for he was describing how he escaped a town that I was just beginning to understand had ever existed.

"Qaraqosh had around fifty thousand people," he continued. "Everyone left that first day, except for thirty or forty of us who stayed. By the next morning, at around two o'clock, we looked around and said, 'Forget it. ISIS is coming, and no one else is coming to save us.' At three thirty in the morning, someone called and said, 'What? Where are you? Get out now because ISIS is entering the city.' At four in the morning, we left. And ISIS really was coming. ISIS was coming from the area of the south, and we were leaving from the north.

"We left with nothing," he continued. "I didn't even bring my liturgical clothes with me. I knew I'd be able to find them again. I only brought my passport and my computer. You don't think about what you can bring when you escape your city at four in the morning."

He tried to explain to me how an entire world left on those two days: mothers and fathers and grandparents and children, priests and nuns, painters and musicians, farmers and students. He described the single road out of the town, crammed with cars; the houses emptying of their inhabitants; the bells of the main church ringing to urge everyone to leave.

"It wasn't just Qaraqosh that emptied out that day," he said. "It was the towns of Bartella and Bashiqa and Karamles, the entire area of the Nineveh Plains around Mosul. We fled to Ankawa in Erbil in Kurdistan, but others from our city escaped to Sulaymani-yah and Dohuk. In Ankawa, we stayed together, sleeping in the streets, in buildings, and in churches, waiting. Then, last year, I was sent to Amman to work with the refugees who were arriving here."

I tried to imagine that waiting—one that had extended from days to weeks to years, a waiting that was happening still. More than two years had passed since that August day in 2014, and still no one had been able to return. "Would you mind telling me a little bit about what Qaraqosh was like?" I asked. I had never even seen a photograph.

Father Elian nodded, and I could see him focusing, fixing his vision on a place far off. "The most important thing to know about us is that we were the largest Christian town in all of Iraq and one of the most ancient Christian towns in the world," he said. "We had nine churches: seven from the Syrian Catholic tradition and two from the Syrian Orthodox tradition. The language of our lit-urgy, of our traditions, and even our spoken language was Syriac, a dialect of the Aramaic language."

He opened up his computer and clicked on a video. Together we watched thousands of young men and women and children wearing bright traditional outfits processing through streets, wav-ing olive branches in the air and singing "Hosanna." "That was our last Palm Sunday in Qaraqosh," he said quietly.

I looked at the people's faces, singing, radiant. In his poem "A Song on the End of the World," written in Warsaw in 1944, the poet Czeslaw Milosz describes the scene at the end of the world, where a man mends a fishing net, and women walk with umbrel-las, and vegetable sellers shout in the streets, and a man binds up his tomato plants. I thought of that poem as I stared at the video of girls singing in the streets four months before ISIS arrived and emptied their town entirely. "There will be no other end of the world," writes Milosz. Qaraqosh was something like that—a world entirely there and then vanished.

Father Elian pointed to a stack of papers on his desk. They contained names scribbled in Arabic and square identity photos paperclipped to corners. He explained that these were the files for all the refugees in his charge—men, women, and children who had escaped Qaraqosh, Bartella and Bashiqa, Mosul and Baghdad in Iraq—along with cities like Aleppo, Homs, and Damascus in Syria. Here was the uprooting of entire populations of ancient Christian communities in the Middle East, an exodus distilled into a pile of bureaucratic papers.

"Look at how many of us we are." He held up the pile of papers in his hands to measure its weight. "We have 1,250 Syriac Catholic families here. Each one of those sheets of papers isn't for one person—it's for a family of four or five people. And the minute one family is resettled, another one arrives and takes its place."

I tried to envision the numbers in my head. Thousands of people from Qaraqosh were waiting for visas while living in Jordan. Thousands of others had already traveled to Europe, Canada, Australia, and other countries to find resettlement. Tens of thousands were still waiting in Kurdistan in Iraq, in camps and temporary housing, unable to return home. An entire city had been uprooted and exiled.

"What do you think will happen to the community?" I asked.

"We're scattering all over the world," Father Elian told me. "Just look at my own family. I have one sister in Canada, one in Slovakia, one in the United States, one in Germany, one moving to Australia, one in Jordan, and one who remained in Iraq. It's difficult to think of a future when there isn't a strong government that can ensure peace. Even if I returned to Qaraqosh, how could I know that the same thing won't happen again?"

I finished taking notes in my notebook and slipped it away in my bag. As I prepared my things to leave, he looked at me and said, with a firmness and a clarity I wasn't expecting, "Now that Qaraqosh has been taken, our language will likely disappear. When the people of Qaraqosh leave for Australia or Canada, who will keep speaking it five years from now? And it's not just the language. Everything will disappear—our heritage, even our ancient liturgy."

We sat for a few moments in silence. I stood up, and he shook my hand.

"Come to the Mass on Saturday at five at the Deir Latin Church in Hashmi al-Shamali," he finished. "If you want to meet the people of Qaraqosh, you will find them there."

2 | HYMNALS

Four days later, I took a taxi to the Deir Latin Church in Hashmi al-Shamali in East Amman. A man sitting on a chair on the sidewalk pointed me to a side entrance, and when I finally found it, I slipped inside. What I found in the lobby of the church felt like another country entirely. In front of me, a middle-aged woman was helping her elderly mother to stand. Children darted through the lobby and paused to light candles. Many of the oldest women seemed to be reaching for support—from arms, church pews, canes, as if the earth itself were unsteady. Nearly everyone was speaking a dialect of neo-Aramaic, a Semitic language that had centuries ago been the spoken language of the entire Middle East but had now all but disappeared.

I found a seat near the front of the church, watching as the pews filled up and the faithful extended into the back lobby until there was no place left to stand. Father Elian approached the altar, dressed in long white liturgical garments and wearing a green stole around his neck, followed by an assembly of deacons and altar boys and girls. All of them had become refugees. He began the liturgy in Arabic instead of Aramaic, in deference to the country and the borrowed church in which they now found themselves, as well as to the scattered refugees from Mosul, Baghdad, and Damascus among them who would not have been able to follow his native dialect of Aramaic.

"Today we begin a new liturgical year," Father Elian announced solemnly during the homily. "We ask ourselves, 'Who is Jesus to me?' In the Gospel, all the disciples give the wrong answer. Only Simon Peter says, 'You are the Messiah, the son of the living God!'"

He paused. "We must also ask God to make our relationship closer. This is the time to begin anew."

It was the final Sunday of October, and in the Syriac tradition, it was the beginning of the liturgical calendar and the sanctification of the church. Now the weeks of Advent leading up to Christmas would begin—a longer Advent than the Roman Catholic calendar I had grown up with and more aligned with the new year of the Jewish calendar, with which the ancient Syriac tradition remained so closely bound. It was a day of new beginnings, and they were carrying their calendar with them. I wondered how long that, too, would last. In any normal year in Qaraqosh, this would have been harvest season. But this was no normal year. It occurred to me that when the physical home is taken away, the liturgical calendar becomes a country in time, for time cannot be taken from us.

Father Elian sat down, and a heaviness settled over the assembly. A woman across from me was weeping, her forehead pressed to the wooden pew in front of her. The choir began to sing, and I listened as their voices filled the room with a song—not in Arabic but in Syriac this time, a liturgical form of Aramaic.

I cannot quite describe what happened next as those consonants and vowels fell from the choir loft and the song landed among us. It was as if the space began to slowly be lit from the inside. One person after another began to sing along in Aramaic, first softly and then with more confidence, until the church was alive with the song of a people who—for a very brief moment—were home again.

When the Mass was finished, I stood in the foyer surrounded by people introducing themselves. A twelve-year-old boy named Marvin told me he had come to Amman from Baghdad. I remembered that joint suicide bombers had targeted the Syriac Catholic Cathedral in Baghdad in 2010, killing an estimated fifty-eight people and setting off a wave of refugees, and I wondered if he had also been in the church that day. Another young woman told me she was from Mosul, where the Christian community had escaped ISIS. Other refugees had escaped Bartella and Bashiqa, villages in the Nineveh Plains emptied out by ISIS in 2014.

I recognized the soloist from the choir walking in my direction, her long black hair pulled back tightly. She wore a red blouse trimmed with lace and a large necklace of black and red beads. I introduced myself, and she shook my hand. "My name is Meena," she said. "I'm from Qaraqosh."

I asked her how long she had been living in Amman. "For just a few months now," she answered. When I told her I was a writer, she pulled a phone from her pocket and scrolled to a photograph of a house. The roof and the second story had been charred black, like someone had set fire to it and then blown it out. "That's my home in Iraq," she said quietly.

By now, the rest of the choir had joined us, and Meena introduced them: Alaa', Louis, and her sister Mirna. Wassim and Sonia, who were married. They were all refugees from Qaraqosh, and they spoke Arabic and English in addition to Aramaic, having been students at the university in Mosul.

"We left everything in a single night: our studies, our homes, everything," Wassim said. "I was an engineer. We waited to see if we could return, but ISIS destroyed everything."

His young wife, Sonia, who was pregnant, stood cradling her stomach with her hands. "We had been planning to get married in Qaraqosh," she added. "I lost all that I had, even my wedding gown."

"Were you all in the choir together in Qaraqosh then?"

Meena shook her head. "There were seven different Catholic churches in our city, and we were all members of different choirs.

But when we arrived here, we found one another. We thought that we had lost everything. But then we understood that we could at least still save a church choir."

"Would you mind singing something for me?" I asked.

They nodded, and we returned to the sanctuary, where they took their places in front of the altar. Meena stood at the center, and they pulled out their cell phones from bags and back pockets. With their liturgical books destroyed, these phones had become their hymnals, and they held the screens in front of them so they could follow the notes.

They sang. Meena's voice rang out clearly, leading them. I listened to them singing a language that could be on the edge of vanishing but was still alive in them, a song they had carried out of war and across borders. The choir sang that song for the onset of a new year, punctuated by *alleluias*. For a moment, all of us were transported to that city whose song had been saved at the end of the world.

They finished. A silence held in the air. We walked out into the night streets together. It was cold; I had not dressed well. They shielded me from the onslaught of cars. Alaa', one of the choir members who had been quiet until now, turned to me. "If you're not too busy," he said shyly, "we'd like for you to meet our families."

3 | THE MAP OF A WORLD

I followed the choir through the streets until we turned off into an alley and entered an apartment block. I thought of the number I had read: that 80 percent of the refugees in Jordan lived not in refugee camps, as is commonly thought, but in urban areas among the local population, often in poverty. Alaa' opened a door on the ground floor, and we all passed through. Inside, a dozen people had crowded around a television set to watch the news. Images were being transmitted by a camera that had been mounted onto a car, which was driving through a city in Iraq. One by one, buildings came into view, many sprayed with black graffiti in Arabic that said *"The Caliphate of the Islamic State."* Some of the houses had been set on fire. Steeples were crumbling. With each new image, the people in the room gasped.

It took me a moment to understand they were watching scenes of Qaraqosh, the town they had escaped two years earlier, which had been liberated by Iraqi forces only days before. This was the first time they had seen their streets since they had escaped. Earlier that evening, when Meena had shown me the photograph of her burned house, I assumed it was an old photograph. I hadn't understood that she had only just learned what had happened to her home.

"This is the way to my house," Alaa' told me, pointing to the scene unfolding on the television. "That was my uncle's apartment."

"Look at the burned buildings!" Sonia gasped.

"Oh, Baghdeda," a woman called out. "All of it is gone."

I took a seat, and Meena sat beside me, translating from Aramaic to Arabic. Every now and then, I could recognize a word with the same Semitic roots as Arabic, but otherwise I was lost.

"Is there something you'd like to ask people about?" Meena asked gently. I didn't know where to begin. I had walked into what felt like sacred space, and I was hesitant to do anything but observe. I told her that if anyone felt comfortable sharing, I'd be grateful to hear a story that might help me to visualize Qaraqosh: something about their trees, their vegetables, their harvests, the names of their churches. Or if anyone had brought anything with them, like an icon or perhaps even a dress . . .

"A dress?" Meena asked. I nodded.

"A dress?" she repeated as though she might have misunderstood me, and I nodded again.

"You need to speak to my mother," she said firmly. "She didn't bring anything from Qaraqosh with her when we escaped. But she saved something of Qaraqosh with what she made."

I didn't understand what Meena meant, and so her sentence stayed with me. *She saved something of Qaraqosh with what she made.*

Meena called her mother from across the room. "Mama, show her your shal!" I turned to where her voice had landed, and I glimpsed Hana for the first time, standing in the back of the room. She was perhaps in her midforties, wearing her brown hair pulled back in a ponytail, a gray T-shirt, and what appeared to be polka-dot pajama bottoms. When she heard her daughter's request, she blushed with a certain youthfulness about her that I would notice from then on.

Others in the room encouraged her until Hana disappeared and then reappeared again, holding a white and red and orange and yellow plastic bag with the name "Al-Shab" emblazoned across it, the brand of a well-known shop for roasted nuts in Jordan. She reached inside the bag and pulled out a folded-up square of red and black checked fabric, which at first did not look like a dress at all but perhaps a tablecloth.

And there it was. The shal. Already I could see threaded colors emerging. She was holding it inside out so that as she unfolded it, I could glimpse what looked like scribbles: the outlines of what might be figures in pink and blue, purple and yellow, a deep shade of green; some pompoms of varied colors hanging on each corner; what almost looked like train tracks of alternating shades. She held it gingerly, still unfolding it, and with each unfolding, more colors and figures leaped out—what might be trees, a heart—all of it still inside out and so giving the impression of a child's drawing scribbled onto fabric. Finally, the square unfolded in half, and as the center of the dress was half-revealed, all was color, color—a line of triangles spanning the dress, the etchings of what looked like figures dancing. I cannot tell you what even that glimpse felt like—for until then, the room had been so heavy, and now into it had erupted this color.

She turned the square around until the front of the shal was finally facing me. She held it high, by the top corners, so that I could only see part of her face. I gasped. Images came into focus: two embroidered churches; a house; a line of costumed human figures extending across the dress, holding hands and dancing; trees. Animals. A word in a foreign alphabet. A saint. A well filled up to the brim with water.

Meena whispered, "This is our history."

It took me a moment before I responded, "But how do you read it?" For it was already clear to me that this wasn't just a dress. It was also a map or a book telling a story.

Meena's mother pointed to the top right corner, where she had sewn a word in Syriac in purple thread rimmed with yellow. "Baghdeda," Hana read out loud. "The name of our town."

"But you're not from Qaraqosh?"

She smiled. "Qaraqosh is the Turkish name for our town—what others call it. But we call it by its ancient name: Baghdeda. You'll see that I wrote it in Syriac letters." I had read dozens of newspaper articles calling her town Qaraqosh, and I was intrigued that for the people living in it, their city had its own private name.

Hana continued, moving from right to left as any book in Syriac would read. She paused at two sheaves of wheat, sewn side by side on pale lavender stalks. Nine spikes of beige were embroidered on each, interrupted by yellow and orange leaves. To its left was a shining golden monstrance holding the Eucharist, and to its left still was a bunch of grapes, bursting out of the fabric in rich purple, even the seeds visible. Finally, two fish and a loaf of bread rested in a basket, a reminder of the scene in the Gospels when Jesus multiplies food for a crowd.

"Everyone in Baghdeda was Christian," she said. "The wheat and grapes might symbolize the bread and the wine used in the Mass, but my father—may his soul rest in peace—was also a farmer. We grew grapes and wheat at my home when I was growing up." I watched as she reflected for a moment, remembering, before she continued moving along the dress, pointing to each image. On the upper left-hand corner, a name had been carefully sewn in Arabic and a date: 2016—that very year.

"That's my name: Hana," she said. "I sewed it in Arabic because all of us also studied Arabic. We lived close to Mosul, and so we had to know how to read and write in Arabic. I was a schoolteacher."

"And the date?"

"That was when I finished the dress," Hana replied. "We had already escaped from Qaraqosh to Kurdistan. I understood by then that we would have to leave Iraq forever. I thought this was something I could carry with me. I started sewing there, for two months. I finished it here, in Amman, just a few weeks ago."

She continued moving down the dress as one might point to images on a blackboard. The Virgin Mary dressed in a blue gown, a halo of stars around her head. Jesus robed in purple. Saint Charbel, a monk in a black cowl, who had lived in Lebanon and was venerated by Christians all over the Middle East. A white dove in flight, a fresh olive sprig hanging from its mouth.

My eyes settled on what appeared to be two large churches sewn into the center of the dress in such a way that they became the focus of attention. The first had been stitched in great detail: a pink tower with what looked like a space for a clock, three golden crosses embroidered on top, and a long red roof with a dome on the opposite end. The nave of the cathedral could be entered by two arched entrances and a series of side doors.

"That's the Church of al-Tahira," she said. "That was the largest church in Baghdeda. Actually, it was the largest church in all of Iraq."

She pointed to the second church, shaped like a star and embroidered in pale lavender, a cross of light on the roof and what looked like a square for an inscription on the front. "That's the Church of Saints Mar Behnam and Sara."

We continued down to the third panel. A series of dancers spanned the width of the dress.

"That's the debkeh: what we danced for any joyous occasion," she said. The figures held hands, still dancing. She had embroidered four old women, wearing the same traditional shal dress onto which they were sewn. Old men danced, donning robes together with a headscarf. A nun in a blue robe and white veil joined in. The bride, wearing a billowing white gown and matching white shoes, a gold necklace and earrings, simultaneously clasped a white handkerchief and the hand of her husband in a tuxedo. On the far edge of the dress, two men in white robes and black vests, wearing white head coverings, played the ney and the drum.

"Who are those men?" I asked.

"They're musicians from Bashiqa," Hana answered. "They're from a different village, and that's why their clothes look different from ours."

It was such an act of attention: earrings and shoes, hand-kerchiefs, hands clasping one another. My eyes moved down the fabric to what appeared to be an almost fairy-tale pink cottage. Rain fell from a cloud above, and two trees, with apples sewn in, were stitched nearby. The leaves of a palm tree bowed beneath the weight of dates. A well was filled to the brim with water.

Hana was quiet. In fact, as I would learn, she was frequently quiet. Almost everything I would ever know about her would first emerge from that dress.

I scribbled down names and details. I still did not understand exactly how this was a dress, and everyone urged Meena to model her mother's dress for me. She disappeared into another room and then appeared again, to the applause of everyone in the room. It turned out that the shal was the final layer in an ensemble. The bottom layer was a yellow garment with long flowing sleeves. A second, more colorful layer on top of that, cut to reveal the yellow sleeves beneath it, was called a zubun. On top of that still she donned a green velvet waist jacket that she explained was a fermana. With no traditional belt, she borrowed an ordinary one from one of the boys in the choir and fastened it around her waist. At last, on top of all of those, she wrapped the shal around her and tied it at the shoulder so that its churches and wheat and women and men dancing were fully visible to all of us.

Everyone in the room had by now momentarily forgotten the television. I felt a tap on my knee. Mariam, eight years old, was holding up a phone and showing me a picture of herself as a small child in Qaraqosh, dressed in a shal. Others took out their phones, holding out images of grandmothers, mothers, and aunts in a far-off city, all wearing shals.

It was late into the night when we said goodbye, and I walked into the cold streets alone. I had tried to write down all the details in my notebook, but I had been so overwhelmed that I had not even thought to write down Hana's last name. Then I remembered that she had sewn it into her dress, and I had taken a photograph.

I had been expecting to find a fragment—a recipe, a song. Instead, Hana seemed to have shown me the story of herself, with her trees and language and memories of dancing. She had walked me through an entire town, now gone.

I returned to Jerusalem, to my husband and two sons. To books in the library and bedtimes and bowls of cereal, to research for other trips ahead. To singing my one-year-old daughter to sleep. Months passed. But the dress would not leave me.

4 | THE ARCHIVIST OF PARIS

In those days, cities like Aleppo, Homs, Raqqa, and Mosul were being bombed beyond recognition, reduced on the news to images of collapsing buildings, shoes left in the rubble, bits of tile. Millions of their inhabitants were escaping all over the world. And now those ordinary objects I had assumed would always exist were also vanishing, and those that remained were now witnesses to a simplicity of life now gone, to homes where people had once lived and now did not, to markets where people had once bought bread and spools of fabric.

I had entered into a moment in which objects that had survived were being called to speak, to tell the stories of the people and cities they had known. I found myself among the listeners. A piece of soap was no longer a piece of soap. The soundscape of the call to prayer would vanish when the one who sang it died. A choir of voices would summon churches left behind. Everything became more than itself: Damascus rose petals, and five o'clock in the evening, when the light used to fall a certain way but no longer did. So I learned that objects could speak or elicit a memory. And I learned that when the places you love begin to disappear, you begin to live in them all the time. You live in those places from a distance—not out of nostalgia but out of necessity so that they will not also disappear from you.

The news for two years had lamented the partial destruction of Palmyra, a Greco-Roman city in the deserts of Syria, by ISIS and their blasting of the statues in the Mosul museum. Or the damage to the walls of Krak des Chevaliers, the Crusader castle near Homs in Syria, from fighting between Syrian government and opposition forces. The people I met did not speak to me of those things, and I did not speak of them either. I was haunted by other images—ordinary things no longer ordinary.

The memory of a classroom of girls in their white headscarves, sitting in a mosque in Damascus, where I used to teach English and that was now closed. Where were they now? Sentences in my last letter from Fr. Paolo, my teacher, who had been kidnapped by ISIS in Raqqa and who did not remain long enough to see my daughter born: *I love the four of you. I long to see you soon.* I sought out bars of Aleppo soap I still found in the marketplace in Amman, knowing that the factories had been bombed and that the soap might soon disappear. I kept speaking the Syrian dialect of Arabic even though I no longer lived in Syria, knowing that if I unlearned it, it would never return, and I would no longer bear the evidence that I had belonged in that country.

During those last days in Amman after I met Hana and the choir, I had wandered the city to take stock of what else had survived and been carried out of war by the people of Iraq and Syria. Bakdash, the ice cream shop from the Old City of Damascus, where young men pounded ice cream by hand, now had a location on al-Manara street in Amman. A Syrian pastry shop that was famous for halawet el-jibn from Homs—rolls of sweet cheese stuffed with clotted cream and topped with pistachios and a dab of rose petal jam—had also moved, and lines of Syrians in exile waited for a taste of home.

There in Amman, I sat in a restaurant with Ibrahim, a bookseller from Damascus with whom I had many friends in common. We talked our way through the neighborhood of Bab Touma in

Damascus, where I had once lived and where he had often gone for walks. The cart that sold fava beans in the parking lot. The toasted chicken sandwiches. The man at the corner who cooked shawarma and pressed the flatbread against the grill before placing a dab of garlic sauce and a single piece of meat at the end as garnish. The Kurdish young men who crafted milkshakes and decorated the rims of the glass mugs with cut strawberries. The ATM that was always broken; the vegetable stand with the Syrian flag outside, flies buzzing over the eggplants; the man who pressed inlaid wooden boxes; the cave where St. Paul was baptized; the woman whose hands, locals believed, oozed oil.

"It's different when you speak to your own people about what you dream of," Ibrahim admitted quietly. "In my home, we had this tree—we had two jasmine trees, and we had an apricot tree—not the normal apricots but mishmish hindi." He was almost whispering. "When my grandmother died, the three trees died with her. I still remember. We had to cut them down."

I paid attention. When something is precious, it even outlasts being gone.

In January, three months after that first trip to Jordan, I traveled to Paris with my husband and three children. We intended to apply for new visas and then to return to our home in Jerusalem. But when those didn't immediately come through, we found ourselves stranded. We rented an apartment, too small for the five of us, and waited for news, calling the embassy day after day. It was dreadfully cold, and I kept my young daughter strapped to my chest to keep both of us warm.

In trains, in cafés, in restaurant kitchens, and in the metro, I recognized Arabic. I had always felt out of place in Paris, though I carry a French passport because of my husband. Now, because of the Syrians, Iraqis, and others who had arrived, I could ask for directions to strangers passing by. And so I did, navigating the city in a way I never could before, speaking in Arabic. My ears, tuned in, picked it up everywhere. When someone responded, we recognized one another, and I could find my way through the foreign streets. *How do I get to the train station? How do I get to the Louvre?* There is never shame in asking directions from someone you know understands what it means to be lost.

Artists, musicians, chefs, and political dissidents from Syria had found their way to Paris during the war. I took a train thirty kilometers outside of the city, where Hassan Harastani, from Aleppo, Syria, was keeping his family's recipe for olive oil and laurel soap alive at a factory for a soap named Alepia. Aleppo soap was so famous that it had spread all over the world on the Silk Road; history suggests that the Crusaders learned about it when they passed through Aleppo and then carried it on as inspiration in creating the famous soap of Marseilles in France. Hassan's factory in Aleppo had been bombed in the war. A Franco-Syrian friend and business partner had urged him to come to Paris, where Aleppo soap remained in high demand, especially now that factories were disappearing. But Hassan had at first refused, unwilling to be classified as a "refugee," and he wouldn't relocate to Paris to make his soap until he received the paper that recognized him as a master craftsman and allowed him proper respect and travel. Now, in a factory heavy with the scent of laurel and with an olive tree planted right inside, I found Hassan Harastani inspecting immense pots of soap. His image was stamped on every product, along with the words Maître Savonnier ("Master Soap Maker"): M. Harastani.

In a music shop near the Moulin Rouge, I met Khaled, originally from Aleppo, selling ouds, short-necked lutes beloved in Middle Eastern music. He informed me that he had lost track of Ibrahim Sukkar, the famous Syrian instrument maker, in the chaos of the war. Now he was trying to track him down for the many customers who were still seeking his instruments. Hanging on the walls of the store I saw ouds and buzuqs and kanuns on display. And I wondered about that too—about the knowledge and strings and songs that vanish when a man does.

I wrote it all down: People carrying their cities in bars of soap, in bits of paint, in ouds, in a dish of eggplants. It was not only one person who did this, but it seemed to be a collective instinct to save what could be saved.

At the same time, the rest of the world around me continued as though nothing at all had happened, with its cafés and shoes in sizes 38 and 39 displayed in windows. Its ticking watches and subway fares and destinations called out, as though they would exist forever.

On our second Sunday morning in Paris, I walked with my husband and children to the Church of St. Ephrem, the Syriac Catholic Church not far from the Museum of Medieval History, for Mass. We entered the side door and again into another world. Though the priest was speaking French instead of Arabic this time, the church, like the one I had visited in Amman, was filled with Christians who had escaped the wars in Syria and Iraq.

When the Mass finished, I was introduced to a young woman and her mother, holding her arm beside her for balance. The young woman was clearly pregnant. When I introduced myself in Arabic, she answered in kind. Her name was Niveen. Her husband served as a deacon in this church, and so every Sunday they traveled by train from the village of Fontainebleau outside of Paris. They had recently been resettled there, not far from the famous castle with its gardens and fountains, the hunting lodge of kings and the playground of Napoleon.

"Where are you from originally?" I asked.

"We're from Iraq," she answered. "From a city called Qaraqosh."

I started at the name. Hana's city. I told her that I had met others from her city who were now living in Jordan. After chatting for a few minutes, I asked her if we might get together so that I could learn a bit more of Qaraqosh.

"You're most welcome," she said and then laughed and gestured at her belly. "You might want to hurry, though. This baby is going to be born any day."

I didn't hurry. There was something in this story that I found difficult to face, and I kept finding reasons to put the visit off. Eventually, three weeks later, I found the courage to call Niveen on the phone, and she answered, inviting us out to their home.

I took the train the next day with my husband and children to Fontainebleau. An hour later, we arrived at a village centered around an immense castle of more than 1,500 rooms, surrounded by fountains and sculpted trees in the garden, where the royalty of France had lived for generations and where Napoleon had resided. When we finished touring the castle, we walked ten minutes down a quiet street, stopping in front of a nondescript apartment block, where we climbed a flight of stairs and walked to the end of a hallway. Niveen opened the door, holding her newborn baby, wrapped in a white blanket and sleeping in her arms. She had fastened a gold ring to his white cap with a clothespin. It was a tradition from her own childhood, she told us, though she was not certain what it meant.

We sat in the living room, decorated with a few French flags. She brought out tea, and I asked if other people from Qaraqosh lived nearby.

"No, there's no one but my mother, who lives beneath us," she said. She paused, and her voice quieted as she wondered aloud if

France had purposefully settled them far from other refugees from Qaraqosh so that they would assimilate. She was lonely, and she worried that because her children had no one to speak their language to, they would soon forget it.

The descendants of every refugee or immigrant who settle in a country with another dominant language risk losing their own. Statistically speaking, the language is usually gone in three generations—with the immigrant remaining a native speaker, the children becoming bilingual, and the grandchildren speaking only the new, local tongue. A language is particularly endangered when one community moves into another in which the power relationship is asymmetrical, forcing them to assimilate to the local language in order to survive. I listened, and I thought of my own family in San Antonio, where my Spanish-speaking mother had felt pressured not to pass the language to us and where my father had not put the ñ on our last name.

In France, the pressure to lose a language is particularly pronounced. The French constitution states that "the language of the country is French," and the French have a history of suppressing even their own local dialects. This attitude was slowly changing, and the country was now at least trying to save its own regional languages. But from where I stood, France seemed more invested in protecting statues from Iraq than Iraq's endangered languages, many of which carried words even older than some of those statues displayed in museums. The linguist Ken Hale famously said that "when you lose a language, it's like dropping a bomb on a museum, the Louvre." I couldn't help but think of his words now. It is easy enough to describe the atrocities of ISIS. It is far more difficult to confront how our own policies of assimilation—whether in France or in the United States, both of the countries from which I have passports—participate in the disappearance of cultures and heritage.

I took in the picture of the Eiffel Tower taped to Niveen's wall and some balloons brought from the hospital. We sat quietly and drank our tea. When it was nearly time to go, I asked, "When will the baby be baptized?" If we were still in Paris, I thought, we might try to attend.

Niveen's husband, Afram, who had barely said a word until then, spoke up. "We haven't decided yet," he said. "But you can be certain that it won't be like baptisms in Qaraqosh. When my daughter was baptized, we slaughtered a sheep."

He pulled out his phone and moved his thumb across the screen until he arrived at a photograph. A nun was standing at the gate of their house in Qaraqosh, dressed in white, smiling above the carcass of a slaughtered sheep, whose blood spilled toward the entrance gate. I asked him if he would feel comfortable sharing a copy of the photo with me as I gathered more details to try to understand what Qaraqosh had been like.

"I can send you a copy of all my photos," Afram replied, smiling.

"*All* of them?"

When Afram and Niveen escaped Qaraqosh on August 6, 2014, they left in a hurry, unable to carry anything with them—with one notable exception. Afram carried his cell phone. As a deacon at the Church of al-Tahira, the largest church in Iraq, he had spent years photographing the Palm Sunday procession, the installation of the red tiles on the cathedral roof, his wedding, and the baptism of his children. The phone he carried out of Qaraqosh contained an invaluable historical archive of what life had looked like in Qaraqosh before all its inhabitants fled and were dispersed.

Here was a photograph of Afram, holding a candle and dressed in the robes of a deacon, standing nearby Father Elian, the priest I had met in Amman. Now they were circling a giant bonfire blazing in a church courtyard. And here was the red roof of a church that I recognized as having been sewn in great detail on Hana's dress. It was the Church of al-Tahira, and Afram himself was standing on the roof, holding up one side of an enormous clock to help install it into the very tower that Hana had sewn. Now here were wedding photos, with Niveen in a billowing white dress, surrounded by old women wearing embroidered shals resembling Hana's. A church shaped like a star—that must be the Church of Mar Behnam and Sara. A black and white photo of villagers harvesting wheat like that embroidered into Hana's dress. A line of men and women dancing the debkeh at a wedding. Beside them, two men donning white robes with black vests. One was playing the drum, the other the ney flute.

I could almost walk the streets of an entire world, filled with all its particularities: its harvest seasons and wedding vows, birthdays and baptisms. Its rooftops broken and repaired, its clocks placed just so, its children praying in a cave and lighting candles. All the details that make up a life.

Hana's dress was real. I had known that, at some level. Yet I had not grasped how precisely she had embroidered those images, how carefully she had attended to details of doors and windows and clocks and dresses, and that those images corresponded so closely to the *suchness* of real lives, lived and now changed. It should have been obvious to me, as it was to her daughter Meena, who had whispered to me when Hana unfurled her dress, "This is our history."

Hana was an artist, a seamstress and an embroiderer. But she was also a historian. She had sewn into her dress a faithful account of what had been loved, and now lost, in Qaraqosh.

It was time for me to return to her and to listen.

5 | A SEWING MACHINE

By the time I settled back in Jerusalem with my family and then made it across the border to Jordan again, nearly five months had passed since my first visit. I had remained in touch with some members of the choir, and they connected me to Hana, who invited me for coffee. I remember the taxi getting lost on the way to her apartment in Hashmi al-Shamali and the driver phoning her to ask for directions. He hung up the phone and shook his head. "Even she doesn't seem to know where she lives," he said.

When we finally found her street, Hana was waiting for me outside. She led me up to the apartment that had been provided to her by the church while she waited in Jordan. It was on an upper story so that you could hear the world passing outside the window, the vendors calling out the price of goods and cars passing by.

She filled me in on the news of the community. Their family's case—Hana, her husband, and her two unmarried children—had still not moved forward at the Australian embassy. However, Alaa'— the young man from the choir who had led me through the streets to that apartment—had already been resettled in Melbourne with his family. All the other choir members were still waiting for news. In the meantime, now that ISIS had been defeated in Qaraqosh, many refugees were worried that they might soon be forced to return to Iraq, even though ISIS remained in Mosul, twenty miles from Qaraqosh, where fighting had been ongoing for months.

Hana stood by the stove, patiently stirring coffee before pouring it into small cups. I told her about my trip to Paris and the photographs I'd seen that so closely corresponded with what she'd sewn. "If you'd be willing to talk about it," I said, "I'd love to understand more about the world of your shal."

She smiled. "Of course. But, please, before anything else, drink your coffee."

I drank. When we finished, Hana left the room and returned with the shal, and she unfolded it as one opens a storybook, laying it out on a table so that I could see the details. Yes, we would read it together. Even in exile, Hana remained a teacher in every way, and she approached everything from now on with a quiet but certain authority.

She pointed to the word Baghdeda, embroidered from right to left in purple and yellow letters, which I knew to be the Syriac language. She began speaking:

From our childhood, all of us spoke Syriani, a dialect of Aramaic. Me, my siblings, our parents and grandparents. In Baghdeda, everyone spoke it. We thought it was a normal language. It was only when we were older that we learned it was special. But we didn't know how to read it or write it down. We learned Arabic only when we entered primary school, when I was around six years old.

As far as Baghdeda as a town is concerned—I can tell you that there was no sea, no water, but it was a rich place for us. The people were kind, and they would help one another. During the wars of the last decades, we received so many Christians who fled Mosul and Baghdad. We took them into our homes—sometimes two or three families were received into a single home. It is a place that none of us will ever forget. We grew up there. We raised our children there. We studied together there. We learned our faith inside of that town.

Hana moved her finger left on the dress, to the cup of wine with grapes and those sheaves of wheat.

> My father was a farmer, and for the most part, he grew wheat and barley. He had large fields. We had two olive trees, pomegranates, seven orange trees, two clementine trees, and fields of okra, beans, onions, strawberries, chickpeas, and black sesame. He planted everything. The largest area of Qaraqosh was land in which farmers sowed and harvested.

Hana had lived in the Plains of Nineveh, historically the agricultural lands irrigated by rains and the River Zab, providing wheat and barley for the empires that grew out of that region. The ancient Assyrian city of Nineveh had existed on what is now Mosul. It was a storied land, where tradition said that the prophet Jonah traveled to warn of coming destruction. His tomb had been an important site for Muslims, Christians, and Jews in nearby Mosul before ISIS detonated it with explosives.

According to tradition, however, Hana's family had not originated from the Nineveh Plains. Like many families in Qaraqosh, they had migrated from Tikrit between the eleventh and twelfth centuries. Originally Syrian Orthodox, these families later became Catholic, keeping many of their Orthodox traditions in the liturgy, including the prayers in the Syriac language.

> We were seven girls and two boys in my family. We had cows and chickens. Every morning, my mother would milk the cows and give us cups of fresh milk to drink. We ate eggs from our chickens. At night, she boiled the milk to make yogurt, and she made fresh cheese.

Grapes hung over a terrace, and from the leaves, she, her mother, and her sisters folded dolma, stuffed vine leaves. From the figs, they processed jam, and their single palm tree provided dates. One day, as a child, Hana asked her mother if she might borrow her shal, the embroidered dress that she saw her wear on special occasions, for a few moments. Her mother agreed. Hana fastened the wool fabric around her shoulder and glided into the garden, where she stood to pose for a photograph among the flowers. The photo, like everything else, is gone, but the memory is stamped into eternity.

Hana turned thirteen. One day, she passed through the house of her aunt and, intrigued by the sight of her aunt's sewing machine, asked to sit beside her long enough to learn how to pump the pedal with her foot and run the needle. After that, she learned how to sew, and from then on, Hana measured her younger siblings for their holiday outfits, dressed them for the Christmas and Easter processions in fancy dresses, and knitted sweaters and booties for the babies newly born.

For Christmas, what they called the Little Feast, she would knit winter clothes. For Easter, called the Great Feast, she would sew light dresses.

As for her own clothes, her father would sometimes take her and her sisters to shop in Mosul to buy dresses for the holidays. When she was older, she was allowed to travel there on her own, where she would wander the streets, taking in styles not available in her village. In Mosul, the people in the streets spoke Arabic, not Aramaic, which is how Hana first learned that the entire world was not like her Baghdeda, that she lived in a particular place.

As a child, she heard villagers talking about their spoken language as if it possessed something important, but she took little notice of it. She was unaware of the scholars who were already seeking out the last speakers of the dialects of Aramaic around the world, trying to record the words that she was speaking in her daily life before they vanished. Narma: a land without stones. Ktawa: a book.

For Hana, her childhood was remarkable only in that, unlike in other families, she and her siblings didn't seem to fight with one another. "We loved one another. We shared the same heart."

We turned to the church she had carefully sewn into her dress: a long nave topped with a dome and a red roof, golden crosses, and entrances on the side. It was the Church of al-Tahira, the largest church in Iraq.

> It was the heart of everything. I always went to church at al-Tahira, where I sang in the choir for twelve years. We celebrated our feasts days there. I was married there. We baptized the children there. And whenever there was any big event in Qaraqosh, it centered around that church.

The construction of the modern part of the Church of St. Mary al-Tahira, or the Church of the Immaculate Conception, ended in 1948. Hana's father-in-law helped to build it along with other men of the village, who carried bricks and donated supplies.

> When they built the church, my mother was a young girl. But it was built from the work and exhaustion of families from Qaraqosh. People who were farmers like my father gave some of their harvest as an offering. Others made the bricks, and they carried them up ladders on their backs. One girl, who was thirteen years old and a friend of my mother's, fell off the roof. But she miraculously survived, and today she has children, and her children have their own children.

On Christmas Eve, what they called the Little Feast, the villagers gathered dry sticks from the countryside and built the great bonfire outside of the Church of al-Tahira, and the villagers warmed themselves around its great light. From the rooftops, it was visible throughout the town, erupting into the winter darkness. The priests circled the fire three times, and Hana sang. She always sang. When the fire died out, the villagers gathered the ashes and carried them home to be sprinkled among the harvest as a blessing.

They lived their lives in seasons. On the Feast Day of Mar Behnam and Sara, Hana traveled to the monastery outside of Qaraqosh, where the priest handed out blessed loaves of bread baked in the monastery's oven and where she visited the sacred spring.

"Behnam and Sara?" I asked. "Who are they?"

"What? You don't know Behnam and Sara?" she asked. "They're the most famous saints of Qaraqosh!" And so she told me:

According to tradition, Saints Behnam and Sara lived in the fourth century, the two children of the King Sennacherib. Sara had a skin disease, and they were desperate to find a cure. One day when Behnam was off hunting, he lost his way. He was somehow led to Saint Metti, who promised him that he could cure his sister of her illness.

Encouraged, Behnam returned with his sister and their forty slaves. St. Metti put his staff into the earth, and a spring of water came forth. Sara washed her face. Her disease was gone! Amazed by what had happened, Behnam, Sara, and all their slaves converted to Christianity.

Yet when they returned to their father, the king, he became enraged with a sense of betrayal. He had his own children killed. But the king became ill with guilt. Eventually he dreamed that St. Metti could help him too. He made his way to the cave, and St. Metti discovered that a demon had possessed him and so removed it. He was converted to Christianity, and he spent the rest of his life trying to fix what he had done.

Tradition said that it was this same father who had built the monastery of Mar Behnam and Sara, with a tomb over the remains of his own children. It was to here that Hana traveled for those warm loaves of bread, a place beloved in the region until ISIS arrived in 2015, set the tomb with explosives, and leveled it to the ground.

But the monastery stood at a distance outside of Qaraqosh, and the people wanted to honor the young saints daily. So they built a new church in their town in the shape of a star, with a long rectangle lintel over the entrance that was engraved with images of the saints and their forty slaves. Hana had sewn the church into her dress, complete with the rectangle over the entrance—not knowing that ISIS had set the church on fire.

The largest feast of the year in Qaraqosh took place on Palm Sunday, when Christians from Mosul and the towns of the Nineveh Plains traveled on pilgrimage to Qaraqosh. On that day, thousands would wear traditional shals and parade in the streets, waving olive branches and singing Hosannah. Hana led them as part of the choir.

I remembered the film of Palm Sunday that Fr. Elian had shown me months before and Afram's photograph of crowds marching through the streets on that same day. Surely somewhere, just outside the crop of the photo, Hana had been leading them in song.

After she graduated, Hana became a schoolteacher in the area of Mount Sinjar, the Yazidi and Muslim region a few hours west, toward the border with Syria. At the same time, a man named Amer had just left the seminary in Mosul, after years of studying to be a priest, and had returned to live with his family in Qaraqosh, where he was working in a restaurant cooking shawarma. One day, he saw Hana. And that was it. His family went and asked her family for Hana's hand.

"I didn't even know Amer." Hana laughed. "This way of meeting was normal!"

She said yes, and they were married at the Church of al-Tahira. Hana showed me the photograph: There she is, dressed in a billowing white gown, a veil pinned to her hair, beside Amer, grinning in a dark suit. Between them is his mother, radiant, her colorful shal embroidered with birds and flowers and people carrying baskets.

"The shal is joyful because you only wear it in joyous times," Hana explained.

When the wedding Mass had finished, all of the guests linked arms and danced.

Hana moved into her new husband's family home, as was the custom. When their first daughter was born, Amer was away in Baghdad. She named her Meena and tied a gold ring to the bonnet on her head, though she did not know why. She gave birth to a boy named Syrian the following year and, five years later, to their third child, a girl named Mirna.

In the beginning, Amer was often away in other cities, working to try to make money in the wake of the international sanctions that were crippling the Iraqi economy. Hana learned to take care of herself and the children on her own. Those were lean years. Then, in 2003, the US forces invaded Iraq, intent on taking down the government of Saddam Hussein. For a brief moment, Hana thought that, if nothing else, at least the economic sanctions that had been strangling the country for over a decade might end. Instead, the United States blundered in error after error. The Americans dismantled the Iraqi armed forces and prevented anyone associated with the Baath party from holding positions in power, in a country where many ordinary teachers and civil servants had joined the party as a necessity. The result was the loss of expertise and the sudden marginalization of many Sunni Arabs, as well as a simmering resentment that would have long-lasting and drastic results. American forces stood back as museums were looted. Al-Qaeda, sensing an opportunity in the chaos, began a series of attacks on Christian, Shiite, and government sites in the country that fueled a spiraling sectarian conflict.

As Christian churches were bombed in major cities like Baghdad and Mosul, and Christians increasingly faced kidnapping and violence, Qaraqosh swelled with Christians from other Iraqi cities seeking refuge. Iraqi Christians also started finding ways to leave the country.

It was during that period that Hana's husband, Amer, understood he had received a badly needed gift while studying at the seminary: he had learned to read and write the Syriac language, which was now in danger of vanishing. In Qaraqosh, it had largely existed as a spoken language. He decided to become a teacher, part of a growing movement to keep their heritage alive.

As thousands of others migrated, Hana and Amer built a new home in Qaraqosh instead, doubling down on the decision to stay. Hana remembers coming home from teaching to supervise the workers. They moved into their new house in June 2006. "We felt released that day," Hana remembered. "When you have a home, you have this sense of relief. We had gone into debt to build the house—we had borrowed money from my sister, from my father, and from Amer's father." She filled the house with their pots and pans and spices—and later with Meena's electronic keyboard and the library of Amer's Syriac dictionaries. They saved so that they could quickly pay back their debts. "We drank our tea without sugar," Hana told me.

The children grew up, and the situation in Mosul became more fraught. At the beginning of May in 2010, hundreds of college-age students from Qaraqosh boarded their morning school buses to head the twenty miles to the university in Mosul. As the convoy of buses headed out, two bombs exploded near a checkpoint in front of them, sending glass shards streaming into the passenger seats. Four people died, and 171 students were injured.

Six months later, gunmen linked to al-Qaeda stormed the Syriac Catholic Cathedral in Baghdad and murdered fifty-eight people.

Some of the parishioners killed were originally from Qaraqosh but had moved to Baghdad for work.

"We became exhausted," Hana told me. Hana and Amer made a decision to focus on their children's educations. They borrowed money to add a second story to their home so that their children could study quietly for their exams. In 2013, workers finished construction on the second floor of their home, with new bedrooms for the children and a table where they could sit with their books. Meanwhile, a group of extremists calling themselves ISIS had begun organizing a few hundred kilometers away, across the border in Syria.

6 | A SONG AT THE END OF THE WORLD

Months passed, and I continued my visits with Hana, her husband often joining to fill in bits of history. I came to understand that, though Qaraqosh was now empty of its inhabitants, it remained alive in the streets of Amman. An entire world had been transplanted. There was Nasir, a famous singer in northern Iraq, who had fled Qaraqosh with his wife and two children and who sang for me in Aramaic, his eyes gleaming as he leaned forward as though he was still performing onstage. War is ruthlessly impartial. It displaces famous singers just as it takes anyone else.

In Amman, I also met Qaraqosh's artist Sami Lalu, whose painting of the Last Supper, resembling Da Vinci's but interpreted to be located in Qaraqosh, had graced the walls of the Mar Behnam and Sara monastery. His stone artworks of Behnam on a horse and Sara descending into the waters of the sacred spring had adorned the outside walls of the monastery. All of this was later destroyed by ISIS. Sami and his wife were now elderly, and each time I arranged to meet him, he arrived to wait for me in the parking lot of a gas station, the only landmark in that part of Amman that we both knew, wearing a suit. At lunchtime on Sundays, they called family members on speakerphone—their adult children's voices entering from France, Iraq, Canada, and Australia, still gathering around a table.

In every case, they spoke their dialect of Aramaic with one another. I wondered how long it would last. I knew that even if the community continued to speak the language in exile, this would not be the same as speaking it in Qaraqosh itself. There is a certain ecology, a diversity within a language that becomes poorer in migration. Even if a language does manage to survive, specific words often only last insofar as they correspond to reality. People who move from a rural area to a city might soon lose the names in their language for mulberry trees they no longer harvest, for the handmade plow they don't use, the hoopoe that no longer alights at the window. The words we know correspond to the world as we live in it. If there is no need to speak a word, then it will no longer be spoken. If it is no longer spoken, it will often be forgotten.

And yet, every now and then, I would hear an instance of remembering that seemed to go against gravity. I spent an afternoon with Matti, a violinist from Qaraqosh who was also now living in Amman. Eventually, he placed his violin on his shoulder and began to sing a folk melody about a young man asking a girl for a dance.

I recognized it immediately. Nasir, the famous singer from Qaraqosh, had sung the same melody for me. "Why is everyone in Qaraqosh singing the same folk song?" I asked Matti.

He laughed. "Who else sang this to you?"

"Nasir."

"Nasir? That's because we're both Syriac Orthodox," Matti said. "This song isn't from Qaraqosh. It's from Tur Abdin." Their families had arrived in Qaraqosh in 1915 after fleeing the massacres of Christians in what is today southeastern Turkey. The Syriac preserved in that song was not the Qaraqosh dialect. It was in the dialect of Tur Abdin, the ancient Syriac lands they had once lived in, a region that had been famous for its music.

Matti's great-grandfather had been a musician. When he escaped Tur Abdin, he carried this folk song with him and continued to sing it in the dialect of the village he left behind. He moved to the Sinjar region of Iraq, where he taught his son how to sing the song. His son taught his own son. When Matti was a boy, and inter-communal tensions began to build in Sinjar, his family moved to Qaraqosh. Sometime along the way, his father taught him to sing the song too.

On August 6, 2014—the night on which tens of thousands of people fled the Nineveh Plains—Matti fled also, carrying his violin with him. When he arrived in Kurdistan, a film crew was waiting there. Seeing his violin, they asked if he might play something. And in the darkness of the collapsing world, he played the violin. He sang the song that he had saved, the song that was saved so that it might be sung, again and again, every time the world ends.

7 | RED BULGUR

Every story of departure is unique. What I came to understand as I spoke to the people of Qaraqosh was that even when it was expected, leaving still somehow comes entirely as a surprise. Who can possibly be prepared for losing an entire life, the particularities of streets and churches and feast days and the dialect of a language spoken nowhere else in the world?

When Hana finally told the story of her own leaving, it was only after I had known her for many months. It was in the afternoon, and she made tea, which she poured into clear mugs. When she finally spoke, her voice was quiet, interrupted only by the drinking of tea and the calling of voices through the open window beside us.

In 2014, the first five months were normal. Meena used to go to the university in Mosul and return. She was studying civil engineering. Syrian was completing his college entrance exams: he finished only the first exam in Arabic, and he got high marks. Then ISIS arrived in Mosul at the beginning of June. On that day, my son, Syrian, was scheduled to have his math exam, but they canceled it. They said they would put it off for one or two days, but by then ISIS had taken over all of Mosul. Syrian had been a good student. He used to wake up at four in the morning to study. I was really sad for him.

It was one of those details of war that those of us who haven't experienced it never think about: the entire trajectory of a life changed because of a missed exam.

In Mosul, ISIS told Christians that they could convert, flee, or be killed, and they painted the Arabic letter ن, for "Christian," on the walls of their houses and buildings as they confiscated them. As they escaped, many sought safety in a place that they knew they would be secure: Baghdeda. The city we know as Qaraqosh swelled with the internally displaced, their presence a reminder of the horror playing out only twenty miles away. Hana and her neighbors waited, assured that Kurdish forces would hold the Nineveh Plains.

Hana awakened early on the morning of August 6, the Feast of Transfiguration, to the sound of mortars falling near the city. In the August heat, her family had been sleeping on the roof to take in the breeze, but the sound of explosions sent the children shuddering and rushing to sleep inside. Only a few days earlier, ISIS had swept in from Mosul and northeastern Syria to converge in the villages of the Yazidis in Mount Sinjar, an hour and a half west of Qaraqosh. People were saying that they had been kidnapping Yazidis on the roads, killing the men and taking the women. If they took Qaraqosh now, would they do the same? What about her own daughters?

Hana considered gathering the family and leaving straight away. Some people in the city had already gone. But she would not make a mistake she had already made once. Just over a month before, believing that ISIS was attacking Baghdeda, the entire family had panicked and escaped to Kurdistan, certain they would never return home again. Yet in the end, everything had been fine, and three days after their arrival, a priest had come into the school where they and others from Qaraqosh were sleeping to announce to them that they could go home again. So they had driven back home. Arriving again in Baghdeda, they had stopped the car at the Church of al-Tahira and rushed inside to thank the Virgin Mary for their safety.

Then Hana, her husband, and her three children had tried to go about their lives. Everything felt more tenuous after that: the electricity cut, much of the water available only from wells, the supplies from Mosul no longer for sale in the markets.

On August 6, 2014, at six o'clock in the morning, Hana slid away from her husband and the children, dressed, and walked the few blocks to attend Mass. The city remained asleep and the shops closed. The pale-blue dome of the Church of Mar Yohanna, with its golden cross, appeared as she approached. She opened the door to see only a few brave locals in the pews who had come for the feast.

She prayed. Behind the altar, the priest lifted the host and spoke the prayer in Aramaic. Sab akhoul meneh koul-khoun: "Take this, all of you, and eat of it." When the service was finished, the priest tried to calm the congregants with words of assurance. "Don't be scared," he said. "There's no need to leave your houses. The Peshmerga will protect us."

Hana returned home that morning by the same path she had taken, turning her key in the lock and opening the front gate, painted gold with vines and flowers, and walking past the clementine tree in the garden. Inside, everyone remained fast asleep. She returned to bed and drifted off. The ringing of the telephone startled her awake.

"You're still sleeping?" her sister exclaimed. "You're still at home? Don't you know what's happening? A woman and two children have been killed by shelling! Don't go out of the house." Hana put the phone down. She wrested Amer and the children from their beds and told them to prepare. The girls began screaming.

"We stayed at home." Hana's voice was even as she told me the story. "I heard the sound of explosions. Boom. Boom. Boom. Boom." Hana continued:

> Amer was saying, "There's nothing. Just noise. Daesh [ISIS] aren't near us." But the children were scared. At noon, my sister called again and asked, "Are you leaving?" We said no. We stayed until the afternoon. I made red bulgur. I still haven't forgotten: I wanted to make something that cooks quickly. We ate a bit. It was summer, so we slept in the afternoon. There was that sound again, but everyone we asked said that there was nothing. The neighbors said there was nothing, but then later we went to check on them, and they had already gone.

> At six o'clock, Amer called out, "Look outside at the neighbors— they're all leaving." We climbed into the car, and we circled the village, and we saw that all of the people from Baghdeda were escaping. We kept asking them, "Why are you leaving? There's nothing going on!" Finally, we returned home. By then, Mirna and Meena were begging my husband, saying, "Dad, let's leave."

> Finally, all five of us left together. Nothing was in the bag but our passports and a change of clothes. We didn't really have money—we had just finished building the second floor of the house, and we still had debts to pay back. We had three hundred dollars, passports, and documents when we left home.

It was six thirty in the evening. The main road was crowded with thousands of cars, sometimes three or four side by side. When it seemed that no one was moving, people began getting out of their cars and walking to the checkpoints. They would have to separate: Amer would remain in the car; Hana would walk with the children.

They trudged ahead. At some point, they heard the sound of gunshots from the direction of the checkpoints, and they dove to the ground. Eventually, someone with a pickup truck offered to transport them to Erbil. They arrived at the Church of St. Joseph at eight in the morning. Amer finally arrived four hours later.

In the space of a single day, the city of Qaraqosh had nearly emptied out in its entirety. The wedding singer and the painter, the mother, the infant, the violin player. The farmer, the seller of hammers and nails, the mother who pours the glass of milk, the tenor, the bass, the alto, the weaver of wool fabric, the one who holds the cross aloft, the pregnant, the engaged, the widowed, the exhausted, the teacher, the student, the bus driver, the girl in love. All that exists in a city left the city, fleeing an enemy they knew was coming but whom they did not see.

Just as quickly, the Christian neighborhood of Ankawa in Erbil in Kurdistan transformed into a refuge for tens of thousands of displaced persons. Christians arrived from Qaraqosh, Bashiqa, Bartella, and Karamleis, sleeping in any space they could find. Hana and her family slept in the church garden.

Days passed. Every morning, Hana waited for a priest to appear and tell them it was time to go home again. After a few days, it became clear that they weren't going home.

Hana and her family moved into the shell of a nearby building under construction. Eventually, word came of apartments downtown, opened by a benefactor for internally displaced Christians on the top floor of a shopping mall. They moved again. Now everyone around her spoke Kurdish, which she could neither speak nor understand.

Her daughter Meena married. ISIS remained in Qaraqosh, and they remained in exile. Christians began leaving the country, lining up inside European consulates and asking for visas, crossing the sea with smugglers. In November 2015, seven people from Qaraqosh, including four children, traveled from Iraq to Turkey and climbed into a small boat in an attempt to cross the sea to Greece. The boat capsized, and all of them drowned. "They were saved from death and then were sent to death," the people of Qaraqosh whispered to one another.

After that, Hana knew they would never dare take the sea route to safety.

She heard that Jordan was allowing Iraqi Christians to arrive there by plane and register as refugees applying for resettlement to countries like Australia. She knew nothing about Australia except that it seemed as far away as you could go on the globe without circling back again to Iraq. Her children begged her and Amer for the family to travel. They would not say no to them. She felt she owed them that much: to let them start their lives over again in a place where they would feel safe.

She was leaving her entire world behind. As the family prepared to travel to Jordan, she knew she would have to find a way to take it with her, all of it: the fruit trees and the house, the water with its well, the flowers, her language, the mother and sister she was leaving behind.

She woke up one morning, grabbed her purse, and walked to the market to search for the closest colors that she could find to the red and black woolen fabric her mother had worn, the fabric of the dress she had once put on in a garden as a girl. She had been sewing all her life, but she had never before made the traditional shal of her village.

Now to choose the threads: Red and gold for the roof of the Church of al-Tahira. Green for the garden her father planted, pale blue for the water of her well. A rosary of white and pink beads, deep purple for the grapes that hung outside of her childhood home. Black for the tuxedo Amer had worn on their wedding day. Three shades of beige to capture the wheat that breathed on the plains near home. Red for the apples hanging on the tree.

How to distill an entire lifetime into a dress? Hana sketched her memories with chalk onto the fabric. Had her house been destroyed? Was the church still standing? She had no idea.

She began to sew. She was only halfway finished on the day they boarded the plane to Jordan. She carried it with her.

8 | THE ROAD TO QARAQOSH

I had known for some time that I would have to follow Hana's dress all the way to its origins. Her stories weren't just asking me to learn about Qaraqosh: they were leading me to it.

I'm not a conflict journalist. But by May 2017, seven months after I met Hana, the road to Qaraqosh from Kurdistan appeared as if it might be safe enough for me to travel. For some time, journalists, priests and nuns, and residents of Qaraqosh living in Kurdistan had been making the trip by day to see what had happened to the city and to their homes and to try to gauge whether it would even be possible to build again. At the same time, the region was still unstable, and ISIS was still occupying Mosul, only thirty kilometers away from Qaraqosh.

I packed a small bag and boarded a plane to Istanbul, where I transferred on to Erbil, in the Kurdistan region of Iraq. Once I arrived at the airport there, I took a taxi to a hotel in the city's Christian quarter of Ankawa for the evening. The name of my hotel was written in Syriac letters: the young man who checked me in was a refugee from Syria. My taxi driver was displaced from Mosul. I went to bed that first night already exhausted.

The next day, I woke up and set out to an apartment across town, one on the top floor of the shopping mall where Hana had once lived. It was surreal to see life continuing mostly as normal, just hours away from where ISIS was still controlling Mosul. There was traffic, and coffee and juice for sale, carpets hanging on display. I rode an escalator to the top floor of the mall. Hana's sister Bushra was still living there, in the temporary apartment where Hana and her family had lived for nearly two years before moving onto Amman, and she embraced me. She had the same girlishness as Hana, the same kind smile and gentle way of being present.

She led me inside. On the wall of Hana's old apartment, several small square pictures of St. Charbel with his black-hooded robe had been taped to the walls. It was the same image that Hana had sewn into the center of her dress.

We walked past the neighboring apartments, and women came out to the hall to welcome me. When they heard about my reason for coming, many showed me their own shals, embroidered with their own trees and homes and images of dancing. A woman from Karamleis, a neighboring village of Qaraqosh, displayed a costume of orange fabric, entirely different from that of Qaraqosh. It marked people as being from exactly that place and not another just a few kilometers away. Some of the women had doctored a metal drum in which to bake their traditional flatbread. Together, they laid out the dough on tables in the hallway of the mall, and the entire experience was of Aramaic and the scent of bread baking, with the hum of shopping audible in the background. I listened to them chatting back and forth in their endangered dialects. This is what remained of a world.

I slept badly that night on a mattress on the floor. The next morning, Bushra and I caught a taxi to Qaraqosh. It was her first time back, and I was grateful to have her beside me. Our driver was also from Qaraqosh, and he played music in Aramaic from a cassette player and had a rosary dangling from the dashboard.

I will never forget the endless road, manned with checkpoints of soldiers speaking in Kurdish then Arabic. It was just as Hana had described it: a single road extending between Erbil and Qaraqosh and seeming to continue forever.

An abandoned Ferris wheel rose out of the plains. We passed over the River Zab. On the side of the road, all signs still pointed toward Mosul.

After hours of being backed up in traffic, we arrived in Karamleis, where the Church of Saint Barbara remained standing. The driver called out to the soldiers. "They're our boys," he told me. He had spoken to them in Aramaic. They waved us through. At the main roundabout, we drove up a dirt road.

Then we were in Qaraqosh. There is something surreal in discovering that the place described to you as a paradise is a collection of houses on plain, flat streets. Church steeples interrupted the landscape. Qaraqosh had become a ghost town. We drove through the eerily quiet roads.

In the center of town, there was only a single open shop, where a man was selling brooms, windows, cleaning supplies for those with the courage to return to their ransacked houses and make sense of them. I remembered what one of my friends in Homs, Syria, had once said to me of her own experience of war: "The first one back is always the man selling the windows."

Black graffiti was still sprayed onto white walls, declaring the caliphate of the Islamic State. The driver stopped the car in front of a gold and silver painted gate. Here was the house that Amer and Hana had built, borrowing money from family and friends and then adding a second floor so that their children would have a place to study. Before I had left for Iraq, they had given me permission to visit and go inside. The family's house still somehow stood, although ISIS had burned it entirely. The driver hoisted himself onto the wall, climbed to the other side, and opened the gate.

The house had been destroyed sufficiently that we had to put on surgical masks in order to breathe. We passed a clementine tree and walked through the front door. Something had been written in black permanent marker on the wall of the house in Arabic when officials had come to survey the buildings of the city, to make records of what had been lost and what could be saved.

The House of Amer [family name of Hana and Amer]: Entirely destroyed.

We entered. The walls and ceiling had been blackened by fire, and I used the flashlight on my cell phone to make my way through the darkness. The floor was blanketed with thick dust, which had blown in through the space where windows had once been and were no longer. Black paint had been splattered onto the walls. A box of medicine, cloth flowers, and plates and pots and spoons littered the floor, along with spices spilling onto the ground.

I remembered Hana's story of the day they first moved in. The way she came home from teaching to watch the builders. The kitchen, where she folded stuffed grape leaves, and baked biryani, and boiled the red bulgur. The rooms where she sang to her children, where she waited by the window for them to return home from school.

The ceiling fan had been burned so completely by ISIS that its three propellers melted downward and drooped toward the floor. In the room beside it, the entire ceiling had collapsed. A small library still held scattered Syriac books that belonged to Amer and what looked like school papers, still waiting to be marked.

We climbed the stairs to the second story. On the floor, the black and white keys to Meena's keyboard lay melted. A clock on the floor had stopped, forever now, at 9:10. I could imagine Hana and Amer's children, Syrian and Meena and Mirna, studying for their exams, the way the clear light would have come in from the windows.

We descended the stairs, and I went to the garden. A single clementine was left on the tree. The neighborhood was empty.

Then we drove away. After just a few minutes, I recognized the red roof from Hana's dress: the Church of al-Tahira. We walked inside to a wide nave, burned and blackened from the inside by what must have been a massive fire. Half of the church's pews, evidently destroyed, had been stashed against the wall in a huge, mounting pile.

I closed my eyes, and into that burned and broken space I imagined Hana as a girl, singing in the church choir; Hana, waiting for the bonfire on Christmas Eve, watching her siblings emerge in the clothes she had sewn for them.

We continued on to a vast open courtyard, which I recognized from the photos of Palm Sunday. On the far end sat the church lectern, from which the scriptures are read. Someone had dragged it outside, set it up, and attached a human target to it. ISIS had turned the long, open church courtyard into a shooting gallery.

I looked up to the red roof to see the clock gone. A cross was dangling from a wire.

Later, we drove to the Church of St. George. The statue of the saint had been beheaded, his cape still swinging in the air. Horror after horror. As we circled the city, I recognized the star shape of the Church of Mar Behnam and Sara. Some of Behnam's forty slaves were visible on a relief over the entrance to the church, behind St. Metti pouring water over the heads of Behnam and Sara. All their faces had been chiseled out.

The only way out of Qaraqosh was by the same single road we had taken.

I do not know what I had been expecting to find in Qaraqosh. Hana had managed to show me more of Qaraqosh with her dress than I had seen with my own eyes. Through her stories, she had taken me to weddings, to the fire burning on Christmas Eve, to her children studying with the light coming in from the window. I had listened to the voices of the choir.

A town without its people is no longer alive.

I spent another week in the Kurdistan region of Iraq, traveling on my own. I passed internally displaced camps housing tens of thousands of Yazidis, who had escaped a genocide at Mount Sinjar. The killings on Mount Sinjar had happened the same week that ISIS took Qaraqosh, and the Yazidis were still unable to return home. I traveled to Lalish, where Yazidis believe that the world first became covered with vegetation. It was a landscape of hills and white conical shrines, where some of the women who had been kidnapped and enslaved but had managed to escape could now come to be baptized, to start their lives over again.

I continued on to al-Qosh, a Christian village not taken by ISIS, where all of the villagers spoke still another dialect of Aramaic, one distinct from Hana's. It was a dusty town, just at the base of a mountain. I wandered through the narrow streets, passing a stone archway engraved with lions, a small church. Inside, men and women and children were praying in Aramaic, some of the last speakers of that dialect in the world. I listened.

When I walked outside again, I saw two women walking arm in arm. I asked them for directions to the tomb of the prophet Nahum, the ancient synagogue where Jews had, for centuries, traveled on pilgrimage from cities like Mosul and Zakho on the Feast of Shavuot. I had heard that, almost miraculously, the synagogue still stood. Passersby pointed me to the house of the family that held the keys, and I knocked.

A young boy answered the door. I asked if I could visit the tomb. He disappeared without saying a word, and I expected that he would return with an adult. Instead, he came back holding what looked like an ordinary house key and handed it to me. I continued looking at him until I understood that I should make my way there alone and then bring the key back to him when I had finished.

I grasped it in my hand, rounded the corner to the entrance of the synagogue, and turned the key. The door opened. I walked into the courtyard and then looked down at what appeared to be a simple stone structure filled in with mud, entered by an ornate door. I walked inside. An iron grill was protecting a tomb covered in a green cloth, which tradition held belonged to the prophet Nahum. Above the doors, inscriptions in Hebrew remained on the walls.

Once upon a time, not too long ago, thousands of Iraqi Jews had traveled here on pilgrimage, placing dried fruit on the tomb to be blessed. Those from cities like Zakho in Iraqi Kurdistan had also spoken Aramaic, part of what was considered to be the most ancient Jewish diaspora community in the world. Behind the tomb complex, I could see the mountain they had designated as Mount Sinai, where every year they reenacted the giving of the Ten Commandments.

I stayed for a long time, sitting among the crumbling stones, breathing in the presence of all those now gone. Most Jews from Zakho had left Iraq in the 1950s in the wake of the tensions following the 1948 Arab-Israeli war, many moving to Jerusalem.

It was getting late. I locked the door, walked around the corner, knocked again, and handed the key to the little boy, whose family was still taking care of the holy place of a community now gone.

I remembered the colors on Hana's dress. It felt like so much was fading and so quickly now. It felt like I had entered this story just in time to watch the vanishing.

After that, I visited Hana in Jordan just twice more—the second time to say goodbye. She and her family were finally being resettled in Australia, where she would soon be reunited with her daughter Meena and son-in-law, who were already there. Where she could finally meet her first grandchild and, later, her second.

In time, they were all resettled in Australia: the famous singer, the violin player, the painter. The singers in the choir. I had witnessed briefly a world between worlds until it, too, was gone.

PART II

FERHAD'S SONG

Al-Hasakeh, Syria → Istanbul, Turkey

Take hold of me, my friend, as one we shall . . .
—Fragment from Tablet V, *The Epic of Gilgamesh*

9 | LOOKING FOR A BUZUQ

A suspension bridge once straddled the Euphrates in Deir Ezor, in northeastern Syria. I know this because I once stood on that bridge. It was evening, in 2005, during my year as a student living in Damascus. I had traveled to the area with a friend to visit the archaeological remains of Dura Europos, where the frescoes of an ancient synagogue had been unearthed in the 1930s after being buried beneath the earth for centuries. Those frescoes, with ancient human faces peering out, were then displayed in the National Museum of Damascus, and I often went to visit them. I had wanted to understand where the synagogue itself had once stood before the paintings were dismantled and carried off, far from their original context.

The nearby Euphrates, ever-present, made the earth greener than I'd expected. In the evening, after visiting the ruins, I had returned to my hotel in Deir Ezor and then walked in the direction of that suspension bridge. Couples, side by side, strolled in front of me. Bicycles sped past. A child held a balloon. The friend who was traveling with me snapped my photograph: the bridge rising behind me, trees visible along the banks of the river itself.

So much would later disappear in the war. Houses, alleys, gardens, entire families.

The bridge was blown up during the fighting between the Syrian government and opposition forces in 2013. For years after, I could not stop thinking of it. I don't know why, of all of the things lost, that bridge came to haunt me. The way those couples walked out onto it as though balancing in midair.

Anyone familiar with war knows that it invites magical thinking. We want to believe there is a pattern to what survives and what dies. We long for some logic—some reason that those frescoed faces from an ancient synagogue lasted more than fifteen hundred years before being unearthed and carted to a museum, while an entire suspension bridge collapsed into the Euphrates. Why something that appeared so sturdy gave out and something so fragile survived.

Now, so many years after I walked on that bridge, it was hard not to succumb to the randomness of it all. Still, after I met Hana, I stayed faithful to my plans: traveling from country to country, speaking to Syrians and Iraqis who had escaped war, trying to learn from them of what had been lost and saved. In the Zaatari refugee camp in Jordan, which had swollen to eighty thousand souls, I found a young man named Ibrahim from Dera'a in Syria still mixing perfume and pouring it into glass bottles. A dance troupe had survived from Homs to still perform at weddings. In England, I met young migrants and refugees from Iran and Iraq who had traveled hidden in the back of lorries, now baking their flatbread in a makeshift community center. In al-Mafraq, in the north of Jordan, a woman held out her phone. "I couldn't bring jasmine with me," she said. "So I brought a photograph of jasmine."

I wrote into my notebooks lists of things that seemed to last: Recipes. Seeds. Perfume. Gardens. Prayers. Languages. Music.

That a bridge might collapse into the Euphrates but a song survive was something I was only beginning to comprehend. The intangible quality of a song makes it both fragile and portable, able to be carried out of war even by those who did not have time to pack a bag or who lost their belongings along the way. A mother without a suitcase might still carry a lullaby.

The Syriac melody the choir saved from Qaraqosh. The folk song Matti and Nasir's ancestors carried out of Tur Abdin when they fled the genocide in 1915, passing it on to their children, who would pass it to their children, who passed it until it was sung in my own generation. The two musicians embroidered into Hana's dress, playing the tabla and the ney. The music store owner in Paris, who spoke of his search for the missing Syrian instrument maker, Ibrahim Sukkar, so that he could continue selling his instruments. Music seemed to be such a part of remembering. It often seemed that music formed the language of memory itself.

At a conference on endangered Syrian music organized by UNESCO, Gani Merzo, a Syrian Kurdish musician, estimated that between 60 and 70 percent of Kurdish musicians in Syria had already fled the war, carrying their songs with them. Each one of these songs contained a story, making this displacement akin to the volumes of an ancient library being dispersed around the world.

I reasoned that some of these musicians must have crossed into Turkey as it bordered the Kurdish areas of northern Syria and would be—along with Kurdistan in Iraq—the closest border over which to escape. And for reasons unknown to me, I found myself drawn to an image of the buzuq—a long-necked lute with a tear-shaped body often used in Kurdish music. I had rarely seen it in Syria—living in Damascus, I more often saw the oud, which has a shorter neck and a wider body.

I knew that the buzuq, with the twenty-four frets along the neck, was especially suited to producing microtones: micro-intervals that fall between the notes I was accustomed to hearing in so-called "Western" music and therefore holding the possibility of revealing new depths of sound. So I decided to go searching for a buzuq. I sensed there was something to be learned in the notes between the notes that I had yet to understand.

I performed a quick online search and came upon a name: Hozan, a young buzuq player who, according to the brief entry I found, had escaped the war in Syria and arrived in Turkey without his instrument. Unable to find a replacement exactly like the buzuqs of Syria, he was seeking funding to craft his own. The fact that he could no longer find his instrument and was willing to go to such lengths to replace it seemed urgent. I reached out to him, and we arranged a meeting.

So it was that I flew to Istanbul, Turkey, searching for a sound.

It did not take me long in Istanbul to become lost. I walked for hours up and down the alleys around the Bosphorus Strait, climbing and descending hills, the same haunting water nearby. A city of eighteen million people was no place to go looking for a fragment.

People had taken to calling the neighborhood of Aksaray "Little Syria" because many of the 500,000 Syrian refugees in Istanbul had found their way there. I sought out the familiar. That was Salloura, a sweet shop that dated back some 150 years in Aleppo and that had now been relocated to Istanbul in the war. Azad, a third-generation pastry chef from Aleppo, stood in a red uniform lined with brass buttons and prepared to scoop ice cream—with flavors like almond milk, clotted cream, and cherry. He had escaped Syria three years earlier. In Aleppo, he had worked in the Salloura sweet shop for twenty years, learning how to craft baklawa, two kinds of knafeh, milk pudding, semolina cake, and the famous halawet el-jibn. "Making sweets is a kind of madrassa," he explained to me. "You slowly learn everything—how to make the desserts, how to sell them, and finally how to work with others."

If there is a spirituality common to the Syrians I know, it is that there are lessons to be learned in the simple acts we carry out each day: from the way you place cucumbers in a bowl, to the moment you choose to pick a lemon from a tree, to the patient details of inlaid wooden boxes, soap that must age before hardening, red peppers that take time to dry on the roof. This quality of loving attention, which I learned and now longed for, had apparently survived the war.

Aleppo had been famous for its pistachios, with their flecks of pink and pale green. An elderly man from Aleppo once swore to me that he used them to woo the women of Milan. Yes, I remembered. The roses and mulberries of Damascus, the milk of the Harran, the dates of Palmyra. Aleppo's pomegranates, quinces, red peppers.

A bridge falls. A cup of cherry ice cream lasts. And who is to say that Salloura, the sweet shop, was not also a library, saving stories—written out in baklawa and dishes of sweets from Homs so that we might remember?

I was coming to the end of my trip, and I still had not connected with the musician, Hozan. In reading more about him, I discovered he was one of the founding members of a band dedicated to saving Kurdish music. We made our appointment, and one evening toward the very end of my stay, I set out. Two hours later, I was still walking in circles, lost this time in the streets of the Tarlabasi neighborhood, once home to Armenians, Greeks, and Jews in Ottoman Istanbul. Now the neighborhood was a mess of alleys and chipped but brightly painted façades of peach and yellow and blue, laundry lines, balconies, and rows of arched and rectangular windows.

I looked in the distance and saw three faces leaning out the window and calling to me. It was already 11:00 p.m. I ran to the apartment block and knocked, and as the door swung open, I stood face to face with a young man with black, curly hair and charcoal eyes who introduced himself as Hozan. With him stood the young, seemingly shy woman with a gentle smile who had been helping me with directions, who now introduced herself in English as Mar, and a young man with golden hair reaching to the middle of his back, a slight beard and mustache, and bright green eyes. His name was Ferhad.

I slipped inside, and we sat in a circle on the floor for a glass of tea. I relaxed, somehow feeling entirely at home. I still remember the music of the spoons against glass, the tiny space crammed with speakers and guitars. We settled into speaking Arabic, and when Ferhad asked me how I had heard about their music, I answered reluctantly that I had actually been looking for a buzuq. We all laughed. He then nodded, as though following a buzuq to Istanbul made all the sense in the world.

After tea, they grabbed their instruments, the conversation turning into a concert, with Hozan playing the buzuq and Ferhad playing the guitar and singing in Kurdish.

Endê were dikana, lê lê lê lê

Hozan's fingers moved up and down the neck of the lute with speed, at moments the notes so close to one another that he seemed to press his fingers together. Ferhad leaned toward him, listening and adapting, smiling when he recognized a resonance between buzuq, guitar, voice. I listened too—to this song carried out of Syria, about a young man in love with a girl he could not have.

When they finished playing, we all took a deep breath to recover before sitting again around the small table.

"You're from al-Hasakeh?" I asked.

"Yes, Hozan and I were born in the same neighborhood in Syria. In the same hospital!"

"And when did you arrive here in Istanbul?"

"Five years ago."

"In 2012."

"Yes. We were in university in Homs when the war began," Hozan broke in.

"When they closed the university, we left," Ferhad finished. "We were at the music program. I studied classical guitar. Hozan specialized in the buzuq."

They had a habit of finishing one another's sentences, which made it difficult for me to write everything down in a way that separated one speaker from another.

In time, Ferhad began to speak without pause, and a silence formed around him to give his words space. And so this story began. It began as a tale about a buzuq and then one about Hozan, who was trying to craft his own buzuq. But in time it became a story about Ferhad. Or, rather, it remained a story about Ferhad and Hozan because it was impossible to think of them as entirely separate. Still, I came to rely on Ferhad's account of what happened to them.

This happened for several reasons—the first being that it soon became apparent that Hozan did not like to speak much, except to jump in and add details to the stories Ferhad was already in the midst of telling. Or to be more accurate, Hozan spoke all the time but through his instrument.

Ferhad, on the other hand, was not only a musician but a natural storyteller. He was a storyteller from a world of storytellers, a land where storytelling is revered as art. And as he began to speak about their pasts—not only about his own but also about Hozan's— it became clear that he would narrate the story from now on. So it was that, once again, I surrendered to what was given to me.

And so we turn to Ferhad—who, you may remember, was that young man with a narrow and pronounced face; long, golden hair; bright-green eyes; and a slight golden moustache and beard. And we turn to that city in northeastern Syria—al-Hasakeh—that he would bring alive for me.

10 | A FIELD OF ASHES

Al-Hasakeh sat in the furthest corner of Syria—its own world and one of the most diverse cities in Syria before the war, the streets alive with Kurds, Arabs, Assyrians, Chaldeans, Syriacs, Armenians, and Yazidis. It is almost equidistant from Baghdad and Damascus, on the opposite border of Syria from Aleppo, nearly a thousand miles from Istanbul. Though al-Hasakeh was technically part of Syria, its place in the borderlands meant that it was impossible to understand the city without taking a wider view of the surrounding countries and their long histories. Al-Hasakeh stood close to the borders of the Kurdish regions of northern Iraq, as well as the southeastern section of Turkey that was once home to Assyrians and Armenians. It was also nearby Mount Sinjar in Iraq—the historical homeland of the Yazidis. It was not far from Zakho, a city in Iraq that once had thousands of Aramaic-speaking Jews, and not even so far from Iran. The stories and languages and memories of the people of al-Hasakeh could not be completely separated from any of these places. Ferhad looked to the nearby Euphrates for his identity, considering his family to be rooted, simply, in Mesopotamia.

Ferhad and Hozan grew up in a neighborhood called Salihiye, a majority Kurdish neighborhood just next to a neighborhood called Gunde Mufti. As a boy, Ferhad was convinced that Gunde Mufti was dangerous, a neighborhood in which any stranger who walked into it would receive a knife in the back. He believed this despite the fact that many of the children he played with came from this neighborhood, and this belief infused his childhood with a sense of seriousness. But his own neighborhood, his own street—that was home, in the deepest sense. It was a neighborhood of characters, every person attached to a story. It was where he belonged.

Salihiye functioned almost as a single extended domicile, and every door opened when he knocked. Some of the houses were built of concrete and some of clay, but they all seemed to be built in the same simple format as his own family's house, which had a wooden ceiling and a few simple rooms. Any open space between the built houses was, to his child's mind, not empty but simply reserved for playing. The neighborhood could be interpreted as a checkerboard of spaces, alternating between those reserved for habitation and those for running and dreaming and kicking the soccer ball, all of it interconnected into a single frame.

So it was that when he was looking for his friend Rody, Ferhad might choose a door at random and ask, "Where is Rody?" and expect someone to know. There was a collective belonging and a collective responsibility—and with that a collective knowing, somehow. Later still would emerge a collective longing, a collective grief.

Ferhad was the oldest child, living with his mother, his father, his two brothers, and his sister. His grandparents had died before he was born. So while other children were sent to stay with their grandparents over the summer, Ferhad went to live with his aunt, who had a house near Tel Tamar, just north of al-Hasakeh and next to the Khabur River—a tributary of the Euphrates, in what is known as the Fertile Crescent, and near the volcanic landscapes of Ard-al Sheikh. Her husband had died, and she raised her many children alone. Ferhad was devoted to her. The area around her home mapped itself into his body, into his childhood, and, much later, into his music.

During the long summer days, he would swim and fish in the Khabur or play with his cousins and the children from Yazidi communities who lived nearby. Once, when he was eight years old, he accompanied his aunt to breed her cow, and they found themselves in a village of Assyrian women, speaking a dialect of Aramaic and dressed in colorful clothes. He understood that his corner of the world was very special, that it contained ancient stories. Yes, he remembered. He knew, even then.

> My aunt had a very beautiful life—and every time I think of her, I realize that it's my dream to live like her one day. She had a cow, and she had a little bit of land on which she grew cotton and wheat, and she had her garden for vegetables, and she made yogurt from the milk of her cows, and she had chickens. She was such a special person for me. Sometimes we were herding her cows to the Khabur River—and every single cow had a name. So many times I remember her talking—I would look around to see who she was speaking to—but no, she was speaking to her cows. She baked bread in the tanur—an oven made of clay—and I will never forget that bread in my entire life. She had a beautiful relationship with fire. From her, I learned to respect fire.

> Sometimes they would dam the Khabur River, and the entire village would come—it was a festival! There were these big bags for collecting the cotton harvest, and you would poke holes in them for the water to pour out and sink them into the places in the river where the water was still and pull them out full of fish. We were covered with mud. There was a green frog with a yellow line on it that we would also catch to use as bait and then let it go in the water—and the fish would see that phosphorus color and jump up so that we could catch them. There was also an eel that we could catch, but for that you had to be very brave. There are rocks, and you have to put your hand under them and then grab the eel when he passes and immediately throw him before he clasps onto your hand with the thorns on his back. But he is very delicious!

With my Yazidi friends, we went to pick mulberries. They were
the white mulberries in that area—extremely sweet. You would
shake the tree, and they would fall. It was really nice. I was stealing pomegranates from the orchards and then running away
from the dog.

Ferhad understood that his life was not only his own life, that it
existed in a chain of lives and a chain of stories. A famous Kurdish
legend called Derwêshe 'Evdî tells the story of a Yazidi boy in love
with a Kurdish Muslim girl; that story takes place along the Khabur River and in the mountains of Abdul Aziz and Mount Sinjar
across the border in Iraq. When he heard it, Ferhad felt proud to
recognize the landscapes as his own. The first time he found a written version of the story and read it, he cried. He still remembers
when the Yazidis he played with moved away, group by group, to
Germany. He was ten years old, and one afternoon, when he went
looking for his friend Sinan, he discovered that he had gone.

Ferhad's family was not religious, and they never spoke about
God. But they kept a Muslim prayer carpet in their house so that
if any guest wanted to pray, they could easily offer it to them. Hospitality remained sacred—this welcoming of others exactly as they
are. Walking in the city, he would hear different languages: Assyrian, Armenian, Kurdish, Arabic. It felt precious. But in time, he
also understood that these differences also held a weight of fear,
that there were some things he should speak about only within his
own community. The knowledge of this saddened him.

During the hot summer months, when he was back in al-
Hasakeh, Ferhad and his parents and siblings would all sleep on the
roof. His mother would fasten a white sheet around the bedposts to
block the morning sun and mark off private space, and he would
lie there and try to count how many stars were framed within that
box. Each time he moved his head, he would need to start again.

He loved being drawn into sleep, his mind completely clear, looking up at the sky, finding the Little Dipper and the Big Dipper.

He can still remember the first time he sang in public. Hozan's older brother Noah had arrived at the house one day, leading a gang of kids. Noah was carrying something—or someone—dressed up and covered in a white sheet. Ferhad was standing in front of the door. They had created the Bride of Rain out of wood, and now they were parading her through the streets, asking for the rain to arrive. Through the streets they carried the Bride—the Bûka Baranê—who would bestow blessings to the houses and wish those who opened their doors good weather in the seasons of their lives ahead. And they were singing, all the kids together:

Up at the house
Underneath at the house,
God give kids for this house,
Give us something for these kids.
We ask God to give us rain!

Ferhad stood in front of his door, all of six years old, watching. Noah laughed. "Why don't you come with us?"

"I started going with them and clapping, door after door," Ferhad remembers. "Some people were offering bulgur; others were giving butter. Some people were throwing water from the back door, and we would run away. We asked for rain; they gave us rain! Every year, we were doing that."

So Ferhad told the story to me: of how they carried the Bride and of how he became aware of this music that carried power. He did not know—and I did not know until much later—that Kurdish children had been carrying out that ritual for centuries. Yes, the very first time Ferhad sang in front of others, he was also participating in remembering. Song could do that: it could carry the past. Even the sky was listening.

The Arabic language arrived in Ferhad's life when he was six years old and started school. He couldn't help but notice how different it felt from his own Kurdish, which is from the Indo-European family and more closely related to Farsi.

The school curriculum was built on the idea of Arab nationalism, which did not involve the Kurdish people or their language. In time, Ferhad learned to read and write in Arabic, with its looping characters, its root system. His Kurdish language became something private, spoken at home or among friends, present in songs—a language he would not learn to write until he left high school.

He knew that it was the same story for others in his classes who had private languages and histories: the Armenians and the Assyrians. He intuited that they—just as he did—must also speak one language with their family and another at school, that they had a public self and a private self.

All this only increased how much the Kurdish language meant to him. It was part of what made him himself, the tongue that came to him automatically in moments of great emotion, whether joy or fear. Kurdish was the language that he dreamed in, that his mother sang in, that he had carried through the streets as a boy. He began to notice that his language—if he listened to it carefully—was itself a form of music.

The area of the Kurds historically extended from what is today southern Turkey to northeastern Syria, parts of northern Iraq, and parts of Iran. Though they spoke different dialects, for the most part Kurds saw themselves as belonging to one another even across borders. For Ferhad's community, passing down the songs, the stories, and the historical landscapes of their people became essential to understanding who they were. In the past, travelers transmitted songs, singing from village to village. The melodies spoke of love, of battles, of mountains soon known to Kurdish children. Most of all, Ferhad came to associate music with joy. Every time that he experienced happiness—whether at their Nowruz festival marking the New Year or at weddings—music seemed to be playing somewhere, the very language of joy itself.

Of course, their history was never taught in school. Instead, the past was transmitted to the children through song. One morning each autumn, at the end of the harvest season, an old woman would approach Ferhad and the other children as they were playing in the open lots and announce, "Today, we have the danûk. You kids will need to find fire for the burning." That was Ferhad's cue that one of his favorite rituals would soon begin.

> We would go all over the neighborhood to find wood, or cardboard, or anything that can be burned. Then we would return to that woman, eager to show her that we had done something important. In the afternoon—the time they call asr—the weather cooled enough to have a fire, and it would begin. They would bring these cauldrons and begin to put the fire under it, and the children would begin to sit in front, each one holding a plate.

> When the smoke started to go up, we would say, "Oh, danûk is starting." It would be more than one woman, but there is one chief; she would be mixing all the time, using a big shovel like a spoon. And we had stories . . . she was telling so many stories . . .

> And then an old man would arrive, singing, making a night of music and stories for us. Sometimes he would sing, and we would repeat his words. He had a very long moustache, and you couldn't see his mouth. You could just see his moustache moving—and all the kids were just staring at his moustache. He would sing a traditional song, and we would sing after him until we memorized it.

When you come to eat the danûk, you come holding your small plate in your hand, singing—like a good boy—and the woman serves everyone the danûk. You could mix it with salt or butter. She was always saying, "Eat it very, very slowly, or you will have problems with your stomach." It was very peaceful.

Later, Ferhad would come to understand that this annual tradition was both transmission and necessity—that the women needed to boil the harvested bulgur for hours before they could leave it on the roof to dry and then store it in sacks for the long winter. Those who lived in his neighborhood were poor, and so they shared everything with one another: food, story, song, or anything that might nourish a child's body and soul so that no one would go hungry. He would remember passing the empty lot in the days after danûk, learning that it was best to wait to play soccer for a few more days. The ashes of those long hours would cling to the earth for some time, staining the bare feet of anyone who walked through it.

Danûk—that dish slowly cooked in a cauldron—was the method by which the children learned the stories, how they were taught the songs, across generations. This was how their history was passed down, as long as the stories were remembered, the songs sung. These children were a living library. They learned, but they also became participants, answering back—and in this they learned that their time, too, would come to teach the songs to the children after them, that all of this was preparation. If anyone asked why so many Kurdish children were gathered, the women could simply answer that the children were waiting for a meal. And in a sense, they were. It was only later that Ferhad would notice how elemental those stories and songs were to his being, to his understanding of whom he belonged to and who belonged to him and to what he needed to be filled up with in order to stay alive.

He grew up. His parents raised him to have a deep respect for every person, no matter who they were or what they did, to read books, to keep his word. His father was firm that he should never profit at the expense of another, that he should always tell the truth. Though they were poor, his parents always bought the children good shoes, and they wore well-made clothes. *You have a few nice things*, his father taught him. *You respect yourself.*

He knew he had been given a special family. His brother Sherzad, wise and kind, often joined him fishing. Then came his sister, Evin, with striking green eyes, who later played the violin. She longed for a sister, but when her mother gave birth one last time, alas: a younger brother, Kani, appeared. She burst into tears. From then on, she would remain the only girl, the beloved sister and daughter. Ferhad knew that it was something unusual, even then— to have been given a mother and father like that, to have been given those siblings. Yes, they loved one another. He was stunned by the gift of it.

Their lives were measured by seasons. Ferhad's mother had a gift for grasping what was beautiful and making it last. She was famous in the neighborhood for her preserves. She'd make jams of eggplants with walnuts; of the juri flower with its pale blush of petals, which in English we call the Damascus rose; of apricots; and even of tomatoes. For the apricot jam, the women would first gather and make a fire together, cutting the apricots and placing them in a huge pot with sugar to be set to boil. Afterward, Ferhad's mother would cover her share and leave it outside until it turned deep orange and carried the taste of the sun.

So it was. Apricots. Songs. A box of stars. A pair of shoes. Microtones. Little things throughout the year, which, stitched together, become a life well lived.

> Every year for New Year's, my mom cut part of the pine tree we had in our yard, and she had special lights and put cotton on it, and she made ornaments from paper—she had beautiful things to do for us. We had a very simple life, but we had love. That was

what was simple in my family. We didn't have much money, but we had love. So much. My mom and dad were so special.

I was always out of the house. My mother would ask, "Why did you go out of the house? Don't you miss me?" And I would say, "Yes, but I am making you practice. . . . One day I will be far away for a long time."

He grew quiet as he spoke of his mother, looking far off, as though to see her. "It's very strange," he finished. "There were so many things that I said, and then they happened."

At the same time, at the end of the block, a young boy named Hozan was growing up. He was a born musician. In the world in which he lived, the buzuq was ubiquitous, part of the landscape, and it seemed that every time Hozan entered into a house, he would find one hanging on the wall, made of pine and walnut wood, with its tear-shaped body and long neck, beckoning to him.

He began playing when he was twelve or thirteen years old, when an artist fashioned a buzuq for his neighbor. When he saw that the neighbor wasn't using it, Hozan procured the buzuq for himself. If I say that Hozan was twelve or thirteen years old when all of this happened, you will understand that this is because he had very little sense of historical time—he seemed to live in his own world and deeply within himself, and so he does not know at what age he began to play music, just as he does not know the date on which he was born.

He does know, however, that he played those first notes on the Feast of Nowruz, the Kurdish festival celebrating the new year each spring, when they gathered and sang and danced deep into the night. From that moment on, he began to advance . . . slowly, slowly. The sound of the buzuq became the sound of his adolescence and the primary language in which he expressed his deepest thoughts.

If he had a teacher in those early years, then it was the famous buzuq player Seîd Yûsiv—from Qamishli in the north of Syria, who was known as the Prince of the Buzuq. Hozan listened to the cassettes of Seîd Yûsiv over and over again, imitating every note and playing it himself, until his friends called him "Abu Zoro," which was also Seîd Yûsiv's nickname.

At some point in boyhood, Ferhad and Hozan became friends. They are not sure when, in part because neither of them seems able to articulate a time in their lives when they were not. Ferhad describes it as a happy meeting of opposites. When the children of the neighborhood played soccer, Hozan darted—alert and quick— through the field, naturally drawn to the ball, frustrating players when he moved in one direction and then dashed in another. Ferhad ran back and forth, somewhat lost. Something in these two personalities needed one another, and they recognized a common gentleness in a world that was often very harsh.

After that, they would wait until the wheat had been harvested, leaving an empty field. Together, they would make their way to the deepest place within the field, and Hozan would play the buzuq in that empty place while Ferhad listened.

Hozan had a difficult life. When he was a teenager, his brother was arrested, accused of being a political dissident. While his brother was away in jail, Hozan's father died. Though the official cause was a heart attack, everyone who knew them suspected that he died from a broken heart. His family was forced to sell their home and leave the city. This meant that for a time, Hozan and Ferhad separated. After that, Hozan slept every night with his hand over his heart—afraid that an arrow might pierce it. He was fragile. Ferhad often worried about Hozan, Ferhad told me—although I suppose that, had Hozan been the one telling the story, I might have learned that they worried about one another.

When his family moved to the countryside, Hozan would visit al-Hasakeh to see Ferhad, and in those moments, their lives became whole again. They weren't ordinary friends, and they recognized that, very early on in their lives. They were sent to one another: nadim in Arabic, "soul friends." Here was a friend you could laugh with, cry with, be fully yourself with—a friend given as a gift and tied up in your destiny. It was a friendship present in their culture at least as long as the earliest known epic in the world was engraved into tablets in ancient Mesopotamia: the Epic of Gilgamesh, which narrated how the arrival of Enkidu as a friend had changed King Gilgamesh forever.

"Hozan was like Enkidu," Ferhad told me.

"So were you like Gilgamesh, then?" I asked. He laughed.

"No, no. Hozan also called me Enkidu. I called him Enkidu. We never said 'Gilgamesh.' Both of us were Enkidu." A friend who was sent by heaven and who is in touch with nature and the animals in a deep way—whose arrival signals that a journey is about to begin.

It was not until he was twenty-two years old that Ferhad began to play the guitar, also by way of cassette. The first time he remembers hearing the guitar was when he was eighteen years old, before he ever saw one in person, via a cassette his cousin bought of the Gypsy Kings playing flamenco music. Immediately he recognized himself in it and knew that he would have to learn to play the guitar—and, hopefully, one day learn to sing in Spanish. It was a kind of instinct and one he explained matter-of-factly: Hozan's very self was reflected back in the buzuq, and Ferhad's own self was reflected in the sound of the guitar. And though the guitar seemed to be a "Western" instrument, Ferhad did not experience it as such. He knew the guitar's origin legend: that Ziryab, the famous Iraqi musician who some say might even have been Kurdish, traveled in the ninth century to al-Andalusia in Spain, bringing the lute with him and later adding a fifth string. What would later become the guitar—like so many other things that might have appeared unrelated to his life—had origins in the landscapes of his childhood. He knew from the time that he was young what the world thought of as separate was often not separate at all. More often than not, we belong to one another.

Though the guitar was not a common instrument in Arabic music, which privileged the oud and the buzuq, Ferhad gave himself over to it entirely. That was Ferhad. Once he understood a thing, he changed the course of his life in order to assimilate it.

Music ran beneath everything. Each year as springtime approached, they would prepare for the Feast of Nowruz, where his family and neighbors would dress in colorful Kurdish clothes, pack an enormous picnic, and travel to the nearby volcanic mountain. There they would watch theater, and nearly every family would bring out their buzuq to play.

For Ferhad, life brought joy after joy, even in difficulty. At weddings, Ferhad would dance sixteen different types of dances, and the storytellers would sing, and relatives and friends would celebrate for three long days. He remembers sitting at the weddings with the other children, each one asking the other, "Who are your seven grandfathers?" And he would name his grandfathers for the last seven generations: Ahmad, Alo, Haj Ahmad, Sêx Junê, Kûto, Mîrzo, Miho.

And at one point as he spoke, a girl might jump up, recognizing that six or seven generations before, they shared the same grandfather. Or another boy might call out his own list of grandfathers, and Ferhad would smile as the boy named one of his own. They weren't strangers at all; none of them were. In fact, they all belonged to one another.

When Ferhad reached high school, his father was belatedly ordered to serve in the army. The family uprooted to Damascus for Ferhad's final two years of school. One day, to his surprise, he opened his front door in Damascus to find Hozan standing there. He had no idea how he had found him or learned of his address, but the two were unexpectedly together again.

When Ferhad graduated, his family returned to al-Hasakeh, but Ferhad and Hozan stayed on in Damascus, working in a factory making plastic boxes to hold fruit. They stapled boxes and smoked and talked all day, overcome by the smell of plastic. In the evenings, Ferhad listened as Hozan played the buzuq, and the music seemed to break through the scent of plastic and smoke in their clothes. No, they were children again, back in that field of wheat, and all was right in the world.

Ferhad eventually returned to al-Hasakeh and entered a two-year trade school to learn how to be the assistant for an agricultural engineer, while Hozan remained in Damascus. It was during that time that Ferhad began to focus on the guitar, inspired by those evenings listening to Hozan. An important oud musician had recently set up workshops in the nearby city of Qamishli, and one of his prized students lived in al-Hasakeh and also played the guitar. Ferhad befriended him, and in time, this student taught Ferhad how to read notes and scales. This young man possessed a book that taught the notes for beginners and sat with Ferhad week after week, taking him through them over and over again.

"Why is this taking so long?" Ferhad remembers asking.

The young man sighed. "You will need time to understand."

Yes, he remembers. He had invited the young man home to meet his family, and the man had arrived carrying a guitar. He was offered a seat in the corner of the house where Ferhad's mother had created an indoor garden, with lush green plants hanging down the wall. The young man played. The whole room was listening.

Ferhad sensed that the stems and branches of the plants were leaning toward the music too.

Soon, Ferhad could think of nothing else but music. In time, one of Hozan's brothers found him a guitar from Russia that he could buy and call his own. He practiced whenever he had a spare moment, memorizing a single melody and playing it over and over again. One evening, he strummed this melody alone in the dark of his room. Finishing, he took a deep bow in front of an imagined audience. His mother opened the door.

"That's it," she laughed. "My son has lost his mind."

By the time he moved to Homs for a third year of studying agricultural engineering, Ferhad was completely invested in music. He heard about a music conservatory that existed in the same university, one where he and Hozan might learn the skills that would allow them to become professional musicians.

He called Hozan and five other Kurdish friends and encouraged them all to apply at the same time, and they agreed. They traveled together to the entrance auditions. Ferhad remembers arriving at the university and seeing the other guitar players holding foot stands, because it was at that same moment he learned that foot stands exist. He spent the next hour trying to find one, to no avail. He arrived at the audition only to see one already in the room, waiting for him. He began his audition by clumsily placing his foot over the stand in the way he imagined he was supposed to, and when he sat down on the stool, he pressed his hands on the chair beneath him first, all of his knuckles cracking. When it was time to sing scales, his voice froze up.

"We'll call you if you're accepted," a woman on the panel said when he finished. He knew they would not. He failed. Hozan failed also. Only two of his five friends were accepted.

Yet he had seen the practice rooms. He had witnessed musicians from all over the country, shuffling through their sheet music. Hozan returned to Damascus to work, and he inquired until he found a private teacher to train him in classical buzuq. Ferhad stayed in Homs and studied privately with a student from the conservatory between his hours working at an ice cream shop. He practiced every free moment: notes and scales and chords, crescendo and diminuendo.

When Ferhad and Hozan took the same music conservatory audition again the following year, they were both accepted. Everything would change. Ferhad knew this already. He would start his studies over from the beginning, losing several years. His girlfriend, who had hoped that they would soon marry and have a family, broke up with him. He didn't blame her.

Now Ferhad had only to return to al-Hasakeh to break the news to his father. To become a musician instead of working in engineering was understood by most people as a demotion. Few he had told so far seemed to understand his passion—why, so late in his life, he had decided to take a new path. As the oldest son, he was also supposed to make choices that would ensure the stability of his family.

It was summertime in al-Hasakeh, the hour in which he and his father often took tea together in the backyard. They sat across from one another at a table, and Ferhad began to speak to him about his desire to study guitar in the university. His father knew how difficult the world could be—and Ferhad had always trusted him to give sound advice.

"You have only yourself to answer to," his father finally said. "I don't want you to blame me or to blame yourself if this goes wrong. Will you be responsible in front of this choice? Will you still believe that this is the right decision ten years from now?"

Ferhad nodded solemnly. And his father, forever wise, turned to his son and gave him his blessing.

11 | MICROTONES

Hozan and Ferhad arrived to their first day of university in Homs wearing what Ferhad calls their "country clothes"—the simple clothes they wore in their neighborhood back home. He had the sense that the colors of their shirts, bleached and faded by the strong al-Hasakeh sun, marked them as belonging to another world. Did those colors even exist in other cities? Hozan wore plastic sandals, not the shoes typically worn by other students of their cosmopolitan school. The year was 2008. When the friends lined up to register for classes, the secretary pointed out that Hozan still carried his government ID from the year 2000. It had never occurred to him to update it.

"How can we register you?" The secretary asked. Hozan had never needed a birthday until then, much less an updated ID. In fact, he probably didn't really have need of music school, either. But Ferhad had asked him to come, and this asking had prompted his understanding that it must, somehow, be important—if only so that Ferhad wouldn't have to do it alone.

So it was that before they even registered, Ferhad and Hozan set out to get Hozan a new ID card. If this detail stays with Ferhad all these years later, it is both because it says something about who Hozan *is*—how content he had always been to exist outside of systems—and also something about the world they were about to enter. It would be a culture shock. In their neighborhood in al-Hasakeh, if you were an hour late for an appointment, it didn't matter much. Everyone they knew had been from the same economic background, and they never felt self-conscious about being poor. Homs was entirely different, and Hozan was much better suited to their previous rhythm of life. If he was willing to finally get that new identity card, then for Ferhad it said something about how much Hozan was willing to adapt so that they would embark on this adventure together.

"You have this friend, you know?" Ferhad explains to me. "You have a friend from school; you have someone who, when you meet him, and you say, 'Come,' without asking you where, he will come. It's very important. Or go! He will come with you without asking where. It's your *friend.* Just come! He will just take his stuff and come with you. Or 'why?' Or 'where?' No, no, just come. It's very simple. This is a friend. You have this in Mesopotamia."

Homs is located on the opposite side of the country from al-Hasakeh, on the banks of the Orontes River, and halfway between Aleppo and Damascus. The third largest city in Syria with 1.5 million people, Homs had its own population of Sunni Muslims, diverse Christians, and Alawites living together. The Old City was home to a number of important buildings: the Church of St. Mary's Belt, or Umm al-Zinnar, constructed of white and black basalt with arching windows, said to contain the belt of the Virgin Mary. The courtyard of the mosque of Khalid ibn al-Walid contained the characteristic alternating light and dark stones of the Mamluk period. There was a generousness about the old markets, a sense of harmony, with mosques built next to churches and fountains within courtyards that offered water to the thirsty.

Their university stood outside of the Old City, straddling two neighborhoods. To the west was the Bab al-Amr neighborhood, and to the east were the Alawite neighborhoods known for their relationships with President Bashar al-Assad, who was also Alawite. Still, everyone went to university together, along with students from the length and breadth of Syria.

Ferhad had never seen anything like their music conservatory, complete with grand pianos, instructors from Russia, violin and cello and kanun players, practice rooms and lessons in theory. "You had a practice room all to yourself. You could learn harmony, theory," he said. It was a world of notes and scales, class times, exams. Ferhad and Hozan had always experienced music transmitted from one person to another, in the call-and-response method they had learned as children. Now they were being initiated into written transmission, where a song no longer had to be remembered in order to be saved. Ferhad, thrilled, saw in this the possibility of recording and transmitting Kurdish oral culture to the wider world.

Hozan, however, struggled to adapt to the rigid structures. He failed his first-year exams. To be more precise, he slept through them. "He had this idea: 'Even if God is waiting for me, I will not give up my sleep,'" Ferhad told me, laughing. "We had a friend who was a really hard worker, reading all of the notes, and Hozan would sit next to him and would learn the entire thing just from listening to him. It drove his teachers crazy."

When Hozan did show up for class, his fingers moved across strings with such deep intuition that the teachers sometimes burst into applause. That was just Hozan: refusing to relinquish his autonomy, his dreaminess, the deepest of himself. He would never place a higher value on what the university taught him than what he had learned from the ash-strewn fields of his boyhood. Those fields, that wheat, his father's voice, his brother: they, too, had been his teachers.

Ferhad had never been on an airplane. In the music conservatory, the world came to him in jazz and blues, Chopin and Bach and Mozart. He studied the Andalusian muwashahat songs still preserved by musicians in Aleppo, met Kurdish musicians from other areas of Syria like Kobane and Afrin. Together, they formed a band called Orient, which they nicknamed "Buzuqs and Other Instruments" because it had so many buzuqs. They were determined to teach the other students about their Kurdish heritage. In the world of music, he was finally given space to voice those stories he had long kept to himself.

> Hozan and I had this balance between us. Sometimes I was taking Hozan to my side, and sometimes he was taking me to his side—I was energetic, and he was tranquil. The beautiful thing between me and Hozan is that we know each other very deeply. When you are being not yourself, I can remind you of who you are. We listen to one another—we had our childhood in al-Hasakeh, and so when something was difficult in Homs, we could just go together to that peaceful place. We had that connection. Like you have someone who knows exactly who you are. You don't have to explain it. Hozan and I, we have this.

During that first year of studies, Ferhad received word that his sister, Evin, hadn't passed her exams in al-Hasakeh to enter pharmacy school. Ever since she was a child, she had wanted to be a pharmacist. She would tease Ferhad, "Don't worry, I'll give you the medicine for free since you're not good at school and won't have any money." But she had come up just a few points short on her exam, and now she would have to repeat the year.

She was his only sister, and she held a special place in the family. Evin—her green eyes with a honey gold in their center, kind and smart, a hard worker, doting on all of her brothers. She had such a sweetness, such a gentle playfulness about her, and he wondered what he could do to lift her spirits. He spoke with his friend who was a musician, and together they walked to the market and selected a simple violin with a pure, deep sound. With the little money that he had, he bought the violin for Evin.

When she first held it, her face took on such an expression of joy. Evin recognized herself in the violin, and she took to it so quickly. She didn't have a stand for her music notes, and so she strung a clothesline across her small room and hung her notes with clothespins, at eyes' length, so that she could practice. She would wake up every morning and play, sing, and write songs. She had such a beautiful singing voice.

Next, Ferhad tried to teach his younger brother Kani to play a few notes on the guitar so that he and Evin might play together even when Ferhad was away at school. Later, he would remember, and he would say it to himself, over and over again, *I brought music into the house.*

A year of studies passed in Homs. A second. A third. Ferhad prepared to enter his final year. He had not yet decided what he would do next. During the summer, he enrolled in a Spanish course in Damascus, dreaming that he might continue his studies in Spain once he graduated. Would he then join a band? Become a teacher? Open up an institute for music in al-Hasakeh so that others could receive these same gifts of learning notes and scales?

Take a moment, pausing, as you read this. Picture Ferhad—his hair down, his guitar balanced on his knee, playing. Listening to himself as he plays. Each note evokes a color, resonating as a language deep within himself.

Then see Hozan, holding a buzuq in his hand—that buzuq he has known since boyhood—and leaning into it, his fingers moving so quickly and so closely together. Watch them lean toward one another, listening.

See Evin, gazing at the sheets of music strung across her room. Moving the bow back and forth on her violin. Singing.

Take a moment. In order to hold the full weight of loss, we must first lean into what was and what might have been. What almost was, until it wasn't.

In December 2010, a Tunisian street vendor named Mohamed Bouazizi set himself on fire to oppose government corruption, leading to protests and the overthrowal of the government. The Arab Spring had begun. Soon, protests broke out in Egypt, leading to massive street demonstrations and the eventual toppling of the government. They continued to Yemen and Bahrain. In Libya, armed rebel forces took the government down. Still, few believed that the protests would arrive in Syria.

In 2011, demonstrations against the Syrian government broke out in Dera'a, in the south of the country. Largely peaceful protests followed in Homs. Thousands of people began to show up in the streets, with university students demanding popular reforms, freedom of speech, and greater participation in political life. Homs was quickly dubbed the "capital of the revolution." Yet any hope that the situation would remain peaceful was short-lived.

On April 19, 2011, the BBC reported that security forces had fired on protestors. By May, the news service was reporting that government tanks had entered the city.

The opposition armed. What had begun as a revolution would spiral into a civil war.

At about that time, Ferhad and Hozan were living in an apartment just at the entrance to the Old City. That crossroads soon became a center of the fighting as it was located directly between the Sunni and Alawite neighborhoods—what became strongholds of the opposition movement and the government. Ferhad and Hozan had moved from al-Hasakeh to Homs to become musicians, and instead they found themselves in one of the most dangerous cross-sections in the world. Hozan once again slept with his hand over his heart, afraid that an arrow would pierce it. They could hear gunfire outside.

"We were sleeping under the window, hiding," Ferhad tells me. "I kept saying out loud, 'We will not die.'"

One morning, they woke up to discover their ceiling riddled with bullet holes. They would not survive there much longer. They moved and rented an apartment in a basement, remaining in a state of denial, certain that the violence would soon pass. The university closed, but still they didn't leave Homs. Ferhad held out hope that the university would open just long enough for him to take the few classes he needed to graduate. Other musicians also stayed on, continuing to play for one another.

One night, they stayed out late, playing music at the house of a friend. It was early in the morning when they stumbled home, drunk. The streets erupted into gunfire. A man in a shop yelled, "What are you doing?"

"We're searching for maté," Ferhad joked, referencing the drink of dried leaves infused in hot water that the people of Homs famously loved.

"Come inside, or go home," the man shouted back.

They somehow found their way home. Ferhad knew it was sheer luck that they didn't die that night. That was the last time he saw any of those friends.

Ferhad and Hozan left Homs for Damascus. They remained in a state of shock. Ferhad tried to remain faithful to his lessons, teaching music in a school. They partied at night. He chose the most beautiful streets to walk on. He noticed every detail: the light, the way food was placed on a table, the pigeons circling the Qassioun Mountain. Looking back, he can recognize that he was saying goodbye.

At first, he told himself they would soon return to Homs. Then one major bomb exploded nearby. Soon a second, on the very street that Ferhad passed on the way to give lessons. His mother was frightened for him. It was time to return home, to return to al-Hasakeh. They would pass through Homs on the way to retrieve their belongings.

Everything was going dark. We were so tired. Civil war was starting. That day, Hozan was waiting for me in the bus station, and I had my guitar in my bag. And when he saw me, he began to cry. "Why are you crying?" I asked. He said, "With your guitar, you're beautiful." It was very dramatic. I knew then that we would not be back for a very long time.

12 | THE SPANISH PHRASE BOOK

In the first year of the war, large swaths of Syria remained largely untouched by fighting. When Ferhad and Hozan returned to their hometown of al-Hasakeh, life was continuing much as it always had. For the first time, however, that normality didn't comfort Ferhad but saddened him—reminding him of how disconnected parts of Syria remained from one another. The divisions in the society were now being exploited to turn communities against one another.

Ferhad felt the need to assure himself that all was not lost. He and Hozan decided to open a music school, to share some of what they had learned in Homs with their neighbors and in a bid to keep their sanity. Hozan offered to teach buzuq, and Ferhad taught music theory: notes and scales, clefs and fas that were, after three years of study, now entirely natural to him. Two of his students were blind, and he taught them how to visualize the notes using their hands, helping them to imagine half notes resting in the spaces between their fingers.

It was something small. A little thing to do in the face of war. For the next six months, they held classes for students as young as six years old. He and his friends soon formed a band. But the fighting in the country wasn't diminishing. No longer a student, which had exempted him from mandatory military service, Ferhad was now of the age at which he would be conscripted into the army.

Ferhad could not imagine killing his neighbors. The entire idea of violence was an anathema to him. He would have to escape, and there was only one way out of the country—with a smuggler. He would leave his entire world behind: his family, his dreams of musical education, the river where he had fished and watched the frog with the yellow stripe leap up, the world of his language, and Hozan, his soul friend, who was a few years younger and for the moment still had time. He packed a heavy bag—with his edition of Mahmoud Darwish's poetry, a Spanish phrase book from his course in Damascus, two changes of clothes, and a pair of his father's sandals. He would not be able to take his guitar with him, for it was too large and cumbersome to carry.

He stood in front of the house, waiting for the taxi to arrive. His sister, Evin, embraced him, sobbing. "I'll be back in one year," he told her, but she cried so hard that a relative finally pulled them apart. As the taxi left, his dog ran after it until they disappeared in the distance.

The smuggler had told him that his bag was too heavy. It wasn't only that it would be difficult to slide beneath the border fence but also that it needed to be light, in case he had to run from border guards. He emptied out the contents, one by one. The sandals. The clothes. The Mahmoud Darwish collection with his favorite poem, "Mural," whose words had been sounding in his heart: "Who has gone to sleep now, Enkidu? / Is it me or you?"

The Spanish phrase book. He knew it didn't make any sense for him to hold on to it. They didn't speak Spanish in Turkey, where he was going. Yet he couldn't imagine letting it go. It had always been Ferhad's dream to one day travel to Spain. He returned the book to the bag.

When he arrived at the border, another young man and two smugglers were there. Ferhad remained calm. They left late at night, running across a river, between rows of corn. He was wearing new shoes that pinched, and he ran through the pain. In the field of corn he changed his clothes, which had become covered in mud. They kept moving. The sun was now rising, and Ferhad looked up, confused at the sight of the color green. In Syria, there had been only desert. But they were on the other side of the border now, and here there were trees.

"When I crossed the border, I had the sense that I had forgotten something," he tells me. "Later, I realized that what I had left behind was myself. That Ferhad, who had lived in a place for twenty-six years, with all of the ways he had loved—I left him there. Maybe he's still there today."

The next years are a blur. I do not ask much about them, and Ferhad does not tell me much. We could say that Ferhad joined what is sometimes called the "lost generation" of Syrian youth: young people dispossessed by the war. When we say "lost," it can refer to the very things Ferhad and so many others lost: family, friends, ambitions, diplomas, a sense of safety in the world. Ferhad lost his community, where he could speak his language and feel completely himself; he lost his river and fields; he lost those markets, where he heard languages as music. It had taken such strength of purpose for him to leave his engineering studies to study music, and now he didn't have a degree to show for it. He had almost no money. He had always dreamed of traveling abroad—but not like this. He already spoke two languages, and now he would have to learn a third to get by in Turkey. He suffered from survivor's guilt, ashamed that he had found safety while the rest of his family, and so many friends in Homs, remained stranded in war. He drank, he smoked. In general, he tried his best to forget.

Hozan left Syria six months after Ferhad and immediately joined him in Istanbul. He, too, did not carry his buzuq with him. He had believed that the instrument he had seen hanging on nearly every wall in al-Hasakeh would be found easily in Istanbul. Only once he arrived did he discover its suchness. He learned that in Turkey, they played something similar, called the saz, but it was not the same.

Hozan decided that he would try to make his own buzuq—his brother had once made a tambur from the door of a bathroom when he was in prison—but the materials were too expensive. Eventually, someone would find a Syrian buzuq from Aleppo, made by master instrument maker Ibrahim Sukkar—and that buzuq would make its way to him in Istanbul. But that brief impulse to make his own—an effort that, for some reason, was chronicled in a short paragraph on the internet—was what would eventually lead me to their doorstep, looking for the buzuq.

Together again, Hozan and Ferhad played music in the streets of Istanbul. For a time, they lived on an island, sleeping in a tent for forty-five days and eating fish and mussels for food. Ferhad was grateful for those childhood days along the Khabur River, which taught him things he could not know that he would need. "Take your entire life as a classroom," he liked to say. He could not have known during those childhood summers what life was teaching him.

Years passed. He watched as Syrians he had known back home crossed through Istanbul to escape by sea to Europe. Others arrived, waiting in Turkey, hoping for the day they might go home again.

One night, during what would have been the Feast of Nowruz back home, Ferhad was drinking with his friends in a nightclub. Nothing felt so far away as the Kokub Mountain in Syria, the fires they had lit, and the songs they sang. Looking around, Ferhad felt a deep sense of sadness. His body and mind seemed heavy, and he sensed a weight in his chest.

"Let's go," he announced abruptly to his friends. He had the impression that everyone in the club was dancing but that no one was happy. "Let's get out of this place," he insisted again.

They left the nightclub and regrouped in someone's apartment nearby. His phone rang. Ferhad heard the voice of his younger brother Sherzad from a thousand miles away, in al-Hasakeh. "Come back," Sherzad whispered.

"What happened?"

"Just come back."

"Is it Father?"

"No," Sherzad answered, but then his voice closed up in his chest.

Ferhad couldn't imagine any other possibilities. Their uncle grabbed the phone from Sherzad. "It's Evin."

Ferhad laughed, incredulous. "What are you saying?"

"There was a terror attack. And she was there."

Ferhad hung up the phone. Evin. His only sister.

He began to shout. He cried out from a place deep within himself, not in his stomach but as though a hole had opened inside of him. He cried and cried so that the neighbors could hear him, and then no one moved for a long time. His friends understood. Someone was gone.

I do not ask Ferhad for the details of what happened to Evin. What I learn is from newspapers and human rights reports across the world, which later published that in March, 2015, ISIS targeted the Kurdish Feast of Nowruz in al-Hasakeh. Two car bombs killed approximately fifty people and wounded more than 150 others. Evin had been among those who died.

When I shouted that morning, I was just looking in the sky, from the small corner of the window, from that room where I was crying. Something crossed me, some piece of Evin came to all of us: me, my mom, my dad, Sherzan, Kani. And I think I got something from her voice—to sing and share my life with her with other people. I wanted to make happiness against the pain, the sadness.

Until that time, Ferhad had played the guitar. He understood now that it was time for him to sing. He needed to find again that voice from his childhood, the voice that had summoned the rain. It was his turn to remember.

Two months later, Ferhad met with a Turkish Kurdish mey flute player in Istanbul and asked her if she was interested in joining him and Hozan in creating a band of Kurdish music. He had often seen another Kurdish musician playing the def—a large, flat, round drum—in the streets of Istanbul, and he tracked him down, too, and asked him if he might join.

He and Hozan knew they wanted to save the songs of their childhood. They thought back to those afternoons, to the hour of asr, when they and the other kids of the neighborhood would sit in front of the woman, stirring the pots of wheat, listening as she transmitted the stories. They remembered the old man who played the songs, asking them to answer in call and response.

Yes, they would call their band Danûk, after the bowls of wheat, and they would sing their ancient songs, updated with a modern flair of trumpets and guitar. So much had been contained in their music: Love stories. Epic poems. Wind instruments, carrying the sound of the high mountains. Wedding songs, celebrating the bride and groom. Verses describing the curve of a woman's body. Songs crossing borders with mule drivers, connecting them even after borders were drawn between them, songs that helped them remember who they were, who they are.

As they began to practice, memories came back to Ferhad, of the weddings, the festivals, the fields of wheat. No, they weren't just saving music after all. They were saving joy.

"We are trying to hear happiness," Ferhad explains to me. "There are many people who are working on the war, making things about the sadness, the loss—okay, that's fine; everyone knows that. But there must be another road that reveals our strength."

He remembered their first concert in Istanbul. He looked out at the crowd. It seemed impossible: Kurds and Turks and Europeans all together. He began to sing the song from his childhood, "Nofa," about a boy in love with a girl he cannot have:

Endê were dikana, lei lei . . .

He looked out. The crowd was dancing.

13 | A DROP OF WATER

With music performances lined up, Ferhad and Hozan soon had enough money to afford to rent a proper apartment in Istanbul. When Hozan was sitting in a café one afternoon, he casually mentioned that he was on the lookout for a place. A man across the room, overhearing him, spoke up and said he had one available. Hozan followed him to take a look. The apartment, on the fourth floor of a house in the city's former Armenian quarter of Turlabasi, had once been a single unit but had since been split into two smaller apartments, the two halves separated by a wall. The available half had been rented for years to a man with a hoarding disorder, who had filled the apartment to the ceiling with his collection of coils and wires, cups and spoons.

Hozan went looking for Ferhad. They wanted to make a payment as soon as possible, before they were tempted to spend the money on something else. Together, they headed back in the direction of the place the man had shown him. Only Hozan could not remember where the apartment was.

They climbed hilly streets and descended them. Ferhad had the sense that they had come so close, only for stability to fall through their fingers. Hours later, Hozan and Ferhad circled back and found the apartment at last. It was worn down, simple, and cheap. They paid their first month's rent. It was now eight months since Evin had passed away.

They couldn't see through the wall in their new apartment to the next apartment, of course. But if they could have, Ferhad would have seen renovated rooms, unlike their crumbling half, and he would have seen a young woman named Mar, who had arrived in Istanbul after volunteering to work with young Syrian refugees on the Turkish border. She had golden hair and bright blue eyes. She was British but had lived most of her life in Spain.

On their first day moving into the apartment, Ferhad sat at the entrance, resting from moving boxes in and out. Mar walked by. "Merhaba," he said quietly in Turkish. Hello. She pretended not to hear him, turned her face, and walked on.

As for Ferhad, when he saw her, he felt a drop of water fall into his heart. That is how he would explain it to me: a drop of water.

"Who are these noisy new neighbors?" Mar often mumbled to herself. She found it difficult to sleep with Ferhad and Hozan playing music at what seemed like all hours of the night. Still, she didn't ask them to stop. That would mean actually speaking to them, and for the moment, Mar wanted to keep to herself.

She formally met Ferhad's little brother Kani first. Kani had recently escaped from Syria and was now staying with Ferhad as he was passing through Istanbul. He was still a teenager and often alone. One day, he arrived at Mar's door, holding an enormous bowl of popcorn, and introduced himself. She accepted it, ate it with her roommate, and returned the empty bowl. He appeared at the front door a few minutes later with the bowl full again. "He must have been making industrial quantities of popcorn," she would later tell me, laughing.

From her time of volunteering on the Turkish border, Mar had experience counseling young Syrian refugees, and so she sat with

Kani. She listened as much as she could. It was Kani who told her about Evin.

At the same time, everyone else around her kept talking about a young man named Ferhad. But she had never seen him, save for that brief encounter. One day, Ferhad came over to have coffee with her roommate and to give her a poster for an upcoming concert of their band. When he saw Mar, he introduced himself. "Where are you from?" he asked.

"I'm from Spain," she answered. A few minutes later, she took out her phone to show him the pictures of the old mill her parents had half-restored, stopping when they had run out of money.

"Perhaps I'll help you fix it one day," he said, surprised at his own words. He blushed. He didn't know where those words had come from. They didn't seem to belong to him. It was as if those words had been given to him.

Ferhad and Mar became friends. She was kind in a world that was often not kind. She accepted him exactly as he was, with the late nights and the smoking and the moments when he seemed to disappear inside himself. She was patient with him. In turn, he recognized that she had been wounded, and he gave her space. He waited for her.

One afternoon, they walked from their house to the open-air market together to shop for groceries. On the way back, she lost her footing, and all the oranges fell from her bag. They chased them down the hill to rescue them, laughing. He recognized the simplicity of it—like stealing pomegranates in an orchard, long ago.

They took care of one another. One day, Mar learned that Ferhad had to undergo an operation. She found herself arranging fruit on a platter to bring to his bedside.

He looked up at her from the bed and asked, "Do you want to stay?" She did.

So it was that Ferhad's world, slowly, began to take on a shape. He finally obtained a working visa that allowed him to legally stay in Turkey. He opened a bank account for the first time in his life. He found a job in Istanbul teaching music to refugees, and as he played his guitar with Syrian children, something inside of him began to heal.

"It was medicine," he says. "Until that time, I was keeping my pain inside and not showing it to anyone. Then I saw those children. One of the girls had lost her father in the war. Another boy was biting his hands to deal with trauma. I taught that boy to play the guitar. The girl began to sing. I saw that it wasn't only me. All of us—we have this pain. My mind started to open. It was good for me to work with kids. I didn't want to teach them how to play music—their situation was really hard, and so in many cases this wasn't possible. I was just trying to give them a small memory that they might return to later. The sense of possibility, that something else might one day happen to them."

Notes between notes. A plate of fruit. A job teaching music. A band. Hozan, still next to him. A life, beginning to regain some balance.

Even so, Mar lived in her half of the house, and Ferhad lived in his with Hozan, and at the end of the day, a wall stood between them. Until one day Ferhad announced, "Come to me, or I will break down that wall!"

And so Mar moved to his side of the house. And that is where I met her.

When Ferhad declared that he would break down the wall, he wasn't simply being theatrical. He was invoking his culture, the landscapes of his childhood, and the meaning of his own name. His parents had named him Ferhad after the hero of the legend of Ferhad and Shirin, a tale that exists in many forms throughout Kurdistan and Iran. This is the version that Ferhad told me:

Ferhad was a farmer in the castle of the queen. The queen was in love with Ferhad, but Ferhad was in love with the queen's sister, named Shirin. Soon, Shirin and Ferhad began to meet. They loved one another dearly.

But the queen said to Ferhad, "If you marry me, then you will be king, and you will live in the castle. How does that sound?"

Ferhad replied, "You are beautiful and kind, but I'm sorry—I am in love with your sister, Shirin."

Angry with him, the queen declared, "I will let you marry Shirin, but only after you open a hole in this mountain so deep that water rushes out of it."

He agreed. From that day on, he hammered the side of that mountain, breaking rock. For years, he hammered. One day, he finally broke so deep into the mountain that water rushed out, and a rock came out onto his chest and killed him.

When they saw the water, all the villagers went running to find Shirin. They called to her, "Shirin! Ferhad brought water!" And she came running. When she saw his body like that, she jumped into the river and killed herself. And when the sister saw this, she went crazy.

It's a sad story, a Kurdish story. But a beautiful one.

Ferhad slowly asked Mar more about her life. He told her about his own, about his journey across a border, with a sack too heavy to carry. He remembered the Spanish phrase book. He found it in among his belongings and asked her if she might help him learn how to speak.

◆ ◆ ◆

Ferhad believed there was not only a meaning but a destiny in a name. Evin means "love." Hozan means "artist." Ferhad means "rock"—the deepest core of the rock, the part that can't easily be moved.

Six months after they met, Ferhad took Mar out to the island where he had spent some of his most destitute months, living in a tent and fishing for his food. He asked her to marry him.

It was in about this moment in their story, a few months after Mar and Ferhad became engaged, that I went searching for a buzuq and knocked on their door. Ferhad and Hozan played "Nofa" for me, a song they had carried out of al-Hasakeh, across the border, and into that unassuming room in Istanbul. I listened. And I knew that as long as they continued to sing the songs, even if there was no one to hear them, those songs still existed. The stories had survived.

After Ferhad and Mar married, they moved to Spain, while Hozan stayed behind in Istanbul. In Granada, Ferhad learned to play flamenco guitar and speak Spanish, and with Mar, they made the first steps in restoring her family's house, just as he had promised.

Then they moved on to England while Mar pursued her studies, and while they were there, they invited me to visit. I met them this time in a small cottage with a garden, where they had rented rooms.

They learned to make room for one another. When Mar saw a certain look come into Ferhad's eyes, she would whisper, "Is a song coming?" And she would close the door and give him space to let the words come in.

It wasn't easy. His dream was to finally finish his music studies, but he would need to become completely fluent in English—his fifth language after Arabic, Kurdish, Turkish, and Spanish—if he hoped to apply to start all over again in England, years after he had escaped Homs in his final semester as a student. For the moment, he was working as a cook in a Lebanese restaurant, manning the kitchen and mopping floors. Those days in Istanbul, when he had sung in front of huge crowds, seemed far away. He had left one world and had not yet found his way in this one.

Every year, on the day of Evin's death, no matter where he was in the world, Ferhad planted a tree or flower in her name. He had not been able to return home for her funeral. This small act—of touching the soil and planting a seed or a sapling—became an act of faithfulness, of rooting himself in her and his grieving family.

He took me out to the garden to show me a magnolia stellata tree he'd just planted, already revealing its white flowers. Evin's trees were growing all over the world, in Turkey, in Spain, and now in a quiet corner of England: two jasmine plants, a pink bougain-villea, daphne flowers, a cherry tree.

"When the moon starts, like smiling, and has a star on one side, I see her face smiling," he says. "That's my theory. I haven't seen it many times, but when I do, I know she's happy with me. And when I do something wrong, I hear her say, 'You need to be stronger, more powerful.' And I hear her when I sing. And when I hear her, I cry."

Sometimes, when he was mopping the floor at the end of a long shift in the restaurant, Ferhad would wonder how his life had brought him, after all those twists and turns, to this anonymous corner in England, mopping a floor in exile. He would tell himself, *This is something that you have to cross.* And he would think back to Istanbul and the moments he was tempted to go back home to Syria, even in the war.

Yet whenever he was tempted to go back, he remembered a book that he had been given long, long ago by a girl he had been dating. They had broken up soon after, but he had kept the book, believing it had been given to him for a reason, that it contained a message for him inside of it. "In this book, a man said, 'If you go to an island, you will cross so many rivers, so many mountains, so many seas,'" Ferhad told me. "'But at least you will be on that island. In the middle of the way, you will be tired. Maybe you will think that you will go back. But don't go back. The distance for going back is the same as for going forward.'"

Ferhad knew that he was not one person but part of a chain. Perhaps one day, he, too, would be listed in the seven grandfathers—the chain of ancestors spoken out by children so that they might remember and understand how they belong to one another. His part was to sing what was his to sing, for as long as he needed to sing it, until someone could hear the songs and pass them down.

He would save what he could save. The melodies. The words, spoken in his language. The memory of Evin, embracing him, tears rolling down her cheeks. Laughter in the last days of Homs, before his friends disappeared. The moment at weddings during his childhood, when he and his friends danced and held one another by their small fingers, moving in circles. The bag full of fish; his auntie, sparking fire, calling the animals by their names. A field of wheat, where at the deepest point he and Hozan could find the silence that gave birth to music. All of this would be transformed into song. All of this would be remembered.

I closed the recorder. The story was finished for now, and we were back in England, the light coming into the room from the garden. Ferhad reached for his guitar, and he began to sing in Kurdish the song he had written long ago now, when he arrived in Istanbul—a summoning:

Lo Hevalo,
Hey, my friend,

Do you remember the warmth of the autumn fire
Next to the pot of cooking danûk?
The kindling we collected
The small plates
The songs and the games
The giggles and the gathering of youngsters
I call you from there
We are still those children
Lo Hevalo
Hey, my friend
Lo Hevalo
Hey, my friend.

He sat near the window, waiting. He did not know when or how, but he could feel it. Hozan would soon be on his way.

PART III

MUNIR'S LIGHT

Mosul, Iraq → Lesvos, Greece

See the beautiful patience of the candle,
Which offers itself as light even as the fire consumes it.
—attributed to Usama ibn Munqidh

14 | A HAIRCUT

From the plane, I could see only water, and more water, and a port town that appeared like a vision, surreal. I had arrived seemingly in the middle of nowhere, with no exit and no bearings.

It was 2017, two weeks before Christmas, and the sun was beating down into the cold. I caught a taxi from the airport to the hotel. The driver asked, "Are you here to visit, or are you here because of the refugees?"

The refugees. I had arrived on the island of Lesvos, home to the largest "hotspot" for refugees in Europe. I had recently read in the newspaper that the nearby refugee and migrant camp of Moria, designed for 2,330 people, had now swollen to more than seven thousand souls. They were only some of the fifteen thousand refugees and migrants from more than twenty countries being held in camps on different Greek islands, waiting to learn their fates. Now it was December, and refugees and migrants were worried they might freeze to death in the coming cold. I could not quite believe that refugees were being abandoned beneath trees to freeze on the shores of Europe, and so I had decided to come.

I had known for some time that I could not write about Syrians and Iraqis seeking refuge from war without confronting the terrible reality of the sea crossings. In Turkey, reminders of the sea crossings were ever-present. I met a Syrian woman whose brother had made the crossing from Turkey to Greece with his disabled son. Their boat eventually crashed, and when they were rescued, the family was placed in a detention center on the island of Kos. In Istanbul, I had interviewed a Syrian art gallery owner who built an entire vault to hold the paintings of refugee painters who were crossing the sea from Turkey, unable to carry their canvases with them and so at risk of losing their life's work. His basement contained the other belongings artists left behind: cigarettes and medicines, suitcases and powdered soup, all of those possessions that no one can carry when they are allowed only the smallest of bags to cross the sea.

Now it was December, the last month of a year in which more than 171,635 migrants and refugees had entered Europe by sea. At least 3,116 had died in the crossing. These numbers were only a fraction of the nearly one million refugees and migrants who had crossed the sea two years earlier, during the peak of the refugee crisis in 2015. In the meantime, sentiment against refugees had hardened in Europe, making it increasingly difficult both to cross and to find settlement there.

The landing at the airport on Lesvos had been jarring, the view from the air revealing clear waters, blue skies, nothing to suggest that I had arrived anywhere other than a tourist island in the Aegean Sea. My hotel stood just on the port with a view out into the water, and I checked in and dropped off my bags before heading for a stroll through the town of Mytilene. The port circles the water at the base of several hills so that the houses, with their red roofs, seem to pile one on top of another. In the harbor, fishing boats swayed side by side, anchored alongside a larger boat that I thought might be for tourists until I looked closer and saw, marked clearly along the side of it, "Border Force."

It was the holiday season. In the town square, a cabin had been converted into a life-sized nativity set, and children scampered inside to have their photos snapped. The statue of a wise man, taller than me, wore a pink suit, a blue cloak, and a green head covering and held what might have been myrrh. Across the square, an even larger figure of Santa Claus was pushing a white sleigh, flanked by two reindeer.

I slipped off the main corniche and into the back alleys of the town, and the quaint streets gave way to graffiti. Something shifted. I spotted two men walking beside two women pushing strollers with two babies inside, the women wearing long black robes and veils. They looked exhausted and scared—and completely out of place. I approached one of them, shyly, and asked in Arabic where she was from.

"From Deir Ezor," she answered. She introduced herself as Bisan, and I placed my hand over my heart in greeting. The city of Deir Ezor in Syria had been under ISIS rule for nearly three years before it had fallen, after ferocious fighting, that November. She seemed confused and overwhelmed. She had been on the island for four months, she told me. They had fled to Turkey and then had been smuggled by boat to Lesvos, where they were currently stranded and waiting to hear if they could continue onto the mainland of Europe.

"We fled Daesh," she said. "We fled the government. We fled everyone."

The sight of a young family plucked out of the throes of war and now wandering the streets of a Greek port town of tourists and locals posing with nativity sets didn't make any sense. She waved goodbye. The war had not left her yet; it was in her eyes. She looked afraid against the backdrop of the sea.

I walked back to the hotel. On the way, I passed two young men absently watching the waves. "Where are you from?" I asked.

One of them answered, "From Yemen." The country was in the middle of a violent civil war, but I'd had no idea that civilians were making it as far as Greece.

"Are there a lot of people from Yemen at Lesvos?" I asked him.

He shrugged. "There's thirty or forty of us." He had traveled from Yemen to Egypt, from Egypt to Turkey by plane, and then by boat to the island. "The crossing is dangerous," he said. "The food they give us is dangerous. It's all bad."

Back at the hotel, I asked at the front desk how I might travel to Moria, the migrant and refugee camp on the island that had become the largest camp in Europe. I expected that a camp with seven thousand people packed inside in poor conditions would be difficult to access, hidden from ordinary islanders and visitors so as not to expose the scandal of it all. But no—the receptionist assured me that accessing Moria was easy. A bus left from the harbor every hour or so, for the price of a euro, and the ride to the camp was about fifteen or twenty minutes long. The bus stop was just outside, near the Christmas trees and the nativity set. If I got lost, I could ask anyone.

Since March 2016, when a European Union–Turkey agreement determined that no one could leave the island until their asylum status had been processed, the entire island of Lesvos had become a de facto prison for refugees and migrants, placed in the wide open in what in normal times had been a holiday destination. Refugees often waited for months on end, surrounded on all sides by the sea that had brought them there but that just as easily might have killed them. Long gone were the days in 2015 when refugees arrived on the island shores and were allowed to pass onto the mainland unimpeded. The horrors of Moria were no secret: newspapers regularly quoted refugees who referred to it as "hell," and Pope Francis, after visiting, had gone as far as to call it a "concentration camp."

The next morning, I waited at the bus stop in the central square. A young man sat down beside me on the bench. He was wearing a red puffy winter jacket decorated with triangles. I asked him in Arabic which bus I might take to the camp, and he suggested that I travel with him. And so I did, climbing on, once it came, a bus crowded with men and women and children from Iraq and Afghanistan and Pakistan and Algeria and Syria and the Congo, each one taking their seat, some looking out the window as the bus wound through the Greek countryside. We passed a soccer field, and the man beside me mentioned that all of the players on both teams scrimmaging each other were refugees.

The young man's name was Ahmed, and I asked him about his life. He was married and had three children. In Basra, Iraq, he had owned a coffee shop, and his wife had owned a beauty salon. His coffee shop had been bombed, and he had decided they'd better go. He was the first of many Iraqis I would meet from the city of Basra, and from them I learned that when the security forces from the city had gone north to fight ISIS, the city had been taken over by militias. Those young men afraid of being pulled into the fighting were making their way to Turkey and then across the Mediterranean Sea, along with others from their country who could finally escape the stranglehold of ISIS in places like Mosul.

Ahmed had attempted the crossing five times before succeeding, and he laughed sadly as he described why each try had failed: the waves had been too high, the raft wouldn't inflate, the Turkish police had arrested them. When he had finally succeeded, he'd arrived at an island prison camp.

Journalists were no longer permitted to enter Moria, and I told Ahmed that I would need to find a way inside the camp. I had read of journalists sneaking in at night or through the holes in the fence that had been cut around the periphery. He shrugged. "You'll enter with me," he said. I laughed, but then I realized he wasn't joking.

The camp appeared in the distance, sprawling, entirely enclosed in barbed wire. We exited the bus and walked up the hill to the main entrance, which was manned by guards. I assumed a posture of confidence, speaking to Ahmed in Arabic loudly enough for the guards to hear. We walked through the entrance to the camp together, and no one looked twice at me.

He shrugged. "I told you," he said.

Perhaps I spoke a bit much from then on: I was frightened. It was freezing cold despite the sun overhead, and I dug my hands into my pockets, shivering. I passed in front of the police, beneath the guard towers, beside volunteers. No one looked at me—in fact, they seemed to look through me, as if I didn't exist. If I had ever needed a reminder that there is no difference in humanity between a refugee and myself—that in other circumstances I could easily be a refugee—then here it was.

We entered into the nightmare of the camp. I was now engulfed in a scene of wire fencing and noise and stench and babies crying. People were living in rows upon rows of white shipping containers, laundry was hanging on fences, and bins of trash overflowed into the alleyways. There weren't nearly enough white containers for everyone, and so every remaining inch of ground was also filled with a tent. People had urinated and defecated under the trees outside rather than using the bathrooms, which were filthy and dangerous. Piles of trash collected beside the tents in which children slept.

Ahmed led me toward a white shipping container, the last in a line of containers standing on a steep incline. Inside, men and women and children sat in a circle, as though passengers in a train car. I ducked inside. Mohammed, from Aleppo, had been living in the camp for more than five months with his four children. He told me their ages: ten, seven, five, and four years old. As they clambered around me, his wife offered me a glass of tea. I could only imagine how precious a bag of tea was, and I drank it carefully.

They showed me their meager daily food rations, described the filthy toilets without water. I asked them about the cold, and they thanked God. In the container, they were at least protected—not like others in tents, who had rain and snow falling directly on their tents without respite. Mohammed told me that he had once complained about the lack of bread, and the guard had shouted at him, "You don't like it? Then go back to Turkey!"

Others in the circle had just arrived that week, at night, and though they spoke to me in Arabic, they were Kurdish Syrians. Mustafa, who had been a shopkeeper in Aleppo, handed over his cell phone to show me a video of his recent crossing. His family had slept for ten days in the mountains before being led by a smuggler to the sea. He pointed to their faces: his wife and children, freezing in their winter hats, crowded into a rubber dinghy, among orange life vests, arms of women holding infants wrapped in blankets, and the sound of waves lapping in the background. He moved ahead to a second video, of the dinghy landing in the port and people falling over one another as they tried to disembark, wailing. In the background, I could hear his voice calling out to his children over and over in Kurdish.

"What are you saying?" I asked.

"I'm saying, 'Don't be scared. Don't be scared. Don't be scared.'"

It was December 2017. The Islamic State had finally been wrested from most of Mosul, from parts of eastern Syria, and the camp was swelling with souls from Raqqa and Mosul and Deir Ezor—those who had been trapped for years and were only now able to escape. Now Turkey was preparing to invade Afrin in the north of Syria, setting off another wave of refugees, including these.

Since the European Union–Turkey agreement, which gave Turkey six billion euros of aid in exchange for stopping the flow of migrants and refugees to Europe, Turkey had been arresting refugees attempting to cross, making the passage difficult and dangerous. Now boats crossed not when the waters were calm but when it was least likely that they would be caught. Many had tried the sea crossing multiple times before they arrived, some robbed in the process.

I was anxious inside of the camp, and we exited. I wandered in the direction of the hundreds of refugees and migrants living beneath the olive trees outside of the camp gates. Some lived there because they could find no space in the camp proper; others, after years of war, were scared to sleep in any enclosed space where they might be trapped and unable to escape. A teacher from Deraa, Syria, guided me around the periphery of the camp. He pointed out human excrement on the ground so that I wouldn't dirty my shoes. Children wept. In a field, men bathed in their underwear with water spouting from a hose. A man sat his friend in a chair, in a field full of trash, and gently gave him a haircut.

I had been to refugee camps all over the Middle East, none of which was as terrible as this. I knew there was no reason for it to be so awful, and so I could only come to the conclusion, as many had before me, that the camp was intentionally awful so that refugees would stop fleeing to Europe. It was a strategy to make the arriving even worse than the staying behind.

Only it wasn't working. People were still selling everything they had to pay for the crossing. It turns out that escaping from war isn't a fiction but a reality and that people will go to great lengths to stay alive.

I wandered to a small encampment on the farthest edges of the camp, where recent arrivals from Deir Ezor in Syria were living together. A group of men were warming themselves next to trash they had set on fire. Alaa al-Din, there with his wife, rubbed his hands together. Nearby, the enormous piles of trash from the camp had not been collected.

"May God give you health," I greeted him.

"It's been a long time," he said quietly, "since anyone has spoken to me politely like that." He had arrived with his new wife to

Lesvos only a few weeks before. He was still confused by how they were being treated.

"When there was a war in Iraq in 2003, and missiles were striking the population, all of the Iraqis escaped across the border to us in Deir Ezor, and we didn't put them in a camp," he told me. "We brought them into our houses, we gave them the same food that we eat, and we gave them the same drink that we drink. We did for the people what no one did for us. We had heard that the European countries are advanced. We'd heard these things on the radio. But all of it was lies. We've seen a different reality. They live in hotels and homes, and they leave a child here—sleeping in the cold at night, with no doctor, nothing."

I strained to hear him over the sounds of children wailing beside us. He moved closer to the fire. "Here, you find four or five people in a tiny tent. In Syria, we wouldn't even put chickens in a home like this. We had a donkey, and in winter we had a kind of jacket we would put on him—and he's not a person! But look at the ticket on my clothing. It says 'Made in Syria' because I'm in Europe, but still no one has offered me any clothes. I'm a person like any person. We left our country. There was no food, no water; there were bombs at night. If they saw anyone, they would kill them. We were caught between two stones: those who attacked us and those who came to liberate us. It never ended. In the end, there was no choice but to leave if we had any hope for a future."

He was quiet for a moment, surveying those wandering around him in the cold. "We don't feel like people," he continued. "I feel like this is a prison, not a camp. We have the same routine as animals. We wake up, and we are fed. And sometimes we wait in the line only to throw the food away because it isn't edible.

"The people who died in Syria—they were ordinary people," he continued. "Teachers. Farmers. A man goes to plant his field, and then suddenly he's dead. Those who were fighting the war—they had somewhere safe to retreat. But the rest of us had nowhere to go. A man would die not by carrying weapons but in trying to go buy bread."

I asked him when he had escaped Deir Ezor. He responded that they had escaped in October, two months before. "We married, and we left," he said.

15 | A CANDLE

When I first saw Munir, he was helping women dismantle their tents in order to move their belongings inside of the camp, where spaces had opened up. He seemed to have an energy around him, and I watched as one person after another asked him for help. The next time I saw him, he was standing beneath the olive trees, beside his blue and fluorescent-green flimsy tent, marked, for some reason, with the number 4019.

Munir had placed his tent on top of a wooden palate, with an additional layer of cardboard pushed as a carpet beneath it, in an attempt to keep the cold of the ground from seeping up. One of those ubiquitous blankets of golden foil that rescuers wrap around refugees when they land had been repurposed: it was draped beneath an additional blue tarp over the tent roof to keep in some warmth. It was a dangerous place to be cold. The year before in Lesvos, five people in the camp had died. In other camps throughout the Middle East, kerosene tanks had exploded, and refugees had lost their lives from inhaling the fumes of burning plastic.

Munir stood out as the oldest in a crew: Mustafa from Gaza, Murtada from Basra, and a few people from the Bedoon class in Kuwait, a stateless group of citizens whom I was also now hearing about for the first time. Lesvos, it seemed, would be a crash course in every major disaster or political tension from South Sudan to

Afghanistan. The island had become a textbook of every crisis as it was unfolding in real time.

This was some gang of boys and young men; there was something kind and exhausted and also schooled in toughness about them, and they laughed a lot and welcomed me. In the camp, they had nicknamed Munir Abu Nur, the "Father of Light," since he had something deeply fatherly about him but had no children. When I met him, he was speaking to Murtada, another Iraqi, and they seemed to revel in one another's company. I recognized in them the realism of a certain generation who had been betrayed by such a vast array of people that they could no longer be manipulated by either political factions or religious ideology. They were done being used.

Munir was Sunni Muslim, and Murtada was Shiite Muslim. The only good thing about the camp, they told me, was that here at least Sunni and Shiite Iraqis could be friends. "In Iraq," Murtada said, "they were trying to get us to kill one another."

The young men had set up camp beneath the olive trees, on a high place. In front of us, in the distance, you could see the sea. When they spoke of Turkey, they liked to point in that direction, as though it were close enough to touch. Down the hill, refugees from countries in Africa lived in their own encampments—countries like South Sudan, the Congo, Ethiopia, Eritrea, Egypt, Algeria, Ghana, Somalia, and Nigeria—as did the refugees from Afghanistan. A tension had built up between the refugees who fled war and those whom they perceived had fled by choice. Stories of fights and of rocks thrown at night were common.

In the meantime, they were waiting for their asylum interviews, which might take months. If someone became sick, he would go into the camp to wait for a doctor, who often didn't speak Arabic.

"You have a cold? Take aspirin! Your stomach hurts? Take aspirin! You've been stabbed? Take aspirin!" Mustafa cried out, and they all howled with laughter.

A young man who had recently arrived from Deir Ezor passed in front of us. He and his wife had built their own tiny tent, barely large enough for two people to stand in. Unlike the other tents in the camp, he had fortified theirs with large concrete cinder blocks. She was pregnant.

Munir waved to him. "Poor guy," he told me quietly. "His whole family was killed."

At the end of the day, I returned to Mytilene and to my hotel with its view of the sea. The kind man at the front desk handed me the key to my room. I did not know what was more troubling—the camp itself with its thousands of trapped souls or the village of Mytilene, where everything went on as normal despite the horrors nearby. Restaurants and hotels, Christmas trees. Hand-painted pottery for sale. A buffet at breakfast, with as many olives and as much cheese as I could fit on my plate.

I returned to Moria the next morning with an appointment to speak with Munir again. I found my way to the olive grove, and when someone called his name, he emerged, disheveled, from his tent. He had stayed awake late, until it felt safe to sleep, and was only now rousing at eleven. He coughed from deep within his chest. It was cold. We sat on the small palate of tent number 4019. People left us alone, as though they understood that Munir needed a space in which to tell his story.

Munir is an imposing man, with broad shoulders and a large build, and still at the same time gentle, quiet. He seemed bigger than the frame of that small tent he had slept in that night, and I wondered how he had found space inside of it. Despite the noise and chaos of the camp, a silence seemed to settle around the story itself, as though it occupied a space and was determined to hold it. I would ask him about Mosul, a city I had never seen with my own eyes.

He made a place for me on his wooden palate and found just the top of a broken plastic table that he could position in front of me so that I had something on which to write in my notebook. I asked him about home. He began to speak, his voice full of compassion.

We're from the old families of Mosul. My great-grandfather was a general in the Ottoman army. We were from some of the first people who lived in the Old City, the area from which Mosul actually emerged. Close to us was the Church of al-Tahira, the mosque of Imam Ibrahim, one of the oldest mosques in Mosul, the mosque of the Prophet Girgis. Nearby, there's the ruins of a castle known as Qalaa' Bash Tabiya, from the Ottoman forts that are old.

He waited as I paused to write and then continued:

When outsiders tried to invade Mosul, they couldn't because they were unable to break through the walls of that fort. I'm talking about Janab al ayman, the right side of Mosul. Nearby, there was also Karasaray—that's a Turkish word.

"Where travelers slept?"

That's right. We were living near the fifth bridge; there were five bridges in Mosul. Another place near my house was the mosque of Imam Abdul Rahman Mohammed—these are all old historical places—and sadly, they destroyed all of it. One of the famous places in our area is Ras al-Kor, and al-Farouk Street, and the area of Shahwan, and the area called Meydan. These are the oldest areas that are now almost completely destroyed. It was the neighborhood of The Hour, which has the Church of the Hour, the most famous church in Mosul that has a clock tower in it.

He spoke every neighborhood, every street name, with a kind of reverence. Nearby, a young boy kicked a can in circles, and the sound of that can pulled me away from the Mosul he was conjuring and back again to our surroundings.

"What was your neighborhood like?" I asked.

The area we lived in was called Dawrat al Mustashfa—we are Muslim, but there were Christians living in three sides around us. There were many Christians in the area. There were Assyrians speaking the Assyrian language, and they used to tease me in their language about my mustache and beard. That's what I remember.

There was no difference between us as Muslims and Christians. We weren't really speaking to our neighbors—if they didn't speak to us, we didn't speak to them. But a woman from the neighboring house, who was Christian, started screaming one afternoon and asking for help. My mom went and asked what was going on. The woman said, "My husband got into an accident." My mom said, "I'll send my son to sort it out," and that's what I did: I took care of it. I vouched for the man, and the man was very grateful, and our relationship became closer. So we started sitting together, eating together—we became a family.

The problems started after 2003, when the extremists started kidnapping people. Some of the incidents happened to my neighbor when mobs took over, and they started asking him for money. This is when we went and sat with them and supported them. But then they left the area because he was scared for his children. This is when the Christians started to leave Mosul; there were a lot of car bombs. I know a person whose life was ruined because of these—he had a permanent paralysis and disfiguration because of it.

"The problems started in 2003?" I repeated as I wrote it down. This was the year of the US-led invasion of Iraq, when in the chaos that followed a wave of sectarian violence broke out, setting off the mass exodus of Christians. He continued:

> Well, of course it began much earlier than that, from the 1990s, when the first war started, and there were the sanctions that consumed the economy of Iraq and the infrastructure. But after 2003, the Christians started leaving.
>
> At the beginning of the war in 2003, some Christians lived with us for a time: a woman and her daughter, and after a while her sister and her sister's son came with them. They were our neighbors, wall to wall. They were scared. Because my father and I were older, we were protection, and while they were with us in our house, no one could dare come in our house. In case there was any attack, they were under our protection. We were at the fifth bridge, where you can see the horizon, and we would go up and see how the American tanks would destroy those who were trying to resist them. They'd strike them, and the firing would happen in front of us, and we would hide.
>
> In 2003, al-Qaeda started kidnappings in Mosul. The Christians got kidnapped because they were peaceful people, and they always negotiated with them for ransom money. The extremists took money from them. After that, the Christians left for Qaraqosh, to Karamleis, to al-Qosh—they went to live there.
>
> There was a long silence.
>
> But even until now we are keeping in touch with them. The girl who lived with us is my sister's friend, and now she is living in America.
>
> There was another church nearby—there were people living inside of the church, and some of their girls would come and stay with us for long periods. And me and my father would purposefully stay at work for long hours so that they would feel

comfortable in our home. At night, I would take them back to their house when it was safe.

By 2006, very few Christians remained in Mosul. These who stayed were protected by their neighbors, who were making sure they didn't get hurt. Their neighbors guaranteed for them that they would be safe. But eventually we all knew it was wiser for the Christians to go outside of Mosul.

I listened to him, sitting frozen on that palate on a Greek island, surrounded by filth and the smell of excrement. It already seemed too much to take that his entire neighborhood, with all its churches and mosques, had been destroyed. But he was also of the last generations from Mosul that would ever speak of those relationships between Christians and Muslims because all of that was gone. A bombed mosque or a church might be rebuilt. But a city without its people will never be the same city again.

The horror of war is perhaps most purely seen in the fact that a certain social order breaks down. Those who were known for taking care of others now, out of a kind of instinct to survive, might be tempted to think of themselves or their families. Those details of humanity, of human goodness, might give way to a kind of need to survive. And a certain despair comes in the inability to predict who will remain selfless, who will think of others first.

And yet there are people like Munir, who, in the depths of war, discover what it means to give themselves to others completely. I asked him if he had studied. He paused for a moment and then spoke carefully:

My situation didn't allow me to study. So I became the candle by which my sisters studied. I tried to give them what I couldn't have. They all completed their educations. All three of my sisters graduated in computer science. It was so dangerous at that time that I had to take them by my hand to the university and wait for them at the door to take them home, despite the dangers. There was a big chance that I was going to die from a bomb, but I was waiting for them.

I was the oldest child. My day was full, from one moment to another. I would take one sister to school, and then I would go back to take one to university. Sometimes I would do my work delivering things in the car. Then I would go to school, take my sister home, and then go to the university to get my other sister. That was my daily life.

Later, I had several jobs—I worked in a gym as an accountant. Then I learned about training and became a personal trainer. Then I left it and worked in a women's clothing shop. I had good manners, and, thank God, women felt comfortable to come buy from me. After that, I worked in a place for medical aid. We would sell first-aid equipment to the hospital. But the guy I worked with got kidnapped and negotiated for ransom, and so I left my job. After that, I worked in communications.

In June 2014, ISIS took over Mosul, and everything changed.

We all stayed home because we were scared of going out. A group of the engineers who worked with me were accused of using the communication towers to work for the government, and they were executed. And I was scared to go out because of that.

I was in the house with my family—my two brothers, my four sisters, and my father—because my mom died; she had a brain aneurysm, and she died in my arms. I had taken her to the hospital, and my father called me, and I told him that she was fine—while at that moment, with my hands, I was putting her in the freezer of the hospital. That was between 2009 and 2010. I had taken her to the hospital with the eldest of my sisters—that sister sacrificed everything to take care of all of us. Even to this day, she hasn't married in order to be the mother figure in the house.

So we stayed at home after ISIS took over Mosul completely. At the beginning, it didn't feel like anything, and people were even able to leave Mosul. But we didn't move because it's hard to leave your house, everything you founded your life upon with the sweat of your own hands. It's not easy to leave everything. And so we stayed in Mosul.

And this is when ISIS started making their own regulations, and new decisions were announced about the dress code, about cutting the beards; there were many things that were forbidden, lots of them, and so we adjusted to this life against our wills because we were forced to, because those who stood against it were killed, and a person negotiates his own life. For those who escaped from Mosul, they confiscated his money, his property, and his house—while those who stayed in Mosul lived under dark injustice. We tried to keep out of the way—really keep out of the way. We didn't go out, and all of the women started wearing a full covering over their face. They had to wear a full cover—for example, my sister was near-sighted, and sometimes she would cover her face and actually fall down.

Munir stopped his story. Some of the men from the camp had come up to show me their food rations—a small box of sticky rice and rubbery chicken that looked translucent and slimy on top. They asked me to smell it. "She knows the food is gross. Please don't put that in her face," Munir told them.

One of the men shrugged. "Either we'll die of the food, or we'll die of hunger," he answered. They wandered off, and Munir returned to his story.

When Iraqi and American-backed forces came to liberate Mosul, it did not feel like liberation to the people still trapped inside of their houses. Mosul was densely populated, and the fighting would be the largest urban battle since World War II: house to house, with civilians stuck in the crosshairs. Twelve hundred Iraqi soldiers died, and six thousand were wounded. That year, the Associated Press would estimate that between nine thousand and eleven thousand civilians were killed in the battles, including a third killed by bombardments led by the US or Iraqi forces. Architectural treasures initially spared by ISIS were ravaged by the fighting. US and Iraqi forces used white phosphorus in urban neighborhoods, with the potential that any ordinary civilian could suffer horrific burnings and die. In the meantime, ISIS was using civilians as human shields. The operation to liberate Mosul would take more than a year.

When a window finally appeared in which they might escape, Munir fled with his family. They knew there was a huge risk in leaving. It was not only that they might get caught in the crossfire but that ISIS considered those from Mosul who fled as traitors and had no qualms about firing on them directly.

The day his family left, they escaped by walking over bodies. A shell fell nearby, and his sister fainted. Munir had been carrying a bag of their clothes, so he dropped the bag and carried his sister.

A car exploded. He felt a piece of something metallic go into his arm.

That was sometime in September or October 2017, he thinks. He was exhausted. His city was destroyed. As the oldest son, he was responsible for his family, and the best hope that he could offer was to travel to Europe and try to bring his family over later.

He traveled north, where he paid a smuggler, which was the only way out of the country for those who had no connections. He joined a group of other refugees, and together they began to walk. He had no idea how long they would walk or where they were heading. They climbed mountains, went down into villages, slept in a valley. He lost his bearings. The smuggler handed them off to another smuggler, who took them to Turkey.

He felt most himself when he could help those families fleeing with their small children. "I'm a helper," he explained to me quietly. He would carry their bags or carry the children when they became tired. Sometimes they were able to travel in daylight. Other days, they had to walk in the dark.

When they arrived at the coast of Turkey—like thousands of refugees before them—they waited for instructions from smugglers on how to cross by sea. The route to Greece was short—but dangerous. Boats often took great risks not to get caught.

On his first attempt to reach Lesvos, Munir climbed onto a crowded rubber dinghy. They made it more than halfway to Greece before the Turkish police captured them and brought them back to shore.

On the second attempt, the waves were too high, and the engine of the boat became flooded and stopped working. The waves carried them back to the coast where they had begun. They arrived wet, freezing in the cold.

The third time, the Turkish coast guard took them again at sea.

The fourth time, fishermen informed on them, and they were taken back.

The fifth time, it was the military, not the coastal police, who caught them.

The sixth time, he arrived.

"But there are people here in the camp who tried nine times before they crossed," he added.

"It took me ten," a young man who was listening called out.
"Thirteen times!" someone else called out.
Munir continued:

Our rubber dinghy approached the coast, and after we entered into the Greek sea, the coast guard noticed us. I speak a little bit of English, so I spoke to the coast guard and said, "Are you Greek?" And he said yes. And I said, "Do you promise me that you'll take us to Greece?" And he said, "I promise." I repeated my words again, and he said, "I promise." This is when they took us up to the ship, and they took us to the port. It was cold, cold. Our clothes were soaking wet. They registered us. And that's the end of the story.

They registered him and later dropped him off at the camp in Moria. He had been pulled forward by the hope that there would be safety—human goodness, waiting somewhere at the end of the journey in Europe. Instead, he was stunned when he saw the conditions of the camp.

"I expected humanity," he admitted. "In the end, I discovered that I was more humane than they are."

He bought his own tent. He waited. When places opened up inside the camp, he helped the women and elderly fold up their tents and carried them inside.

Then he returned again to his tent outside of the camp gates. He was claustrophobic. It was better beneath the trees.

16 | THE SMALL KINDNESS

I left Moria and returned home for Christmas. I traveled to northern Iraq again in the new year, but I was too exhausted, and I couldn't work, and so I returned home again. The image of Munir and that group of boys wouldn't leave me. Munir had left me with only the fragment of a story that I couldn't quite follow: I would not go to Mosul, and even if I could, too much in his story had already been destroyed. I knew that I would not return to Lesvos. Sometimes the unasked questions must become part of the story, too. So much of the aftermath of war seemed to be the bewildering act of attempting to make history out of shards, moments, and things that will never make sense, even if all of the information was available.

I didn't hear from Munir again until Easter, when he sent an electronic card wishing me a happy Easter and letting me know that he was okay. I received another message the following Christmas, a year after I'd traveled to Moria. After years of living in the Middle East, I recognized these small greetings not just as messages. They were deliberate acts of resistance, ways of keeping alive intercommunal relations between Muslims and Christians that were vanishing in Mosul and across the region. Inherent in each was the message: "What is important to you is therefore important to me."

I tried to read what I could of Munir's Mosul—the city he had breathed alive for me in his stories within the camp. I soon learned that archaeologists had long overlooked Mosul's importance, seeing it as a place to sleep as they explored the nearby Assyrian ruins of Nineveh. What they had missed was a remarkable urban landscape of interdependency, where mosques and churches had been built nearby one another, where Sunni and Shiite Muslims, Christians, Jews, Assyrians, Armenians, Mandaeans, Shabaks, Turkmen, and others had historically lived side by side. Mosul had been cosmopolitan, with a vibrant university, a library, and beautiful old Ottoman houses in the Old City.

If the physical space of a city tells us something of its character, then the story of Mosul was one of coexistence—of an organic belonging, to one another and to history. The inhabitants of the Old City even spoke their own dialect of Arabic—called Moslawi—which contained words in Kurdish, Persian, and Turkish. The language was itself a spoken memory of the city's location as a rich cultural crossroads of trade.

It was also holy. For Jews and Christians, Mosul was the location of Nineveh, described in the Old Testament, and the home to ancient Jewish and Christian communities. Muslims called it the City of the Prophets, for it held the tombs of five Muslim prophets: Jirjis, Daniel, Seth, Jonah, and al-Khidr—evidence of the sanctity and wisdom that had long emerged from within those city walls. Some mosques held the tombs of holy men and the descendants of the Prophet Mohammed. Throughout Iraq, many Muslims, Christians, Jews, and Yazidis had long believed that visiting the tombs of saints and holy people could be a source of blessing, or baraka. The Old City of Mosul had been living evidence of that tradition. The fact that these shrines were so embedded within the architectural fabric of the city itself meant that this blessedness could not be separated from the details of daily life—walks and trips to the market, glasses of tea. Munir's neighborhood had been imbued with blessings. I remembered the way he spoke the names of each shrine, each market, with utter care.

When ISIS took over Mosul in June 2014, they set out to sys-
tematically destroy its history of religious tolerance. Members of
ISIS carried the most extreme interpretation of Salafi Islam. Abu
Bakr al-Baghdadi, the self-proclaimed caliph of the Islamic State,
stood on the pulpit of the city's storied al-Nouri Mosque to declare
the beginning of the Caliphate. Then ISIS set out to destroy the
memory of any other Islamic traditions that had ever existed in
Mosul. They ordered the local Christians to convert, pay a tax, or
leave, upon pain of death. Thus ended a community of Christians
who had lived in the city since the fifth century; it was also the end
of relationships that were part of the city's character.

Physical destruction followed. For ISIS, shrines and tombs were
evidence of idol worship. They would set out to erase the evidence
of any mosques built over the tombs of saints, those holy people so
many of the Muslims of Mosul had long believed blessed their city.

So much media coverage had focused on ISIS' destruction of
ancient archaeological treasures that I had not quite understood,
until I met Munir, just how much the focus of their attention had
been on demolishing Islamic heritage. During their years in Mosul,
ISIS would destroy at least forty-five different historic monuments,
most of which were Islamic shrines. On July 24, 2014, they detonated the mosque of the Prophet Jonah with explosives. The next
day, they blew up the mosque of the Prophet Seth, and the Prophet
Jirgis. Later, they would blow up the mosque of al-Khidr. Though
I had known this in the abstract, I had not comprehended con-
cretely how much people like Munir had suffered—not only personal losses but the loss of places intimately bound up with their
spiritual lives as Muslims.

ISIS destroyed eleven sites in Mosul associated with the descendants of the Prophet Mohammed. They blew up the Church of
al-Tahira, near Munir's house. During all of this, Munir remained
in Mosul, his city crumbling around him. As the extent of the
destruction became apparent, even as the city was too dangerous

to physically access, an organization called Monuments of Mosul in Danger used aerial footage to get a sense of the scope of devastation on the ground. Scholars cataloged the monuments in Mosul with satellite photos of before and after their destruction, adding dates.

I listened to Munir's voice, collected in our interviews, and later, transcribing the recordings again, I noted the names of the places in his neighborhood. Then I searched for them on the aerial maps created by Monuments of Mosul in Danger. It was only then, months after I met Munir, that I understood the extent to which he had been summoning up an entire world that had been already gone by the time I'd met him, in order to name it out loud, in order to remember. *The Church of al-Tahira*: flattened. *The mosque of Nebi Girgis*: gone. *The mosque of al-Saray*: finished. *The mosque of Imam Ibrahim*: disappeared. I stared at photographs at what had once been Munir's neighborhood. The shells of buildings. Domes collapsed. Piles of rubble. Yes, all of it gone.

Munir remained. He carried all of it within him. I had heard the city in his voice.

In a place like Lesvos, you begin to understand what a man can carry with him even when everything else is stripped away—and sometimes the only evidence left of its survival comes in a story. It was only in relistening to Munir's that I could recognize a pattern to how he told them. There, among the bombs, a sister brought to the door of her school. A neighbor helped. A suitcase lifted and then a sibling. Children carried on the way to seek refuge. English spoken on a boat. A tent folded up and lifted for an elderly woman. A plastic desk placed in front of me. A Christmas card sent across the silence.

I found this sentence I had scrawled into my notebook after meeting him that first day: *It is only the small gestures that make Moria bearable.*

He was a man who saw only darkness around him and so decided to offer his own inner light. "I would be their candle," he had said of offering himself so that his sisters could study. That was what I was learning: that when all else is taken away, then we have no choice but to create what we will carry.

It was even in the meaning of his name, Munir. *Luminous*.

As I write this, years later, I still haven't recovered from what I saw on Lesvos: human beings treated like animals, left to freeze beneath trees. A few years later, the population would peak at an astonishing twenty thousand souls before the camp burned to the ground in September 2020, almost three years after my visit.

I will never forget the vision of Munir, speaking in his eloquent Arabic, walking me through, in our imaginations, the destroyed streets of his home from the front of his tent in the cold. His kindness. His politeness. The way it felt so surreal among the cruelty of the camp. The way I learned from him that a kind word can be a deliberate act of resistance.

I think back to the faces of those I met: a mother and daughter from Raqqa who had witnessed executions. Parents and children who had crossed to Lesvos on a flimsy rubber boat. All those who risked their lives, expecting to find compassion on the other side.

I was not the only one who struggled with what European countries were doing to refugees fleeing war. Many journalists became so devastated by what they witnessed happening on European shores that psychologists carried out a study, determining that many were suffering from "moral injury" as a result of their work, often feeling guilt over their inability to step in and help. Journalists weren't so much having PTSD after covering places like Lesvos because they weren't in physical danger. But many instead found themselves in a kind of moral danger as their worldviews collapsed. The enemies in this story weren't just foreign governments or distant militias. It was their own governments, their own neighbors turning refugees away. Journalists and writers who were parents were especially in danger of experiencing moral injury because when they saw children who didn't know how to swim and who had just crossed on flimsy boats, they had some knowledge of how terrifying that must have been.

And what does a writer do, after all? We don't hand out blankets, or act as translators, or work as lawyers, or drive rescue boats. We attempt to witness history. And this did not seem to be helping anything at all. For no matter how many journalists showed up to write about it, the situation on Lesvos only got worse. For me, it challenged the very notion that people will respond to situations of injustice if only they learn about them.

Lesvos was my wakeup call to modern refugee policies more terrible than I could have ever imagined. While people fleeing war have a right to seek safety, the European Union appeared to find creative ways of making sure that they never arrived on their shores. It wasn't only the deal with Turkey that incentivized the stopping of boats before they reached Greek waters. The most dangerous route to Europe had become the route from Libya, and the EU paid and trained Libyan coast guards to intercept those migrant boats, with thousands dying and others sent back to detention camps or to be sold as slaves. The "Dublin laws" insisted that refugees who managed to cross into Europe had to settle in the first country that they were caught and fingerprinted in, which meant that refugees aiming for Germany were threatened with being deported to Romania if they were caught and fingerprinted there.

In an even more cynical act, the EU realized that the easiest way to justify deporting refugees was to declare their home countries safe, regardless of whether this was a reality. The EU signed the "Joint Way Forward" pact with Afghanistan in 2016 to seek the country's cooperation in returning refugees—despite the fact that Afghanistan was then one of the most dangerous countries in the world, making deporting refugees there illegal and against the principle of non-refoulement enshrined in international human rights law.

The cruelty was not only limited to Europe. The year I visited Lesvos, the number of refugees resettled in the United States decreased to one third of those resettled the previous year—despite record numbers of people fleeing conflict worldwide. Families regularly risked their lives crossing the southern border of the United States as migrants and refugees, with many dying in the sweltering heat. Those who did cross were often treated with indignity, with children sometimes even separated from their parents.

In the year I traveled to Lesvos, 2017, Australia was accepting refugees like Hana and others from Qaraqosh. Yet 78 percent of the refugees Australia accepted from Iraq and Syria that year were Christians, despite the fact that Christians were only 15 percent of Iraq's total population of registered refugees and 1 percent of that of Syria. In the meantime, the Australian government had built detention centers on offshore islands to house other migrants and refugees who attempted to reach their shores, in a practice that came to global attention when, by sending out text messages, the Iranian Kurdish poet Behrouz Boochani composed a book about the horrors he saw as a prisoner taking place on Manus Island.

It can be easy enough to see the so-called "refugee crisis" as a story that is primarily about other people's lives. On Lesvos, I finally understood how much it is about all of us. It is about our own unwillingness to see refugees and migrants as our neighbors, our friends—or even as ourselves, for it was increasingly obvious to me that any of us could be refugees in other circumstances. It is about our refusal to admit that the ways in which we welcome refugees and migrants can contribute to their mental health outcomes, and the ways in which we reject them can contribute to their isolation and despair. It is about our willingness to exile to islands those people we would rather not confront with our own eyes, even if it meant leaving children out in the cold.

There is one more story about my time in Lesvos. On my last day on the island, I flagged down a taxi.

"Where do you want to go?" the driver asked. I handed him a piece of paper with a name scribbled on it: Kato Tritos.

He knew what I was looking for. "No one goes there," he said grimly and went to consult with a group of other drivers nearby. "That's fine," he said upon returning. "I think I remember where it is."

I don't remember how long we drove through the countryside. I can still picture the trees, the green open spaces, and the smell of the sea from the open window. Eventually he slowed down in front of a locked gate. I got out of the car.

"It's okay if you just wait here," I said, and he nodded. I jumped the fence, my jacket catching on the jagged wire. The air was crisp, but the sun caught on the grass in front of me. In the distance, a great open green field among olive trees came into view.

As I approached, I could see the mounds of earth, in awkward lines. Then the graves were visible, rows of stones placed on the green winter earth.

Where had the dead been from? What had they been hoping to arrive to? I was standing over them now. Some of the earth had been newly upturned. Earth you could smell. Some of the stones had names written in Greek. Some were in Arabic. A few in English. Some had been marked with the year of death at sea. So many graves were from 2015, when millions fled Syria.

Some had ages: Two years old. Six years old. Some mounds of earth had nothing at all, not even names. On those were no sign of a life lost save for a ring of stones and a marker and earth still wet from recent rain.

I stopped in front of two gravestones. Jalal Molla, four years old. Alaa Jajo, six years old. Both dead beneath the waters on November 14, 2015.

I wanted to vomit. I sobbed and touched the cold ground. I felt my body torn between being frozen and wanting to escape, and I held on to the earth to keep me rooted to those names, that place. Those children.

Then I wiped my eyes, making my way back to the taxi, and climbed the wire fence. The taxi driver inspected me, bewildered by my tears.

"What's the matter?" he asked. "Were you looking for someone you know?"

PART IV

GHADIR AND ADNAN'S PHARMACY

Aleppo, Syria → Amsterdam, Netherlands

The coffee of Aleppo is omnipresent.
Every person will ask for it to be prepared differently, and so when
people come to visit, it takes a long time to make the coffee.
　　　　　　　　　　　　　—Aleppan artist Samer Tarabichi

17 | THE SHADOW WALL

Amsterdam is a city of water, which snakes between streets, where boats are anchored among the houses. Gulls fly low, the shadows of their broad wings crossing the lines of red roofs. I had not visited Amsterdam in two decades, and I had forgotten everything about it: the curve of the canals and the bridges that cross them, the bicycles ringing by, the tulips and sunflowers spilling out of baskets in street markets, and a heaviness I could not name.

The window from my room on Anne Frankstraat looked out to the tram line, bicycle racks, and brick houses painted in gray and rust, brown and pink. Rows of their windows stared blankly in my direction. It was the old Jewish quarter, where Sephardic Jews from Spain and Portugal had settled in the sixteenth century and Ashkenazi Jews a century later. The streets were haunted with memories: the Portuguese synagogue, the theater used as a deportation center during World War II, the orphanage where the girls and their attendants had been sent to Sobibor to be exterminated. By 1944, more than 100,000 Jews had been deported from the Netherlands to be killed. Among them was Anne Frank, whose voice spoke to me from the street signs, from the map as I found my way back to my room at night.

Everything felt damp, the air always heavy, and even the quiet was loud, suffused with birdsong and the whirring of bicycles speeding by. I did not belong there. It was not a place to grieve. More than once, I was pulled from my thoughts by a bicycle darting past. In any case, I was not there for the city. I was there in search of another city, displaced into this one.

I had arrived in Amsterdam in search of Aleppo, a city I had known well before the war. There's something jarring about seeing the people of one city in an entirely different one. I had not been prepared for the heaviness, or the order, or the feeling I would have meeting Syrians speaking their dialect among the canals and bike lanes. Tailors who had escaped Aleppo, whom I watched patiently sewing shirts in the former jail Bijlmerbajes, by now painted and transformed into a café and pop-up hotel run by refugees. A Syrian chef from Aleppo who sat at a picnic table beside the canal, reminiscing about his mother's rose petal jam.

Something in their voices made me remember. Images of alleyways, orange juice, the public park with fountains nearby the old hotel where I used to stay when I visited. If I closed my eyes, I could still remember small details of Aleppo. The entrance to the old covered market, with the reams of fabric stacked high, stripes and solids and sequins; the carts of green plums; the idhan from the Great Mosque; the restaurants, with their radishes cut to look like flowers; the green olive oil and laurel soap piled in stacks that you could smell, even at a distance. The red peppers left on the roof to dry, the Aramaic and Armenian and French and Arabic sung in churches, the men delivering coffee and tea with sprigs of mint through the streets, the pomegranate trees and inner courtyards, the old waxed cars, the train station with trains that traveled all the way to Istanbul. Everything had a suchness, a detail, an attention.

By the time I arrived in Amsterdam, millions of the inhabitants of Aleppo had escaped the war as half of the population of Syria became displaced. The old covered market had burned to the ground. The city's most famous minaret had collapsed in on itself. The instrument and textile and soap factories had been bombed. I know there is no easy way to measure a city once so vibrant and now so gone. Sewing machines silent. The call to prayer erased. Reams of fabric gone up in flames.

From my room on Anne Frankstraat, I could walk out and follow the street along the park until it narrowed alongside the botanical gardens. Residents had planted flowers hanging down brick walls and spilling from their pots: lilac and roses, wisteria, honeysuckle, lavender. Ten minutes later, I arrived at the Nieuwe Keizersgracht canal, the sidewalk beside it lined with metal plaques engraved with names. I kneeled to read: De schaduwkade. The shadow wall.

Each plaque corresponded to a house on the opposite side of the canal. And every name represented a person taken from that house to be murdered because they were Jewish. Nieuwe Kiezersgracht 3; Bajla Lederman, fifty-eight years old, killed on 11-12-1942 in Auschwitz; Frieda Weintraub, twenty-seven years old, killed 30-09-1942 in Auschwitz; Szmul Toronczyk, seventy-eight years old, killed on 23-07-1943 in Sobibor; Abraham Wurzel, forty-five years old, killed on 23-07-1943 in Sobibor; Bajla Toroncyzk-Orbach, seventy-one years old, killed on 10-06-1943 in Amsterdam; Ire Goldmark, fifty-one years old, killed 28-05-1943 in Sobibor.

I read the names out loud, more than two hundred in all. The windows to their rooms had once looked out over where I was standing. Across the water, a man was now unchaining his bicycle to head to work. A woman was watering her plants.

There are cities in the world that contain ghosts, that will always contain ghosts. For a long time, I had believed that a city is no longer that city once its inhabitants are gone—that the people of the city are its very soul. But perhaps I had been wrong. Perhaps the city remains, inhabited by shadows. Perhaps the people, even if they are gone from their city, remain.

Two days before I left Amsterdam, I walked to Park Frankendael, an old wealthy estate house surrounded by trees and open spaces. Beneath one of these trees sat Adnan and Ghadir with their two young sons, who were laughing and practicing their Dutch.

The meeting had been arranged by a mutual friend, who had suggested that Ghadir and Adnan might tell me something about what they had brought with them from Aleppo, where they had lived until 2015—a city to which they were very much attached. And there they were. Ghadir immediately put me at ease with her smile. She was wearing black jeans with white sneakers, a comfortable white long-sleeved shirt with a blue shawl draped over it, and sunglasses perched over her white headscarf. Adnan was wearing a blue polo shirt, jeans, sunglasses. Their boys wore shirts with the same stripes and monsters my own sons wore at their age, which seemed to be about five and seven. Had I not been told, there was nothing about them to signal where they had come from or what they had survived. But then Ghadir spoke, and I could hear it immediately: the dialect of Aleppo, with its clear, musical notes, the words lilting at the end, which sounds almost like singing. I sat down on the grass beside them.

"What are you writing about?" Ghadir asked.

"I write about what Syrians and Iraqis carry with them," I answered. "Tangible and intangible things. Like the soap of Aleppo. Or rose petal jam. The jasmine of Damascus. Or the muwashahat music."

Ghadir smiled. "I'm sorry, I wish that we could help you," she said. "But all we ever had in Syria was a pharmacy."

The sun sank into the quietness of the moment and seemed to fill it. "Then would you like to tell me about your pharmacy?" I asked.

She glanced at Adnan, who laughed. "Which pharmacy?" they both asked at once.

"The first or the second?" Ghadir continued, her eyes sparkling.

"Both of them?" I suggested, leaning in.

So together they began their story, about the first pharmacy and then the second one—the pharmacy they had rescued out of the ruins of war.

18 | QADR

In Aleppo, there had been expectations. Of course there had been expectations. Ghadir had been raised to expect that when a man planned to propose to a woman, if he could afford it, he should first purchase an apartment. He should not only purchase it but furnish it, filling the rooms with sofas and tables and chairs, with beds and carpets, and later with plates and cups and spoons. It was not so much the dwelling itself that mattered but the symbolism of owning it. For this was a way of communicating that a man was ready to take on the responsibility of a family, that he had already established himself in the world—and that any woman who married him would never have to worry about a roof over her head or food on the table. Yes, owning a house or an apartment was a way of offering security.

So when Adnan graduated from pharmacy school and decided not to buy a house but instead to buy a pharmacy in Aleppo, it was not a simple decision but one that had the potential to change his entire life. When he later fell in love with Ghadir, and he told her that he had purchased a pharmacy and so would only be able to rent a house for them, he was not wrong to fear that she might dismiss him as unserious because of this decision.

"Is that okay?" he had asked, and she'd reacted with delight, totally supporting him. Yes, of course he had been right to buy a pharmacy. He sensed that she was not only declaring her support for his dreams but also announcing her own independence of spirit. She was not looking for security so much as a real relationship of equals, a partnership—one in which she would not depend on him for support but that they would depend on one another. Yes, Adnan would simply rent a house because they both agreed that he should own a pharmacy. From the beginning, the pharmacy would be so much more than just a pharmacy. It would be their way of declaring their trust in one another—their decision to support one another in all things.

Adnan and Ghadir had both grown up in Aleppo, just seven hundred meters from one another, although they never met as children. Only when both were studying to be pharmacists in Jordan did their paths finally cross: she with her ready smile and he much quieter but still amicable to everyone he met. Both agreed now that Ghadir was the better student of the two: focused, ambitious, rushing through her studies. She had been only thirteen years old when her father had been diagnosed with a serious heart condition. Though she had been tempted to remain in Aleppo, her father had sent her away to her studies in Jordan, assuring her, "I will stay alive to see your diploma in your hands."

So she had traveled to Jordan and studied with immense focus, hurrying to make sure that her father would be able to hold her diploma before his health took a turn for the worse. When her classmates headed to cafés after lab, she stayed behind and studied. When the summer months arrived, she enrolled in extra classes so that she could finish in four years instead of five. In a country in which it was still rare for a woman to be allowed to study alone, away from her family, Ghadir recognized that her father had given his daughters a gift. Her sister, who was fifteen years her senior, had studied pediatrics in France before moving to America, and Ghadir looked up to her. She dreamed of one day joining her, of traveling around the world.

Adnan was different. His mother was a doctor, his father an engineer, and they, too, valued education. But he was the only son in his family, and his parents had placed their hopes in him remaining in Aleppo and owning a pharmacy. He had always imagined he would live close to them, in the city where his large family was well known. Like Ghadir, he was also brilliant but not quite as sure of himself.

Later, they would struggle to remember exactly how they had met. At the university in Jordan, they belonged to the same circle of friends. Once or twice, they were partners in studying for exams. Yet Ghadir was so focused that she seemed unaware of much outside of studies. It was only when they graduated and returned to Aleppo that they joined the same local course to certify their pharmaceutical degrees in Syria. There, they recognized one another. He saw something in her, in her brilliance, her ready smile, and a kindness that radiated from her.

"How can you explain it?" he would later say. "It's the most complicated and the easiest thing in the world. When you love someone, you love them."

They exchanged phone numbers and began to talk. Soon, Adnan knew that he would need to state his intentions to her family. They were part of a new generation that could choose their own partners for marriage, but there was still an element of the family that needed to be involved. It would not be appropriate for him to continue speaking to her like that unless he was serious. Ghadir also had feelings for Adnan, but she wasn't ready to commit just yet. She knew that marrying Adnan would mean remaining in Aleppo, and she had already scheduled an appointment at the American embassy to apply for a visa. She still had a dream that she might live abroad with her sister, might see the world.

Were they engaged? Well, they were talking about getting engaged. At the same time, Adnan could not understand why she had kept that appointment at the embassy. She, too, couldn't make sense of it. She was torn between her childhood dreams of travel and this young man, whom she had not planned to meet at all.

Adnan had always believed that when someone comes into your life—when anything beautiful comes into your life—you should seize it right away. Who knew if it would pass and never return again? Still, he trusted in her ability to choose the best path for what her life would be. At the same time, he couldn't help but worry about this appointment at the embassy.

She took the bus to Damascus, and all went well. After she showed the invitation from her sister, the officials asked her to return for a second appointment. And so she did, and this time the officials told Ghadir that her visa would be approved in the coming days—just as soon as she returned and showed them a plane ticket for the United States. "Congratulations," they told her. At last! She had worked so hard, handed her diploma to her father, and now she would join her sister, eventually enrolling in a program to specialize in a higher field of pharmaceutics.

Yet her stomach had been hurting for the entire appointment. She walked out of the embassy and ran to the closest pharmacy to purchase medicine for the pain. She took the bus home, and by the time she arrived, she could no longer walk. Her family rushed her to the hospital.

Teratoma of the ovaries: that is what the doctor called the pain in her stomach. She underwent surgery to remove the tumor growing inside of her ovaries, remaining in the hospital for five days.

She was exhausted from surgery. She noticed what it felt like to have her family nearby while she was hurting. She spoke to Adnan, hearing his voice. She remained at home, trying to rest. When she was well enough to walk again, she called the embassy, explaining that she had been in the hospital, missing the window to buy her plane ticket. They told her she would need to start the process again.

Something spoke to her heart, and she listened. She trusted in the life that she had been given already, and she trusted God. This seemed to be qadr—destiny—God's way of communicating to her what the right course of action for her life would be, where she would experience the most fulfillment. What she desired was already here. She would remain in Aleppo and marry Adnan.

In the meantime, Adnan continued to use the money he had saved up for buying a house and instead used it to make payments on owning the pharmacy. He was only twenty-five years old.

The seriousness of his decision soon became concrete. When Ghadir introduced him to her family, her mother was full of questions. Why didn't he own a house? Wouldn't it have been better if she had chosen a man who was already established—who had a career and a home?

As for Adnan's family—he was their only son, after all. His mother worried about him. On the one hand, Ghadir seemed like a perfect match. She herself was a doctor, and she couldn't very well object when her own son was drawn to a woman with a similar education to her own. Ghadir had excellent morals and came from a good family. Her faith clearly guided her. It was more that it had all happened so . . . quickly. He was still so young. He had only just purchased the pharmacy. Shouldn't he wait until he had gotten the business off the ground?

He considered his mother's point of view. He still had years in front of him before anyone would expect him to get married. Yet whenever he questioned his own judgment, he remembered Ghadir's appointment at the embassy. He knew that if he did not propose now, then perhaps Ghadir would pass him by.

Both families had similar values, with lives rooted in the cosmopolitanism of Aleppo. Adnan's parents, though Muslim, had studied at Catholic grade schools. Ghadir's father's best friend was a Christian, and growing up, Ghadir had attended weddings and parties in churches as easily as she went to mosques. Her father had studied for five years in London and had supported her older sister as she studied for her doctorate abroad. He had encouraged Ghadir when she traveled to Jordan. On both sides, there was anxiety, hope that both Ghadir and Adnan would find a marriage partner rooted in the openness and appreciation for diversity that both families shared. Would Ghadir be able to keep working? Would Adnan's dreams of building a successful pharmacy be sidelined by a family?

On the other hand, Ghadir's parents recognized that she was twenty-five years old and knew that she had never expressed an interest in anyone before. She seemed so relaxed in this man's presence. Adnan was not just a potential husband. He seemed to be a partner, an equal—a friend. When her father recognized that, he encouraged her: "The important thing is that both of you have diplomas. I won't be frightened for you."

The tradition in Aleppo was that Adnan's mother would visit Ghadir—and if she liked Ghadir, then Adnan would accompany her on the second visit. So it went. A first visit. A second visit. The third time, Adnan's entire family came to visit Ghadir's, and they took the first step toward marriage. They read the Fatiha, the first chapter of the Quran, making a formal promise.

Not long after the ceremony, Adnan's mother began to feel tired. A week later, they rushed her to the hospital. She had come down with pneumonia and an infection from hepatitis B. Adnan remained at her bedside. She had just enough strength to whisper a few sentences a day. She confided to her only son, "I know you felt that I didn't want you to choose Ghadir, but I was frightened for you. Finally, I know that you are wise and know how to make decisions. I'm with you in this. Go on with your decision. And tawakkal al Allah—put your faith in God."

She slept. Then awakened. Called over her son. "Marry Ghadir," she whispered.

She passed away during Ramadan, and it marked its way into the calendar of their lives—this holy month of sadness and of blessing, of hunger and of gift. They mourned, waiting almost a year before the wedding took place. Because the family was still grieving, they decided that the wedding would be small, only close family members. Ghadir wore a long white dress with gloves, a veil, and a tiara and held a white bouquet of roses. Adnan stood beside her, smiling, in his black suit and red tie.

Years later, when I asked Adnan why he loved Ghadir so much, he laughed and shrugged his shoulders. "That's difficult and easy. No one can answer that," he told me. "Love is something that happens from inside. No one can give reasons for it. It's something you feel with a person, without reasons. Of course, there are reasons why it will work or not; there are social reasons, family reasons, or spiritual reasons. Why did I love her? Because I loved her. Just."

When the wedding was finished, Ghadir gathered the photographs of that day and pressed them into a book so that they would remember.

19 | MORNING PRAYERS

The first pharmacy stood on a busy street in the neighborhood of Seif al-Dowla, a popular working-class area in East Aleppo. It was the perfect neighborhood in which to own a pharmacy—the kind of neighborhood where people couldn't easily afford to visit a doctor, so they would head to the pharmacist with anything from headaches to burns and cuts and scrapes, stomachaches and viruses.

Adnan had first purchased it when his mother was still alive, choosing the neighborhood because her laboratory was located nearby. He had imagined she would send customers in his direction, men and women who would show up mentioning her name. But now she was gone. His placement at exactly that pharmacy was now forever tied to her absence—and so, too, his nagging feeling of being just a little bit out of place.

He had purchased it from a man who had run the pharmacy for over a decade, a pharmacy he no longer had the energy to continue. Adnan had taken on the place complete with shelves of medicines never sold. In that way, it didn't feel entirely like his own. But he also knew that it held promise simply by being where it was. The pharmacy stood on the pedestrian passage on the way to the vegetable market, surrounded by shops. You might look at that pharmacy on your way to buy carrots and remember that you were out of shampoo, or that you needed a toothbrush, or that you may as well take a moment to fill your grandfather's prescription for heart medicine.

On his first day, Adnan carted in his framed diploma from his pharmaceutical studies in Jordan and hung it on his desk behind the wall. He placed the ninety-nine names of God in calligraphy in a golden frame—a gift from his family on the day he opened.

He would name the pharmacy after his family's name. That name would stand emblazoned over the entrance, together with the picture of a bowl with a serpent wrapped around it, that international symbol of medicine and healing. His own name was typed neatly at the bottom of the sign. Yes, from the beginning, it was not just a pharmacy. It was bound up in how he saw himself, in whom he belonged to and who he wanted to become.

One morning, during Adnan's very first weeks at the pharmacy, Sheikh Ahmad arrived. Wearing a long white abaya and a skull cap, he leaned over his cane and looked around. He must have been around seventy years old, his hair and beard white and shining, and he spoke in a whisper. He didn't seem interested in purchasing anything, and Adnan felt uncomfortable as he lingered there. He soon left.

In the meantime, Adnan tried to root himself in an unfamiliar world. Nothing in his studies had prepared him for the practical work of running a pharmacy. The pharmacy walls were lined with cream-colored shelves with glass fronts, behind which were rows upon rows of medicines. At the back of the pharmacy sat his desk, behind smaller glass shelves filled with more bottles still. He arranged and rearranged bottles. He tried to keep the accounts in order. He sorted the medicines that had already been in stock when he arrived, slowly throwing out any past their date, trying to find a system so that he could easily find them.

The entire space felt dreary, antiseptic, and so he attempted to add color: a section of cosmetics, diapers, formula. He set up a display near the entrance of colorful sippy cups and pacifiers, teething rings, and orange and green shiny plastic toilets for children to train on. He added a cartoon sticker of a cigarette on the front window that warned customers not to smoke. He dreamed of making it not just a pharmacy but a destination, one that would balance medicine with lipsticks and blush, lotion and soap—the kind of space where people might drop in not just because they had the flu but because they wanted to pamper themselves.

Though the previous owner had retired, his young assistant had remained, and Adnan decided right away to keep him on. A teenager, Ahmed had worked at the pharmacy since he was a boy, delivering medicines after school to help support his two sick parents. He knew every house in the neighborhood and every customer by name, and he soon felt like a younger brother to Adnan, a bit of family he could look forward to seeing every day. Ahmed would slip through the pharmacy door after school and ask for orders to deliver—a kind of pharmaceutical equivalent of the paperboy. When Adnan saw his shy laugh, his seriousness and compassion for his family, suddenly he felt more rooted in the pharmacy himself, more able to confront the stress of holding it together. Ahmed gave him comfort in those first overwhelming years, never judging him as he stumbled through orders and struggled with customers. Adnan had begun to admit to himself that he had been raised in a bubble, out of touch with people from other social classes, and he realized he would have to learn to connect to his neighbors if there was to be any hope that the pharmacy would work.

The neighborhood slowly welcomed him. Neighbors sensed his out-of-placeness and began making space for him. After a few months, Zakariyya, the kindly dentist whose office was next door, began to make a habit of sliding into the pharmacy before the day began to share a cup of coffee with Adnan. This, too, rooted him, anchoring his days with a small kindness.

Before long, Sheikh Ahmed returned. This time, Adnan didn't feel uncomfortable, for he had now learned about him from others in the neighborhood. For years, Sheikh Ahmed had been the muezzin of the neighborhood mosque, calling the adhan from the minaret five times a day, but in the last years he had lost his voice. Now, as a Hafez al-Quran—one who had memorized the Quran in its entirety—he walked up and down the street each morning, speaking in a near whisper, teaching shopkeepers and others who were interested in how to recite the Quran. He did this for free, as a way of serving the community. Adnan understood that this was why he had entered the shop that first day—to quietly ask Adnan if he, too, would like to study the Quran with him.

The next time Sheikh Ahmed entered the pharmacy, he approached the counter and held out his arm. Might Adnan take his blood pressure? He suffered from hypertension, and he needed to regulate his blood pressure to reduce his chances of suffering from a heart attack or a stroke. This time, he did not bring a Quran but futayr, the small salty pastries baked in ovens on street corners and eaten for breakfast all over Syria. Adnan saw it as a peace offering.

The next day, when he asked to have his blood pressure taken, Adnan saw Sheikh Ahmad differently. He was always wearing the same thing—a long, tailored white thobe with a collar, a pen in his pocket, and a smile in his eyes. His moustache and beard were always neatly trimmed. He had a kindness, a light that emanated from him. He put out his arm. When Adnan finished, Sheikh Ahmad quietly recited a few verses from the Quran in his whispering voice.

Adnan repeated them, stumbling over the pronunciation.

"Good! Good," Sheikh Ahmed encouraged him. From then on, his days in the pharmacy would begin with prayer.

The pharmacy absorbed the rhythms of Aleppo itself. It was a night city. People tended to stay up late and then sleep into the morning so that many shops didn't open until 10:00 a.m. Adnan left the house at 8:45 in the morning and arrived at the pharmacy by nine, sitting behind the front desk and writing out a to-do list: medicines that he needed to order, customers with monthly prescriptions to be delivered, diapers almost all sold out. He tried to finish any paperwork, to sign any documents needing signatures. At nine thirty, Sheikh Ahmed would arrive, put out his arm to have his blood pressure taken, and then teach him a few verses of the Quran, his quiet voice in Arabic sending a calm into the unopened store, reciting the verse from al-Baqara: "On no soul does Allah give more than it can bear."

He'd stay for thirty minutes, and when he left, Adnan would open the door for the day to begin, the hour blessed. Customers would arrive. Parents on their way to work or dropping their children at school. Grandparents stopping in during a morning stroll. Workers injured on the job. He listened and prescribed medicines without pause until 3:00 p.m., when every shop closed in Aleppo for a siesta. He opened again in the late afternoon, finishing only at ten at night. After a few months, when business picked up, he hired another assistant—someone who could take his place so that he could spend extra time with Ghadir—and, after a time, with their newborn sons.

Almost exactly a year after their marriage, Ghadir gave birth to their first son, Samer. A year later, she gave birth to their second, Jamil. When Jamil was still a baby, she accepted a job teaching pharmaceutical students at the university, leaving the children with her mother while she taught during the day. But she missed Adnan, and whenever she had a few hours to spare, she would prepare lunch and drive it to the pharmacy, always adding a double portion to share with young Ahmed. She'd sit beside Adnan and keep him company between customers. He loved her cooking. Stuffed vine leaves and melokhiyya: chicken in a soup of mallow leaves. Her bulgur in tomato sauce and especially kubbe: meatballs cooked in a shell of semolina, a specialty of Aleppo.

Later, Ghadir and Adnan would refer to those times as the "golden years." Mothers and fathers and neighbors and grandparents rotated through the door of the pharmacy with their ordinary problems—ordering pills for indigestion, diarrhea, anti-vomiting, or weight loss. They bought aspirin and diapers, lipstick and herbal tea. Those with heart problems arrived each month to fill their prescriptions. The teachers from the nearby school showed their insurance before placing their orders, and the parents of students passed by with all of the ailments that children have: colds and runny noses, flus and fevers. Adnan listened, advising how many hours they needed between doses, making sure they didn't mix prescriptions. Ahmed gathered packages and raced off to neighboring houses to knock on doors and deliver them.

Every year, Sheikh Ahmad went on Umrah pilgrimage, bringing back prayer beads and zamzam water from the blessed well. In time, he suggested that Adnan begin to memorize the entire Quran. And so he started, learning passages in the mornings, practicing as he moved bottles on shelves. Young Ahmed also began to memorize verses. And so their prayers blended into the details of everyday life, of filling prescriptions and dusting shelves and unpacking boxes. The pharmacy took on a rootedness, a calmness, a sense of purpose in the neighborhood. Adnan and Ghadir bought a new car. They paid their debts.

And Ghadir's father, who had been so worried for his daughter, could finally rest easy.

The war broke out in Syria in 2011, reaching places like Dera'a, Homs, Damascus, and the surrounding countryside. Still, Aleppo remained largely untouched for the entire first year. Many people speculated that the city cared more about commerce than politics and that the primary focus of the merchant city would always be on keeping borders open and trade expanding. It was a major tourist center and a crossing point into Turkey, and though it was the country's largest city, it was on the opposite border from Dera'a, where the war had begun. It was easy enough to believe that the city would be spared the violence.

Yet those who said this underestimated how disenfranchised the city's working class had become, how frustrated they were at the economic disparities between ordinary people and the ruling class. People like those who lived in Seif al-Dowla, who went to the pharmacist for everything from cuts and scrapes to blood pressure, unable to afford the doctor. The protests began first in the rural areas around the city—much as they had in Damascus.

The first major clashes took place in Aleppo on July 19, 2012, in the neighborhood of Salahadin, which soon became the local base of the Syrian opposition against the government. Ramadan began the next day. On the third day of Ramadan, Adnan was making his way to the pharmacy for work when his cell phone rang. It was his assistant, who reported that gunfire was erupting somewhere near the pharmacy. Adnan told him to lock up the pharmacy and go home. Better to be on the safe side, he thought, and so they closed for the day.

By the end of the week, war had come to Aleppo, and the pharmacy was now on the front lines. In other words, it was gone.

A life was there, and then it vanished. Adnan would never go back to work behind the counter at the first pharmacy again. He never even knew which side destroyed his pharmacy, the government or the opposition. He also understood that this not knowing didn't matter in the least because knowing wouldn't have changed the goneness of it all.

He had invested his savings into buying that pharmacy, and he no longer had money to pay the rent on their apartment. They didn't just lose the pharmacy—they lost their home too.

20 | THE GARAGE

2012. That was the year a fire swept through the ancient market of Aleppo, a UNESCO World Heritage site extending more than twelve kilometers. The fire swallowed hundreds of shops and destroyed the most preserved continuously used ancient market in the world. Carpets and spices and walls of textiles and inlaid boxes and beautifully restored homes were all burned in a single evening. The whir of tailors went silent. It was as though someone had set fire to the soul of the city.

Adnan, Ghadir, and their two children joined thousands of others from Aleppo and crossed the border into Turkey, carrying their suitcases. Ghadir thought that since her sister was living in the United States, they might obtain visas and move there during the war. They woke up early in the morning in Istanbul, and the four of them headed to the American embassy to ask for an appointment. The children were still small. When they arrived, the line to get inside was snaking all the way down the street.

"It was impossible," Ghadir told me. "I was with the children, and I couldn't imagine waiting in that long line with them for an appointment. I was so scared to make a decision. And it occurred to me that with my sister in the United States, *I* might be able to travel with the children but that we would have to leave Adnan behind."

The reality of the war hit her all at once. And now it was all too much. They couldn't afford to remain in Turkey for long, and even if they could stay, their children might not have access to schools. They couldn't go abroad without the risk of being separated as a family. And what about her parents? Ghadir was overwhelmed.

And so they packed their bags and returned to Aleppo. They crossed the border again to try to make their way in the war—which seemed impossible, except that it was also home.

Even as Ghadir and Adnan were returning to Aleppo, friends and neighbors were leaving. One of those was Adnan's uncle, who left behind an empty house, located in a neighborhood in West Aleppo. He suggested to Adnan and Ghadir that they move in, keeping it occupied and safe from squatters. They had few other choices. The decision would at least put them closer to Adnan's family if they needed support—which they certainly did. Samer was a toddler. Jamil was still a baby.

So they carried their bags across the city and moved into an unfamiliar home in an unfamiliar neighborhood, joining thousands of others from their city who had now become internally displaced. "It was the beginning of the war," Adnan told me. "We had no idea what anything meant. What was that noise? We had no idea what we were supposed to do in the face of this reality."

Fall passed. Winter arrived. There was no longer regular electricity. They layered their clothes. Ghadir pulled one shirt after another over the children. On days when the electricity came on at two in the morning, she would wake them up just so that they could have a warm bath.

It snowed. Then it snowed again. She felt like it snowed all the time. She told herself that she and Adnan were their children's reference point and that if they appeared calm and connected, then the children would not even notice how much had changed. Ghadir continued to teach. She was now the family's sole income earner, even as the Syrian currency collapsed. When she returned home, she put the children to bed and then went to bed at seven because the house was so cold. There was no gas, no internet, little food. Everything felt dangerous. She was exhausted.

As for Adnan, he went to bed early, too, because he felt there was nothing left to look forward to in the day.

Nearly a year passed. Adnan spent his days lying on the couch. Ghadir had never seen him like this. He had been so full of energy, throwing himself into the details of the first pharmacy, stocking shelves and encouraging young Ahmed to stay in school, drinking coffee with Zakariyya, reciting his prayers. She couldn't bear to see him lose his confidence.

2013. That was the year the stunning eleventh-century minaret of Aleppo's Great Mosque—a symbol of Aleppo—was toppled to the ground during fighting. The call to prayer, which had floated from the minaret for some nine centuries, disappeared from the city's soundscape. By June, the UN estimated that ninety-three thousand people had been killed in Syria and millions displaced.

That was the year Adnan's father, who had remarried in the wake of his wife's death, also left the country for safety in Turkey. He had owned the garage that was attached to the house that they were now living in.

Days passed into days. Ghadir was not entirely sure on what day it was that she walked past the garage and noticed the shape of the door. Rather, she looked through the door in her memory, trying to see the breadth of the space inside. How large *was* that garage? How many people might fit comfortably inside? She could imagine a desk. Shelves. Tiles on the ground. Neighbors walking in and out.

Yes. The garage seemed to be just about the same size as a modest pharmacy.

It was an absurd idea, and she let it pass. But when she walked past the garage again, the idea persisted: shelves, rows of medicines, and Adnan at the front desk, listening to customers.

They had lost almost everything on the day they lost the first pharmacy. The only important material possession that remained was their car, which they planned on either using if and when they had to escape or selling if they needed emergency funds. Wisdom held that anyone in Aleppo who had lasted this long should at the very least hold on to their savings. It was hardly the time to invest in a project, much less to build a pharmacy in a garage in a city already at war. They would risk losing the very little they still had left. Besides, Seif al-Dowla had been known for its pharmacies. But this neighborhood, located in a wealthier part of Aleppo with houses far apart from one another, was exactly the opposite. Families were smaller, and their neighbors were accustomed to visiting the doctor when they were sick. A pharmacy probably wouldn't even work here.

Still . . . the streets were becoming dangerous. At the very least, a pharmacy would mean that their neighbors wouldn't have to walk far when they needed to buy medicine. This alone might save some lives. So many of the doctors had already fled the country that it wasn't so easy to get medical care. And hospitals were being bombed. Who would want to go to a hospital now? And with the price of gas being what it was, who could even afford to drive to one?

Besides, even if some pharmacies in the city had survived the war so far, that didn't matter much to their neighbors. The government had set up a checkpoint at the entrance to the neighborhood, and everyone had to pass through it to get out. Getting to other pharmacies in East Aleppo was increasingly difficult, made possible only on the Bustan al-Qasr crossing, and people weren't always allowed to bring the medicine back through the opposition checkpoints.

The more she thought about it, the more it seemed—to Ghadir, at least—that war wasn't the time to be practical. It was the moment in which you had to discern what gifts were yours to give and then find a way to offer them. And Adnan was so talented. It would be a way for him to get back to doing what he did best: helping others.

One night, they sat down at the kitchen table for dinner. Ghadir delicately brought up the idea to Adnan of building a second pharmacy.

He hesitated. He had wondered if he would ever start a pharmacy again. He had even asked himself whether the garage might be transformed into a small pharmacy now that his father had traveled abroad, leaving him in charge of the space. But every time he started to consider it, he reminded himself they were in the middle of a war. It didn't make sense to start something new while everyone else was leaving.

If he was honest with himself, he wasn't sure he had the strength to give his heart to another pharmacy when chances were high that he would lose it all over again. So he told Ghadir it wasn't practical.

"We *live* during the war," she insisted in response. "We don't wait for the war to end in order for us to live our lives. The war won't end. We have to *do* something."

He wasn't sure. But the next day, he opened the front door and walked to the driveway. Lifting the garage door and peering inside, he imagined where they might place the counter.

Maybe they should just start. Anything was better than just waiting for the war to pass.

Still, it was a garage. Really a garage: with the smell of oil and grease. And there was an obvious obstacle to starting a pharmacy: an eggplant-colored Santa Fe 4 × 4 parked inside.

The car belonged to a friend of Adnan's father—let's call him Yusuf—who had asked Adnan's father if he could park his car inside the garage to keep it protected from missiles. His father had agreed and then left for Turkey. Now, months later, the car remained in the garage, with the war only escalating. Yusuf wasn't even living in Aleppo any longer. He had left for another city, seeking treatment for heart problems.

Had it been another place, another time, there might have been no problem with Adnan asking Yusuf to simply return to Aleppo to remove his car. It wasn't even his garage, after all. But Adnan's father had offered protection, had offered it within a code of honor, and it was not easy to withdraw such a thing in a place like Syria, where the social contract meant that these agreements deeply mattered. Besides, when Adnan called his father in Turkey, Adnan's father wasn't exactly crazy about this idea of his son using what little money he had in reserve to turn his garage into a pharmacy. A garage! Maybe it was better that the car remained parked inside. It could prevent Adnan and Ghadir from making a terrible mistake.

Adnan called Yusuf, begging him to move his car. The man's answer was firm: the garage belonged to Adnan's father, and only his father could ask him to remove it. Yet by now, Adnan and Ghadir were determined. Ghadir's father had already thrown in his support, offering to lend them money to buy their first medicines. The only thing that stood in their way was the car.

Adnan called his father every day in Turkey, trying to convince him. His dad, in return, promised to phone his friend to ask him to take his car out of the garage. This entire process took perhaps a month. In the meantime, Adnan squeezed around the car to inspect the walls, to measure the floors, to determine where the bathroom would be, pressing himself against the wall and extending the tape from one end to the other.

"Yusuf was saying, 'I'll take the car tomorrow.' . . . We were looking where we should install the tiles, but everything we needed to do was in the space now under the car, and he was saying, 'Tomorrow! Tomorrow!' I wanted to get started," Adnan told me, laughing. "In the end, he returned to Aleppo and took his car. He was upset with us, but what could he do? In the end, the place didn't belong to him."

It was Ramadan, 2013. Prices were skyrocketing. Supplies were running short. During that month, the UN would announce that at least 100,000 people had been killed in Syria.

They would begin.

21 | THE EYES OF CREATION

There is a way of looking through the world, of discovering something hidden within it that is not immediately visible. Ghadir calls this the "eyes of creation." She discovered that she could look into the broken city and recognize among the ruins not only what had been lost but also the materials to build something new. What appeared at first to be destroyed was often not finished yet: a severed shelf might be rescued to be hung on a wall, a broken table might become a front desk, every screw and nail salvaged might support a beam or hold a door in place. She found herself thinking about the ruins of her city. Might there be a door somewhere? A chair that might be mended and used again?

Adnan had just received word that the part of the street in Seif al-Dowla that held his first pharmacy was now controlled by government forces. They were allowing people who had owned shops there to show their documents, pass through the checkpoints, and check if anything remained. Adnan drove to Seif al-Dowla, showed his papers, and was allowed to pass through.

He had known it was gone. But he found that it was different, to see it with his own eyes. The neighborhood had been almost entirely destroyed by fighting between government and opposition forces. The façades of houses were blown out, and windows had become gaping holes. Apartment floors collapsed onto those beneath; some had been torn in half. Walls were riddled with bullet holes, electrical wires had been left exposed, laundry was hanging among the ruins.

He stood in front of what remained of the pharmacy. The cream-colored shelves still lined the walls; his desk was still there. But all the glass had been shattered, and the medicine, in its entirety, had been stolen. The floor was littered with empty medical boxes, random sheets of pills half-used, a calendar torn in half, broken glass. The walls were dotted with bullet holes. He took everything he thought might somehow be of use for the second pharmacy— the iron from the walls, the broken shelves, the table—and he piled what he could into his car.

He stood where Sheikh Ahmed had sat beside him and recited the Quran, where Zakariyya had slowly sipped coffee, where young Ahmed had collected orders before delivering them to the now-collapsed buildings. Everyone was gone. An entire world had been taken.

He took his diplomas off the wall.

Because of the war, everyone seemed to be out of work. Shops had been bombed, or their owners had escaped, and no one had money even to buy the essentials. Those who wanted to survive had to become creative, to take on whatever odd jobs were available. An electrician named Abu Ibrahim didn't have work—who needs an electrician in a city without electricity?—but he knew how to put in tiles and work a tape measure, and so they hired him to help them create a pharmacy in a garage. Then they hired someone with a pickup truck for the day, which could haul in bricks to build the makeshift bathroom. They lugged a toilet and then set to work on the dirty tiles that had covered half of the original garage, kneeling on the ground and scrubbing them clean.

"The thing about a pharmacy," Ghadir said, "is that it needs lots of money, lots of work, and lots of medicine. In a time of war, there's no money, no workers, and no medicine. The tiles on the ground were dirty, and so we scrubbed them by hand with a wire brush. Half of the garage was tiled; the other half was grass."

Adnan and Abu Ibrahim would work from eight in the morning to eight at night. "I was really happy," Adnan remembered. "I had been without work for months, and I was happy to do anything, even manual work."

"It had been a hard year," Ghadir added. "I brought them breakfast, lunch, and dinner, and Abu Ibrahim became part of the family during those months. I was still teaching at the university. My mom would come to the house to help with the kids, or I would drop them at her house when I went to the university."

Entire areas of Aleppo had been destroyed by airstrikes, barrel bombs, fighting. Thousands had left the city. Adnan's cousin had once opened a restaurant that didn't succeed. So they took the sign from his old restaurant, contacted a graphic designer, and filled the old sign with the name of their pharmacy. They would name it after their new neighborhood. The name of the pharmacist listed on the sign this time would be Ghadir's.

When the time came to stock the shelves, Adnan and Ghadir made the trip out to the central warehouse, where pharmacists sourced their medicines. Adnan remembered when he had previously stocked up on medicines, buying in bulk as all major pharmacists did. Now, they handpicked one or two of everything they might need: medicines for headaches or to keep wounds from festering. They left the expensive medicines behind. They couldn't afford them until someone ordered them.

"We didn't want something perfect," Ghadir told me. "We wanted okay."

"We weren't obsessed with quality," Adnan added.

"We were trying to make something that *resembled* a pharmacy," Ghadir said, "even if it was only a garage. It was Ramadan, and we would go to the family house and eat iftar, and then after the dinner we would return to the garage and start displaying the new medicines we bought, putting them on the shelves. Instead of placing them sideways, I would put them facing out—so that it looked like there were lots of boxes when in reality there were only a few. There was no décor, but we tried to put something from our souls so that people could see some beauty. We were really happy. I was like a child—the boxes felt like Legos in my hands."

They opened the pharmacy on the first day of Eid, the holiday marking the end of Ramadan. They knew that all the other pharmacies would be closed for the holidays, and so it was the perfect time for their neighbors to discover them. They were still putting on the finishing touches and placing medicines on the shelves, but they left the metal grate over the entrance half open so that pedestrians could see inside. People out for a walk after iftar peered inside and asked, "You're opening a pharmacy here? That's great!"

And, somehow, it really did look like a pharmacy—not just a garage turned into a pharmacy but a proper pharmacy. The front desk from Adnan's old pharmacy had been filled with new glass. The metal grate at the entrance distracted from the garage door behind it, which lifted up and down. And Ghadir had displayed everything just so: a few dangling toothbrushes, a single jar of Vaseline, two large bottles of rubbing alcohol, boxes overlapping sideways or stacked in pyramids. They handed out candies to children passing by on the street, telling them, "Come back as soon as you can!"

A woman ducked beneath the grill and handed Ghadir a piece of paper. She announced, "My husband is sick. He's old. This is his medicine. I'll need it every month."

She lived next to the pharmacy, but they had never met her until then. She drove a KIA Morning, and so until they learned her name, that is what they called her: *Morning.*

When she left, Ghadir turned to Adnan. "You see?" she said. "Our pharmacy is going to work."

The next day, their families arrived to celebrate the opening. They ordered medicines they insisted they needed, though Ghadir knew otherwise. Adnan's sister noticed that an entire section of the pharmacy was still empty. "I'll buy enough shampoo to stock all of those shelves," she announced.

When Eid finished, Adnan and Ghadir began their work at the pharmacy full time. In the middle of a war, the pharmacy provided some rhythm to their lives, some agency. They woke up in the morning, took the kids to preschool, returned, and opened the pharmacy at 9:00 a.m. They drank their first cup of coffee under the tree in the front yard so that people would see them, and they offered a cup to their first customers. As it was, the tree partially covered the entrance to the pharmacy, and Adnan had even wondered if he should cut it back entirely to make the pharmacy more visible. But he could not bear to cut back anything that had managed to stay alive so far. So he cut back only a few branches, just to make the sign for the pharmacy visible from the street.

By now, Ghadir was no longer teaching but was at the pharmacy full time. After morning coffee, they would look over their stock to see if they needed to replace anything. It was wartime, and they decided that it was best if Ghadir went to buy the medicines. If Adnan was driving, there was always a chance he would get kidnapped at a checkpoint, or forced to serve in the army, or that the car would be stolen. But soldiers and militias were more likely to leave Ghadir alone.

And it was also better, all the way around, for Adnan to stay at the pharmacy. He had more experience at the pharmacy, whereas Ghadir was more of an academic and was new to the world of prescriptions and pills. She was still learning how to work in a pharmacy, and he carried with him his years from the first pharmacy in Seif al-Dowla, which was contained in so many small ways within this one, not only just the shelves.

The opposition controlled one side of the area where they lived in Aleppo and government forces the other, and so the two sides fired at one another over the neighborhood. The fighting occurred most often at night, so they learned to work during the day and to close early if fighting started again. The situation grew worse. Three pharmacies in their area turned to two as people fled. Ghadir kept a bag with her and Adnan's passports, money, and copies of their diplomas just next to the door in case they needed to escape.

So many of the pharmacists in Aleppo had already left that people became accustomed to arriving at a pharmacy and finding no one knowledgeable working there. At the second pharmacy, they entered the garage entrance to find the opposite—two highly skilled pharmacists, always on call. The men would ask for Adnan, and the women would ask for Ghadir, feeling more comfortable confiding in her. When the fighting erupted, they would close the metal grate, rush inside the house, and put the kids in front of *Tom and Jerry*.

Ghadir believed that if she just tried hard enough, she would protect the children somehow, and they would never know that a war was going on around them. All they would remember was that front yard, and the presence of their parents, and customers coming in, asking to be healed.

They learned to make do with what they had. By now, there was almost never electricity, and so Adnan figured out a way to charge the batteries they needed for the LED lights by connecting them to their car battery. When that didn't work, they used their cell phones to read prescriptions in the fading light.

More importantly, they felt the need to attract customers, which was almost impossible under their current circumstances. They needed a strategy. Perhaps *strategy* is not the right word because the rules of the second pharmacy were less a plan than a statement of values. The strategy was simply a decision between the two of them about who they wanted to be in the midst of war and what they wanted their little garage to represent. Already they sensed that it might be more than just a pharmacy in a garage: that it might be a reference point, a place for their neighbors to turn to as the world unraveled around them. They wanted to offer as much as they could to them, and so they had to consider what resources they had available. And once they had considered this, they realized that the resources they could offer were simply their inner resources, their very selves.

They did not write them down, but they agreed on what the guiding principles of the second pharmacy would be. Even today, Adnan and Ghadir can repeat them to me:

1. Be available: Unlike prewar pharmacies, they would open their pharmacy early in the morning and close late at night. In a moment in which everything remained so uncertain, they wanted to imagine a place that people could depend on. Perhaps if their neighbors simply saw that the pharmacy was still open, despite everything, this might put them at ease.

2. Be attentive: They would make coffee for their customers, always offer a chair for them to sit in, and encourage them to rest. They would ask for their customers' names, learn the names of their children, and follow up during the week to see if they were feeling better. In a moment in which so many people were displaced and separated from family members, they wanted the pharmacy to feel like home.

3. Be dependable: When a customer asked for something they didn't have in stock, they would invite them to return a few hours later. In the meantime, Ghadir or Adnan would procure the medicine from another pharmacy and sell it, without a markup. They would take on the risk of travel so that others wouldn't need to.

4. Be kind: That was the foundation of the pharmacy. They wanted to salvage some memory of what Aleppo had been known for before the war: relationships, small gestures, hospitality.

It was the beginning of a vocation. They didn't care about money anymore. They wanted to offer something that had become rare in war—a place where people could let down their guard, could talk about their problems, could be received as they are. They felt they could offer some kind of stability. It helped to give them meaning for why they had stayed while so many others had left.

And so it went. They opened early. They closed late. Their children, who were growing up, sat across from one another in the front yard, playing pharmacy, handing one another the empty pillboxes and saying seriously, "This one will make you feel better. Make sure to take it once in the morning and once in the evening."

That year, Aleppo became so dangerous that they no longer went for walks in the evenings. The collected family on Adnan's side who remained in Aleppo all lived in the neighborhood, and they, too, would gather in front of the pharmacy to eat and drink coffee. It became a kind of extended home—the way people might have met in a family restaurant before the war. Adnan's uncle, his sister, the cousins would all come to chat. Neighbors often felt overwhelmed by the war that surrounded them, and it calmed them to pass by the pharmacy and see it open, even if they didn't buy anything. Adnan and Ghadir made keeping the pharmacy open such a value that they would sometimes eat their meals inside it, leaving the front gate half open in case someone needed to shout inside.

Aleppo had become the front lines of the civil war. If you went to buy bread, you didn't know if you would come back again. The neighbors were becoming exhausted. By then, no one had a family in which people hadn't left the country. They were mourning their sons, their daughters, their parents, their siblings. They would come in to buy aspirin, and Ghadir would ask, "How are you?"

It was not an easy question to ask or to answer. She would offer them coffee. Listen. Smile. Take a bottle from the barely stocked shelves or set out into the war-torn streets to buy it from another pharmacy.

What should I do? My daughter is making me upset . . .

What should I do? I feel like my son never comes to visit anymore . . .

What should I do? My husband left the country, and now I'm alone with the children . . .

"They just wanted someone to talk to," Ghadir told me quietly. "Someone to whom they could say, 'I'm tired.' This was medicine for the soul."

Ghadir no longer thought of this as simply a job. She had been given a space, a small garage, in which to be present for other people in their hour of need. Customers would arrive, talk with her for a quarter of an hour about their problems, and then leave without purchasing medicine. Something else was happening there.

Adnan patiently recorded their neighbors' medicines in a notebook they kept at the counter. It became one less thing for people to think about. They could enter the pharmacy and quietly ask, "Could I have my medicine?" Adnan or Ghadir would find it for them, knowing not to ask what that medicine was. It was like ordering "the regular" at a neighborhood café. The very fact that the pharmacists knew what they needed made them feel safe. It felt like someone had been waiting for them.

During that first year, an elderly man entered the pharmacy and came to collect the medicine he'd ordered. When the time came to pay, he realized he didn't have enough money. Ghadir knew from the type of medicine that his situation was serious. "Just take the medicine," she said, smiling. "You can pay me when you have the money."

Such a small kindness was not unusual in a place like Aleppo, a city that had been famous for kind gestures before the war. Yet the war had changed all of that—not because people were cruel but because they were desperate.

The man returned only two hours later, money in his pocket, to repay Ghadir. But even though he could now repay her, something had shifted in him. "I'm so glad that you gave me the medicine without money," he told her.

For the next few months, new customers kept coming into the pharmacy, saying to them, "I'm a friend of the one who couldn't pay for his medicine. We heard about that." Now those people were returning Ghadir's kindness with their own kindness. She realized that the man had given her a gift—an opportunity to remember who she was, to remember who all of them were.

"When I helped the man, it wasn't because I wanted to be successful," Ghadir tells me. "It was because I was discovering what it really means to be a pharmacist."

2014. More than half of the healthcare facilities in Syria were no longer functioning. Many of the residents of their neighborhood had escaped. Now those who had been displaced from other neighborhoods in Aleppo moved into theirs, filling up empty houses. The neighborhood became a mix of people and populations from the upper, middle, and lower classes, from eastern and western Aleppo. Adnan turned to his years at the first pharmacy in Seif al-Dowla and remembered the lessons he had learned from Sheikh Ahmed, from Zakariyya. He could feel comfortable with everyone who entered the pharmacy. He could recognize the shame and grief of those who had been internally displaced from other neighborhoods and be quietly present to them because he remembered his own family's experience of having been displaced and uprooted from their home.

Now almost no one could go to the doctor. Many doctors had left; the hospitals were bombed. Ghadir and Adnan became the closest thing to doctors, with customers asking about everything from heart issues to high blood pressure. Ghadir would sometimes call her sister in the United States, who was a doctor, for advice: "What do I do?"

More than once, they had to flee to bomb shelters and wait for danger to pass. When they emerged, it was to find new customers from other neighborhoods, who said, "We heard you are kind. We thought that we would visit."

"It was dangerous for them to come," Ghadir said. "At that time, whenever I went to go get the medicine, I knew I might not come back. Maybe there would be a missile. There was never any safety. There was so much death."

Mostly people would talk about their friends, their siblings. "I'm tired; I don't know how I'm going to continue," they would say. And Ghadir would respond, "It's not your fault; you're not doing anything wrong. It's wartime, and it's dangerous—everyone is tired. I'm also like you."

One day, a young man in army fatigues showed up, held Ghadir up at gunpoint, and demanded her supply of codeine. Like so many other young people around them, he had become addicted to drugs as a way of medicating against the horrors of war. She told him that she didn't have any.

"Go and find some," he demanded.

She called her brother, pretending she had another pharmacist on the line, and asked for codeine. When he heard her trembling voice, he sent for help.

Adnan and Ghadir were still trying to make things seem as normal as possible for the children. They wanted Fridays to still feel like a day off, so in the evenings, they closed the pharmacy at around 9:00 p.m. and took the children in the car for ice cream in the neighborhood. Aleppo was famous for its ice cream. It was something for Samer and Jamil to look forward to.

One Friday evening, they were joined by Adnan's uncle. They returned to the house around 10:00 p.m. There was no electricity, and so they made their way inside in the dark, holding the tired children and tucking them into bed.

Half an hour later, the children still hadn't fallen asleep when Adnan and Ghadir heard an explosion somewhere near the house. Then a second—this one so close to their house that the walls seemed to tremble. Ghadir didn't know what to do. The windows were open, and she heard someone outside saying, "That house belongs to the pharmacists." She put on her jacket and rushed outside, thinking someone must have been injured and needed their help. Instead, she saw their car smoking, crumbled into a heap. A missile had landed directly on top of it.

In war, everything becomes more than itself. And in that way, the car was not only a car. It was the only major possession they had managed to save intact from their life before the war, the only valuable material possession they still had. The car, for whatever reason, had become the way Ghadir had convinced herself that everything was going to be okay, that they would be able to escape when it was time.

Khallas, Ghadir thought to herself. *That's enough. That's enough.*

The neighbors came out of their houses to comfort her. She looked around at her devastated neighborhood. Dozens of rockets had fallen. All she could think about was the children.

Adnan called someone to take the car away. The next morning, it was gone. When the children woke up, Ghadir told them their dad had sold it.

"Only thirty minutes had passed from the time we parked the car to the time the rocket landed," Adnan told me. "We kept thinking, 'We'd just been there.'"

"It was like a message to us," Ghadir added. "It's time to go—"

"Like a warning," Adnan broke in, "that at any moment, everything could be lost."

"I had always felt like God was protecting us," Ghadir said. "Nothing had happened to my husband or the children. But when that happened, I also felt like God was speaking to us and saying, *You need to act*. And I felt that everything we had accomplished so far with the pharmacy meant nothing so long as the kids weren't safe."

From now on, their focus would be on how to get out of Aleppo alive.

22 | HOLDING THE KEYS

2015. That was the year Russia officially intervened on the Syrian government side of the war. From then on, the scale of violence, including aerial bombardments, increased dramatically. It was, by all accounts, a turning point in an already terrible war.

2015. That was the year Alan Kurdi, a three-year-old Syrian boy dressed in a red shirt and dark shorts, was photographed face down on the beach, as though sleeping. His body had washed up after the boat that was carrying him to Greece capsized off the coast of Turkey, his small shoes still fastened to his feet.

2015. That was the year a truck full of the dead bodies of migrants was discovered on the side of a road in Austria.

2015. That was the year more than eight hundred migrants crowded onto a single ship from Libya that sank in the Mediterranean.

2015. That was the year nearly a million refugees fled to Europe, with thousands losing their lives in the sea on the way.

There are small details that don't seem important at all until a time of war, and then they do. Errands put off, papers left behind, tiny details that upturn the trajectory of a life. I had heard about these details during my years of traveling and speaking with

WHAT WE REMEMBER WILL BE SAVED

refugees—stories of diplomas left behind, papers showing owner-
ship of property lost, final exams missed.

For Adnan and Ghadir, the detail was their passports. Adnan
had renewed his, but Ghadir and the children hadn't finished theirs.
In the meantime, a bomb had landed on the place where passports
were renewed.

"It was something you don't think about," said Ghadir, "and
then it stops your entire life."

Perhaps it was for the best. In any event, it was clarifying. There
was no way they were going to put the children on a rubber boat to
cross the sea, and that was the only way to Europe from Aleppo. So
they made the difficult decision: Adnan would travel without them
to Europe and find a way to help Ghadir and the children to follow
afterward.

Adnan tried not to think of what lay ahead. It was the most
dangerous year to cross the Mediterranean, and yet he felt certain it was even more dangerous to remain in Aleppo. At least he
had some control over the conditions by which he would travel to
Greece. Death in Aleppo felt entirely random.

Adnan begged Ghadir to take the kids to Beirut, Lebanon, and
wait for him there. But Beirut was expensive, and there was no
way for her to work—no place to keep the kids in school. No, they
would remain in Aleppo, and she would run the pharmacy alone,
even among the bombs.

Adnan packed his bags, and then he changed his mind again.
Would he really go? It seemed impossible to leave Ghadir and the
boys alone in the middle of a war. Still, he read the news. Europe
was soon expecting a million refugees, and the borders wouldn't
stay open for long. Ghadir told the boys that their dad would be
visiting his father in Turkey, that he would return home to them
soon.

But they knew, somehow. The last night they slept next to him,
holding on to his legs, refusing to let him go. At 4:15 in the morning,

Jamil, their youngest son, woke up. "Dad's going?" he asked. He began to cry and cry.

The following morning, as Ghadir embraced Adnan, she assured him they would all be together in a month's time. He handed her the keys to the pharmacy. She thought, *All of the responsibility has fallen on me now.*

Adnan traveled to Beirut for two days and then on to Turkey, where he stayed for a month, visiting his father, whom he did not know if he would ever see again. That was the nature of war, of exile—you could no longer assume that any meeting wouldn't be the last. Borders and papers and seas now separated those who had once lived upstairs, next door. All their lives were becoming fragmented.

Adnan called Ghadir one day and said, "Tomorrow, I'm going to a place that I don't know, and I won't be able to speak to you until I'm in Europe."

So it was really happening. She tried to stop him, to ask him to come back home, to insist that what mattered was that the family remained together, but it was no use. He had already paid. He had even given the smugglers extra money to travel on a rubber dinghy with fewer people on it, to reduce the risk of it capsizing. That night, in a place they didn't know, the smugglers loaded Adnan and other refugees into a boat. He was relieved to see that it wasn't crowded, just as they had promised. Then, just when it was about to leave, the smugglers returned, held them at gunpoint, and filled the boat all the way to capacity with new passengers. There was nothing he could do about it.

He sent Ghadir a message: "I'm going."

The boat set out to sea. Soon, the shore was vanishing behind him. Adnan thought to himself, "That's it. This might be the end of my life." It felt like a trip from heaven to hell and hopefully to heaven again. Heaven because the possibility of safety was finally on the horizon for his family. Hell because he might drown seeking it.

It was perhaps an hour between Turkey and Greece, but it felt like one hundred hours. It was so dangerous—we were many people in a single boat: we had children and elderly people with us; we had people who didn't know how to swim, and the one who was steering didn't know how to steer a boat. The person who put the engine and the petrol—he was also someone who didn't specialize in this. In the end, they just wanted us to leave from that place so they could take our money.

When we reached the halfway point, and then when we saw that we were closer to Greece than to Turkey, we started to feel a bit better. Then, when you see the island in front of you, and you think, *Oh, I would be able to swim from here to there . . .*

Ghadir was waiting to hear from him. Twelve hours passed. She called Adnan's sister, who was abroad. "Call the ambulance in Turkey," she said. "Tell them there's been no word of my husband since yesterday."

They were all waiting: Ghadir; Adnan's father, his sisters. They were texting one another with all the anxiety of losing a husband, a brother, an only son.

HAVE YOU HEARD FROM HIM?
ANY WORD?
STILL NO WORD?
NOTHING?

Ghadir tried to contain her rising alarm. Finally, when Adnan arrived on the shores of Greece, he found a cell phone that he could borrow and called Ghadir.

She heard his voice. He tried to explain what happened, but it didn't matter now. He had survived.

The week when school started again, the children were only able to go for two days. They spent two nights in a shelter. Their city had become one of the most dangerous places in the world. On some days, Ghadir could keep the pharmacy open for only two hours. She felt they could die at any moment.

By now, all the clean water had gone. Ghadir spent some of the little money they had buying water from the private vendor who circled through the neighborhoods. Nearly all the fresh vegetables had disappeared from the markets, and the idea of a cucumber or a tomato became a fantasy. It was harder and harder to access medicine. She asked the trader who traveled back and forth to Lebanon to bring vitamins for her children so they wouldn't be malnourished, and she paid him double to make sure he didn't forget.

One morning, she was sitting at the counter of the pharmacy. A woman walked in, her two children trailing behind her, a boy and a little girl. She looked frightened. Ghadir tried to set her at ease with her smile. "We're traveling to meet my husband. He's already left Aleppo," the woman confided. "Can you tell us what we'll need to take with us?"

It was not a question. Ghadir sensed in it something else—the woman's hope that Ghadir could somehow offer them safety, protection. She mapped out the road in her imagination that the family would have to take to safety. She pictured the waits at the checkpoints, the change in temperatures, perhaps a lack of access to clean drinking water.

"I'll give you something if the children experience motion sickness," she said calmly, pulling a box off the shelves. "There might be temperatures you're not used to as well, so we'll put in some medicine if you get a stomach bug or need rehydration. There's something if anyone catches a fever." She packed everything carefully, along with bandages for cuts and scrapes. The woman seemed her age, her children the same age as her own, and she could not help but wonder why she was staying put and this woman was leaving. How much longer could she and the children possibly survive?

For weeks, the pharmacy had been filling up with Aleppans fleeing the country, many on their way to attempt to cross the sea to Europe. They had heard from those who had already arrived in Europe that it was different there; you couldn't just walk into a pharmacy and buy prescription drugs the way you could in Syria. Abroad, only doctors could prescribe many of the medicines they took for granted. And what about the journey? How would they even find a doctor who spoke Arabic? What if they couldn't afford medicine by the time they arrived?

Ghadir was left to imagine herself into others' lives, to send them off with bandages and first-aid kits, with pills to stop nausea and motion sickness, with months of medicines for people who suffered from heart conditions. She scribbled the names of medications in English for them to fold into their bags, to carry in plastic across the sea, to show to new doctors if they arrived on the other side.

In the meantime, Adnan traveled to Amsterdam, where he knew that many of the people spoke English in addition to Dutch. He imagined they might be able to start over there quickly because he and Ghadir and the children already spoke fluent English. It wasn't like Germany, where they would feel like strangers and spend years studying the language before they could work. Here, at least, they would be able to communicate with others from the very first day. When he registered, he told officials that his family was in grave danger and urgently needed to get out of Aleppo. They placed him in a camp for refugees.

He waited. He called home every day. The boys still did not know why he had left. "When are you coming home, Daddy?" they asked.

At the pharmacy in Aleppo, everything reminded Ghadir of Adnan. She had never run a pharmacy alone, and every detail was imbued with his presence: the tiles, the shelves, the written notes in the notebook. The customers all asked for him, and when she told them that he had gone, they whispered, "What a pity." At night, she promised the children they would all leave the war and join their daddy soon.

> Every time I would say, "We'll go in spring." Then spring came, and we hadn't gone yet. "Why?" they'd ask. "Oh, because you need to finish school." Then we'd say, "No, we'll travel on the Eid." Then the Eid would come, and we'd say, "No, on the next Eid." . . . The days would continue, and still we didn't go. We waited ten months . . .

By then, the main roads were closed. There was no milk. "I was so scared. If I heard that a bomb had fallen, even if it was far away, I went to their school and brought them home," Ghadir said. "If a bomb fell when I was out getting medicine, I became like a crazy person . . ."

Once she opened the pharmacy door a few minutes late. A customer was already standing at the door, waiting to check on her: "Why were you late? Are you sure that you're okay?" It had become like that. If a store didn't open, it might mean the person who owned it was gone.

Now it was the customers who took care of her. Umm Ala,' eighty-five years old, still came every twenty days to get her medicine. She stayed an hour and a half with Ghadir. But other than that, she never left her house because it was difficult to move. Ghadir would tell her, "I'll bring your medicine to you." But she said, "No, I want to come and get it." She lived close to the pharmacy, and she would come so slowly, struggling to walk.

There was an old woman who was a doctor, and she would come by too. There was Ismail, seventy years old. He was so respectful and dignified. He said, "I always come, just to take the medicine from you." He would touch his heart. When he came out of the hospital from a heart attack, he came to take his medicine, even before he arrived at home.

Those old people who always came, they would pass by even if they didn't need medicine, to ask about the children. It was too dangerous to visit her parents. Adnan was gone. The customers had become family.

"Today, if I could return again, I wouldn't have done it," Ghadir told me, referring to the choice to agree for Adnan to go ahead. "It was too difficult, especially for the children. The children didn't understand why their father left them, why we were in the war and he was far away. They didn't understand any of this. My youngest son, Jamil, was always asking, 'Why did Dad leave us? Why did he leave us on our own?' It was the hardest thing. And with Adnan, we had no idea when he would get a residency and when we would be able to join him."

Ten months after he arrived in Amsterdam, Adnan's family unification papers came through. They had been hastened by the fact that everyone in Europe now knew that every day someone remained in Aleppo increased the chances of their dying in the war.

Adnan called Ghadir. By then, the news had become so impossible that she could hardly believe it was true.

She had to scramble. Her father had to write a letter, giving her permission to travel without her husband, and then she had to leave within a certain window of time. She needed to close the pharmacy, decide what to do with the medicine.

Then pack. The children each carried a backpack with a note-book, some crayons to draw with, and their favorite toy. She took the photo album that contained their wedding photos. Adnan's old computer, which had other photographs. All she cared about saving was their memories. She had learned that everything else was perishable.

On the last day, she closed the pharmacy and locked it behind her. They left Aleppo at five in the morning, making sure to wear their simplest clothes so that they wouldn't get robbed or kid-napped on the way. The road to Lebanon was dangerous. Even the taxi driver told them that he couldn't guarantee they would arrive safely.

They drove through checkpoints. The driver paid at each one. They arrived at the Lebanese border at twelve in the afternoon, and they waited there until seven at night. It was over one hundred degrees. The kids were crying because there was no water, and the car wasn't moving. They arrived in Beirut at nine in the evening.

The next day, Ghadir, who had made an appointment at the embassy of the Netherlands, took a taxi there and waited for her interview to obtain their visas.

Adnan was supposed to meet them in Beirut so that they wouldn't have to travel to the Netherlands alone. He boarded a flight in Amsterdam. When he was transferring to his next flight in Greece, he showed his documents to officials, and they stopped him.

"You didn't come to Europe in a regular way, did you?" an offi-cer asked him. He conceded that no, he hadn't, that no "regular" ways had been available to refugees.

"You can get on the plane to go to Lebanon. But if you leave, we won't let you back into Europe again." He had no choice but to return to Amsterdam.

Back in Beirut, Ghadir didn't have a cell phone. She took the children to the airport, and they waited at the gate until Adnan's plane arrived. They watched as every single passenger entered the gate. No Adnan.

That was enough. For her. For the children. It had become entirely too much.

It took everything she had to find the strength to go to the embassy of the Netherlands later that week, to collect their visas, and then to fly alone with the children, five days later.

Ten months had passed since Adnan had left Aleppo. Ten long months. Months that had included his passage on the sea. Months that had included Ghadir left behind with her children in war. Months of Adnan begging the camp officials in the Netherlands, day after day, *Please help me. Help me to save my family.*

They passed through the arrivals gate in Amsterdam. Adnan ran to the children and embraced them. The oldest, Samer, collapsed into his father's arms. But Jamil moved away. From his perspective, his father had abandoned them to the war.

There was no way to explain that their father had risked his life in order to save theirs. To do so would only be to explain other, even more frightening realities. And that was when Ghadir first knew. She had done everything she could to protect her children, to make their lives normal, to pretend the war wasn't happening. "It was for nothing," she told me. "I didn't protect them from anything. All along, they knew everything that was happening around them, and there was nothing I could do about it."

They were placed in a camp. Every time Adnan left the room, even to go to the bathroom, Jamil cried. "Are you leaving us, Baba?" he asked. They stayed for a month and a half until they were transferred to a house perched on the edge of a canal, where the seagulls passed with their broad wings, casting shadows over the roofs.

A year passed. Another. The children went to school. On the weekends, they walked to Park Frankendael, full of trees and open spaces and children playing soccer. And that is where I met them, sitting in the park, the boys laughing and practicing their Dutch.

As we ended our conversation, I remembered what they had said when I asked them what they had saved, the way Ghadir had looked at me with her warm smile.

I'm sorry; I wish that we could help you. But all we ever had in Syria was a pharmacy.

A few months later, a friend of mine from Amsterdam was visiting me in Jerusalem. When Ghadir found out, she sent something with her to give me. It was half a bar of Aleppo soap, the stamp in Arabic still visible, sliced so that you could see the green inside of aged oil and laurel leaves. I had no idea how she still had it—whether she had carried it with her or someone else had given it to her. I held it close and smelled it, and for a moment I was walking again through the streets of Aleppo, the whir of sewing machines in the air, and the smell of coffee and soap, and the Arabic that sounds like music. It was all still there.

Everything was not lost. I had permission to know that now. Or perhaps everything was lost, but from the knowledge of that, something could still be built. I could see Ghadir, opening the garage, setting the coffee cups on the counter. Arranging the bottles on the shelves in just such a way that anyone who saw them would believe those shelves were full.

PART V

QASSEM'S FAMILY

Mount Sinjar, Iraq → Germany

> *The world didn't last for Majnûn and Leylê . . .*
> —"Eyshê Balê," traditional Yazidi song

23 | THE STORYTELLER

The nuns were entering and leaving the main gate of the abbey, their black tunics very nearly sweeping the floor. One of them climbed onto a bicycle and pedaled away. I had arrived that afternoon from a long journey of two airplanes, a train, and a bus, the last of which had dropped me at the end of a long road in the middle of the forest. I walked for ten minutes before crossing a bridge and seeing the abbey come into view, a moat directly in front of it, the abbey itself all stone and red roofs, surrounded by a vast silence and trees leaning over the water. I slipped into the chapel in time for afternoon prayers, when the cloistered nuns emerged from the back of the church, singing German hymns in an unexpected and glorious harmony.

I had come to this convent in Germany because the nuns were giving asylum to some of the most vulnerable refugees in the world. That afternoon, one of the nuns, Sarah, an American who had lived at the convent for a decade, led me around the grounds. Two young men crossed our path near the bridge; one of them was pushing a wheelbarrow. She spoke to the one with the wheelbarrow in his native language, and he shyly put out his hand. I introduced myself in Arabic, and he smiled in surprise.

Later, we walked to the kitchen of the guest house, where two young women were baking kleicha, an Iraqi pastry of dates and cinnamon wrapped together in tiny rolls. They invited me to join them, and as I rolled out dough, I noticed the tattoos on the younger girl's arm. They were both Yazidi, members of a small and highly persecuted religious minority from northern Iraq. The youngest, barely twenty, had survived the genocide on Mount Sinjar in Iraq that had been carried out in 2014 by ISIS.

I was terrible at making kleicha; I cut all the pastries much too large, and they teased me good-naturedly. They laughed together, speaking in their language and remembering to translate for me into Arabic every now and then so that I wouldn't feel left out.

He arrived that first hour, that same man I had seen pushing the wheelbarrow. Young, in his early twenties, I think, but it was hard to tell. He was confident but also hesitant, as if always reading every situation for clues. He pulled up a chair near to where we sat at the table, next to where I was rolling out dough. He surveyed me for a moment.

"I have heard that you're a storyteller," he said.

"I'm a writer," I replied quietly.

He nodded, pausing for a moment. Then without me asking, he began to speak to me about their mountain. The younger of the two women was his sister, he said, and they had spent nine days together on Mount Sinjar, fleeing Daesh, or ISIS, who was pursuing them and trying to kill them. Later, they had spent twenty-nine days trying to escape from Iraq to Germany. They had arrived in the country a few months ago.

European law said that they should be sent back to the first place they had been caught and fingerprinted on their journey, which in their case was Romania, where they had been arrested. But there was no way they were going back to Romania. Their parents and two brothers were already in Germany, and they were desperate to stay with them. For the moment, they were stranded in asylum in this remote convent, hoping to eventually change their status and appeal in the courts through German law for family reunification.

He was telling me everything in a rush, in Arabic, and I did not even know his name. It struck me that, in the middle of a German forest, besides the few other Yazidis there and that American nun who had learned their language, he had likely not met anyone in a very long time who he could speak to.

"Will you still be here after evening prayer?" I asked him.

He laughed wryly, amused at the idea that he could be anywhere else. They were stuck there, risking arrest by German authorities if they left the church compound.

I returned that evening after the prayer. And the next, and the next. We sat on two benches across from one another, beneath a tree whose branches shielded us from the sky, beside the field where horses grazed. Germany disappeared, and he channeled the tradition of their Yazidi storytellers: storytellers he had listened to since he was a boy, who recounted the tales of the past and so transmitted them to future generations. In Sinjar, those storytellers had hailed from certain families, and they would visit each Yazidi village to tell them of their past. But everything was different now. He would tell the story because he remained to tell it, and it still needed to be told. He would tell the story so that I could tell the story, so it would be remembered.

A rabbit hopped by us. Laughter came from an open window. I was pulled into the experience of story, memorized and told night after night until it becomes part of the body and can be carried forth. We were no longer in a convent in Germany but at the base of Mount Sinjar, on that day in 2014 when everything changed.

24 | A HOUSE OF CLAY

It was August 3, 2014, and they were coming. He had known they would come, sooner or later, and yet he could not quite believe it. He rose from the terrace where he was sleeping and looked down to see figures scrambling in the street below. He raced down the stairs. The pigeons: he rushed to leave water in their coops. His father was calling for them to hurry.

He ran to the front of the house and climbed into the truck, with his parents and brothers and sisters and aunts and uncles and cousins, all rushing to lift themselves into cars, the houses around him emptying out in a rush of feet, scrambling, in the rising August sun. He forgot to grab enough food. He forgot enough water. Later, he would hear that a woman forgot her child, sleeping in bed.

Then they were gone.

That was the last he saw of the house: a glimpse from the truck, rumbling away. The house of clay and branches, of memory and sound, of footsteps and bread, the pigeons waiting to be released from their cages. The house where he had loved Khonaf. The house where he had slept beneath the forgiving sky.

In that house of clay, Qassem had grown up with thirty-six members of a single family: his father's parents, their four sons, and in turn their sons and daughters, who were his cousins. For the first years of his life, all thirty-six of them lived in a single extended house, eating and sleeping and running into one another, until the long legs of the children could no longer fit, much as they tried to squeeze them. When he noticed his children growing up so quickly, Qassem's father decided to build for them a second house, this one of concrete, on the opposite side of the garden but still in full view of the first house. Between the two homes, eggplants and cucumbers and tomatoes and parsley grew, the green spaces alive with sheep and cows and chickens and dogs and eventually two peacocks, and with the laughter of children. That square contained the entirety of Qassem's childhood.

With the new house completed, Qassem and his siblings carried their belongings from the first house to the second one, but in the end, he loved what was made of the earth. He found himself drawn back to his childhood house of clay, the ancestral home, the house of full belonging. He spent his days moving between one house and the other, as did his brothers and sisters and cousins, sleeping some nights in the new house and others in the old, so that any outsider who stumbled in would have had no clear idea which house belonged to which family or even whose children belonged to which parents.

All of this was meant to be so. His grandfather had always told him they were not four families but one single family, that cousins may as well be brothers and sisters. All of them were part of the same soul. Arguments were to be mended like scraped knees, as quickly as possible. God was watching over them and wanted them to stay together, to remain one.

Once, in a night of his boyhood subsumed by summer heat, when Qassem was perhaps eight years old, he fell asleep on a mattress laid out on the flat roof of the ancient clay house, his body one in a line of boys and men and cousins all sleeping in tangled rows beneath the stars. He could remember the order, even now, years later: his body, then his older brother's, his cousin's, and then his grandmother, who suffered from rheumatism and whose feet the boys had taken turns massaging before she slept in order to ease her pain. On the opposite side of the roof, his father had slept alongside Qassem's other brothers, and his sisters slept still farther down. An entire roof covered with family.

That evening as he'd slept, Qassem had, for no reason at all, stood up in his dreaming beneath the star-studded sky and begun walking in his sleep. He had put one foot in front of the other, winding his way somehow among the sleeping bodies, and he had walked right off the roof.

His sleeping body had fallen through the air, landing with a crash in the neighbor's garden. The impact jolted him awake, his head pounding. Blood poured down the side of his face. Barking dogs advanced.

The neighbor's door opened. "Are you missing someone?" the neighbor called out to the neighboring sky.

There was a pause before Qassem's father called back from the rooftop, "No, everyone's here."

The dogs. The earth against his mouth. The voice again calling out to the roof, "Are you sure you're not missing someone?"

Qassem heard his uncle, from the second line of sleepers, yelling, "No, everyone's here!"

The dogs were circling now, almost upon him. He felt his own voice, stunned, attempting to call out, but he was unable to find the strength. Then he heard his brother's startled cry: "By God! Where's Qassem?"

"Qassem! Qassem!" Footsteps, descending in the dark, advanced toward him, and his body was being lifted into his father's arms. There was the bumpy drive to the hospital miles away, the throbbing headaches that would return to haunt him. Later came the family decision that even in the heat, they would no longer let Qassem sleep on the roof for fear he would walk off again.

Years later, when Qassem told me the story, he recalled that night not with sadness but with wonder, a roof stamped with a thousand nights of all their bodies lying next to one another, indiscernible in the dark.

"To be honest, there was nothing more beautiful than that," he said. "So much family bound up in one another that you couldn't even tell when one was gone."

Tel Qasab, located in the Mount Sinjar region, barely appears on a map. The village where Qassem grew up contained a collection of earth and mud and concrete houses sprawled across a piece of land nestled in the farthest edge of Iraq, between eastern Syria, southeastern Turkey, Iraqi Kurdistan, and Arabic-speaking Mosul. Around his village lay the heartland of the Yazidi people, at the base of the Sinjar Mountain—a land they had lived in for generations, one of shrines and stories. In these lands lived his family: Qassem's grandparents and his parents, his four brothers, three sisters, aunts, uncles, cousins, and his ancestors. The bodies of their ancestors were buried in the white conical mountain shrines on the nearby mountain slopes, where Yazidis believed they had lived since the beginning of creation and where they said Noah's ark had finally settled after the flood.

Qassem resembled his siblings—average height; lean; strong features; a sunburned, chiseled face marked by high cheekbones; short-cropped hair; and hazel, almost greenish eyes that shone when he laughed and clouded over when he was gloomy, which was often. A moustache, as most Yazidi men in Sinjar have as soon as they are old enough to grow it, and a slight beard with reddish flecks.

Qassem had never left the Mount Sinjar region. The land provided his family with olive trees, wheat and barley, and vegetables and animals, the earth for their houses, and even the stones for the game of five stones, the ancient variation of jacks that he played in front of his house as a boy. He had rarely ventured farther than his school, which was a few miles away and to which he walked on a long path. Sometimes he'd get caught in the rain, the water dampening the pages of his lessons.

Qassem loved animals and felt at home in nature, bound to the earth and to the sky. He had always befriended the birds that hovered between them. The Yazidis pray in the direction of the sun, recognizing its rising first thing in the morning with outstretched palms. He felt himself drawn, always, toward light. As a boy, he and the other children would build a fire and take turns leaping over it. Years later, when he had forgotten so much, he remembered the fire.

"Every child would try to count the stars," he told me. "Sometimes I would wait an hour just to see a shooting star, to try to guess where it was going."

He did not know how old he was. In Sinjar, you were as old as the day your family decided to register your birth officially. His grandfather had registered his birth nineteen years before that August day in 2014 that they had fled for the mountain—several years after his actual birth, in order to postpone the date he might have to one day serve in the army. Serving in the army was mandatory in Iraq, and his father and grandfather had spoken of the war years often when he was a child. They described those eras when the country had gone from war with Iran to war in the Gulf, when boys disappeared into battle and were never heard of again—and all for nothing. Better to not let the world know you had been born at all.

So Qassem had happily grown up, ageless—until it had been time to start primary school. Then his grandfather realized that his official papers made him too young to enroll. Now they were faced with a different dilemma; he would not have his grandson not learning how to read.

The only solution was to once again forge new identity papers for him, this time with a birthdate making Qassem *older* than the first ones claimed he was—though he would now have to walk to a school far from his house so that the principal wouldn't recognize him. So he walked, suffering from the rain that soaked him on the long journey there and the boys who teased him for traveling such a long distance. In the end, Qassem carried several papers with several birthdays, and none of them was his actual birthday at all, of which he and his family no longer had any idea. The day soon would come when he would have to venture across the border out of Sinjar and into the land of time, but that day had not come yet.

As far as Qassem was concerned, he was a boy like other boys: one who loved pigeons and sticks and the smell of bread, who played soccer with a ball of old cloth tied together. He and his siblings shoveled the earth with their hands until they compacted a high mound, and then they set a long, rough log atop it so that by balancing on each side of it, they could seesaw for hours. Qassem did not even know that he was Yazidi or that such a thing existed. He was just a child in a world of other children.

For those first years of his life, Qassem passed his afternoons kneeling in the dusty ground beside Khonaf, a girl who lived in the home built beside the eastern entrance to his family's sprawling compound. Together, they constructed houses of found stones. After the rains, when the hard clay softened enough for them to manage it, they built an entire village, complete with cars and a police force and horses, sheep, and donkeys to be tended. On other mornings, she challenged him in a game of five stones. She could throw a stone in the air and swipe the four others from the ground before the first one landed again in her palm with a quickness that made his heart leap. How did she do that?

One day, after kneeling all morning in the dirt beside her, Qassem returned to his home to find his grandmother working alone. It was his chance to tell her. "I want to marry," he announced.

She looked up from her cooking. "Who is it that you want to take?"

He declared it with all the seriousness a small boy could summon. "Our neighbor, Khonaf," he said. "I saw her with my eyes, and now I want to marry her."

He expected a nod, at the very least, or even a smile or an embrace. But his grandmother's response had been swift. "That's not possible," she told him.

Then she paused. For a moment, he thought she might reconsider. "Sure, you could marry her," she conceded. "But we're a large family, and you wouldn't be able to live with us any longer. There would be no room. Where would you go?"

Where would he go? He remembered that their cow had recently died and had not been replaced, that there was a room left open in the stable large enough for a mattress. "We'll sleep where the cow used to live," he decided. "It will be wonderful." But he knew somehow that they would not sleep with the animals and that there would be no marrying Khonaf after all.

To Qassem, the Sinjar region was the world in its entirety: olive trees and open sky and the nearby market, with its bundles of clothes and toys, the animals he tended to. He collected pigeons, acquiring exotic varieties with big breasts or feathers that covered their eyes, opening the doors to their coops in the morning before school, feeding them and letting them out to fly.

Tel Qasab was not their original village. For generations, Qassem's ancestors had lived with thousands of other Yazidis on the slopes of the mountain of Sinjar itself, among the ancient shrines called mazars and holy places and the wells that provided water for animals and agriculture. There, the Yazidis had passed down their traditions by word of mouth, through the storytellers and the qawwals: sacred singers who journeyed to their villages every year, making sure that no story or lesson was lost. They learned the stories of the seven angels, present at creation, of the holy men in each generation who protected them, the goodness they must practice and the evil they must avoid. A world was transmitted this way, through families, but it demanded that they stay together so that none of the past would be lost.

During the period of Saddam Hussein, the Yazidis of Mount Sinjar had been forced to resettle into collective villages at the mountain's base, where they were cut off from the shrines of their ancestors and sent to school to speak Arabic and learn to read and write. There, they became Yazidis who spoke a language that Qassem and his family call "Yazidia" (but that scholars consider to be a dialect of the Kurdish language) to one another and wrote and spoke in Arabic at school. The land that they lived on was valuable, and the Sunni Arabs encouraged them to identify as Arabs; the Kurds encouraged them to identify as Kurds. But Qassem, as a child, was told firmly that they were a world of their own. "You're Yazidi," his grandfather told them as children.

When the government of Saddam Hussein razed their ancestral villages, the Yazidis of Mount Sinjar did what they had always done. The storytellers and singers took the memories of their destroyed villages and turned them into stories and songs so that they would not be forgotten, and they sang them whenever there was a feast day, a gathering, a funeral. Once a year, Qassem and his family still faithfully set out on a pilgrimage to the mountain of their ancestors and visited the dead in the ancient shrine of Mazar Amadin.

There, he and his family would picnic among the tombs of their relatives. Qassem would first watch from a distance as the women went out ahead, wailing and weeping over the tombs and calling out to their missing loved ones. When they had finished, he walked past the wishing tree with the pieces of fabric tied to its branches, toward the white shrine, kissing the door before entering.

On the wall in front of him hung portraits of the dead, their faces meeting his gaze as if to speak to him. Then a long line of shiny, knotted bolts of fabric: pink and white and yellow and gold, draped and knotted. His tiny child's hands had struggled in tying the fabric once in a knot, then untying it. A second piece, tied again, and then untied. Only the third piece was tied and then not untied. With this piece of cloth, he made his wish.

A wish, a vow. Something in his heart told him that God witnessed this prayer in a special way, and so he prepared himself for days in advance, purifying his heart. He made a point of entering each year's pilgrimage with his beloved aunt Nada. She no longer lived with them in the grand house, for she had moved to the opposite side of Sinjar since she'd married, but she joined them every year for the pilgrimage to the family shrine. She loved Qassem as her own son, perhaps because she'd never had a son of her own. She had a daughter, but Qassem knew that she was dreaming of having a boy.

That is why he entered the shrine holding her hand, and he prayed for her. He learned on those days that he could offer up his heart for those he loved. Qassem didn't ask God that his aunt become pregnant with a boy: he didn't presume to ask God for anything directly. He trusted that God wrote everything that happens in our lives for a reason and that surely God knew what was best. And so Qassem prayed to God with this sentence, spoken quietly in his heart: "Please grant my aunt happiness."

All of Sinjar felt sacred to Qassem. The men dug up the earth and made the bricks for the old houses themselves, of clay and straw mixed with water, left under the sun to dry until they formed hard blocks. They fashioned ceilings out of woven mats of straw, which kept the air cool in the summer and the walls heated in winter. After the rains, they covered the outer walls anew with the special clay of the mountains, a fidelity that required an annual pilgrimage to gather it in the region of Zilaliya. The earth was holy, and they lived in it.

Outside of Sinjar, throughout Iraq and northern Syria and southeastern Turkey, where they were known, the Yazidis were sometimes called the People of the Peacock Angel by the Muslims and Christians who lived around them. Members of a monotheistic faith with a rich oral tradition, they believed that when God had sent to the earth seven angels at the beginning of time, the highest one, Tawus Melek, had taken the shape of a peacock and in turn became protector of the Yazidis. The neighboring tribes, suspicious of the Yazidis and the secrecy with which they guarded their faith, sometimes accused them of secretly worshipping the devil in the form of a peacock. As an oral culture, they had no sacred book to prove others wrong.

So the Yazidis were targeted in persecution after persecution for centuries. When al-Qaeda gained strength in Iraq following the US invasion, they set off four coordinated bomb attacks in Sheikh Khudr in 2007 that killed hundreds of Yazidis. The community called these persecutions firman—and the tradition said that there had been seventy-two such incidents against the Yazidis throughout their history. That was yet one more reason Qassem and his family stayed put at the foot of Mount Sinjar in that far corner—because they could be safe there.

By the time he was around seventeen years old, Qassem had dropped out of school. He saved the money he earned from working long hours with his family's company doing physical labor. He didn't want much: to tend his animals, to remain with his family, perhaps to marry one day. He collected goats and dogs and birds and a cow. The neighbors teased him. "Why don't you get a camel?" they joked as the courtyard become more and more crowded with livestock he collected. He assured them that if a camel were to be had, he would purchase it.

Instead, he and his uncles bought two peacocks, enormous and pompous, that strutted back and forth between the family's two houses. The men of his family built a special coop to contain them at night. The neighbors gathered, and with Qassem, they waited for the peacocks to unfurl their plumes—the metallic blue peacock suddenly opening into turquoise and green feathers glinting in the sunlight, the eyes of those feathers looking knowingly in every direction.

This went on for a time until the peacocks persisted in their squabbling every early morning, so loudly that the neighbors no longer cared about their holy associations. They would shout from their windows, "Sell the peacocks! Sell the peacocks!"

When I met him, Qassem looked back at his childhood in Sinjar and seemed a bit bewildered by all the heartache and beauty, the way it was all jumbled up in a single story.

Now it was August 3, 2014, and ISIS was attacking the village. Word had come to Qassem's family that the road to Iraqi Kurdistan, the one by which they might escape, had been cut off completely. The few Peshmerga stationed in their village had abandoned their posts and fled. Where would his family go now? The road to Mosul had been impassable for two months now, ever since the Islamic State had taken the city in June. The only remaining escape route was out to the mountain of Sinjar, blocked on the other side by the border to Syria: a mountain fully exposed in the desert sun.

> When we left, we took a bit of bread, just a few simple things because we had no idea that it was going to be like that. We were wearing plastic house sandals because it was summer. The sun was so strong. We had taken with us only a bit of water because we knew there was water in the region that we were fleeing to.

He would try to explain to me, and to himself, that no one can possibly comprehend the magnitude of leaving as it happens. It was perhaps eight in the morning when they left. The sun was rising, and soon it would be well over a hundred degrees. The road passed first through their ancestral village and then through a spring in Qiniyeh, where they would need to stop for water if they hoped to hide in the mountains for more than a day. They drove quickly toward the mountain. But when Qiniyeh came into view, the men rushed out of the trucks and collected only a bit of water, lacking the courage to stop for long. Who knew how much time they could spare? The men returned to the trucks, and they continued driving toward the mountain, heading to a high place where they might have a vantage point on what was taking place below, where ISIS was taking over their villages. It was decided that the elderly, women, and children would be deposited to safety, and then the young men would descend to the spring at Qiniyeh in the evening on their own. They headed toward the natural place to seek protection: the holy shrine where their ancestors were buried.

In the distance, as they approached the shrine, Qassem saw the shape of the white earthen cube, topped by a spherical cone pointing heavenward—that shrine he had known since boyhood. Mazar Amadin stood near the base of Mount Sinjar, and it was the resting place of Qassem's ancestors, each one buried facing the rising sun. The shrine itself, stark and serene, might have been an extension of the mountain.

ISIS was attacking not only Tel Qasab but all of the surrounding villages, and Mazar Amadin was the closest refuge, the first high place where his family could hide and still survey the area below. They had parked the cars a distance away and approached the shrine on foot. Other Yazidi families fleeing there arrived at the same time, scrambling. His grandmother could barely walk because of her rheumatism. They escorted her into the coolness of the shrine.

The August heat was scathing, and they rationed their little water. From the corner of his eye, he could see the sacred tree, covered with white pieces of cloth, where women like his aunt had prayed for children. He was certain they would remain at the shrine only one night, at most, before returning to their houses. The Peshmerga would certainly return to retake the villages from Daesh, and then they would all go home again. There were animals to take care of, birds to be let out for their evening flights.

At four or five in the evening, the sound of shooting echoed through the mountains, but no one could say from where.

By evening, the water was nearly gone, and the children were thirsty. Qassem's older brother Seyfo, his cousins, an uncle, and a handful of other men climbed back into two trucks—one red and one white—to head down again on the road they had taken from Tel Qasab, to the source of water at Qiniyeh.

Qassem thought back to home. Surely the animals would be shifting nervously in their pens, also parched with thirst. His pigeons would be expecting food. He tried to remain calm so that his sisters wouldn't be frightened.

He could faintly hear the familiar grinding of wheels against the unsteady ground as cars approached. The men were already back from the water source but much too early. Something must have made them turn around. Qassem rushed out to meet them.

"We were halfway down the mountain when we saw them running toward us," his uncle cried. "A woman, holding her baby. Her other two children were trying to catch up with her. She stopped the car and warned us, 'They killed my husband and his brother. Don't go down there. They're killing all the men and taking the women and children to a place we don't know.'"

They had hurriedly lifted the mother and her children into a car, turned around, and raced back to Mazar Amadin without having reached the spring. Now they had no water.

Night was falling. They waited, parched, in the nearing dark. It didn't make any sense. In Mosul, when Daesh had invaded two months earlier, they had given the Christians the choice to convert or to flee. He understood why they would want the territory of Sinjar, as it contained the roads connecting Mosul and ISIS forces in cities like Raqqa in northeastern Syria. But why would they start murdering Yazidis?

Over the ridge, a shape came into view, slowly taking on features. Qassem recognized his brother's friend Osso from their village, his face covered in blood. He had been wounded, but somehow he had made it up the mountain. A gash sliced the side of his cheek. He was trying to tell them something, but Qassem couldn't quite make out the words. *They killed my father*, he gasped. *They killed my two brothers. They took my brothers' children, and their daughters and their wives, and my mother, and my sisters, and threw them in cars and took them to a place we don't know.* Osso had pretended to be dead beneath a pile of corpses until he could escape.

Qassem couldn't understand it, still. Those who fled behind them from their village on the road to Qiniyeh, those neighbors who had no cars or who had run out of gas and who had fallen behind: had they been slaughtered or kidnapped? It seemed surreal—impossible. How could it be that Osso—their schoolmate, who his brother Seyfo had played soccer with every day, whose wedding his brother had just attended—had just lost his entire family? Qassem had often passed his sister Hana at school. Was she gone too?

Osso stumbled off, and Qassem heard his voice in the distance, carried into the passes, wailing, warning everyone he met, the men and women and children huddling in the crags of the mountain: *Don't go down the mountain. They're killing and kidnapping everyone.*

His father searched for his cell phone and dialed the number of their neighbor from Tel Qasab. The two families had long been friends, and he knew he could trust him even though he wasn't Yazidi. Muslims and Yazidis lived together in Tel Qasab as well as other villages in the Sinjar region, inhabiting different quarters but working together.

Qassem's father spoke the grim truth aloud: they were trapped on the mountain and would not be coming down again in the coming days. It was too dangerous. "Please open the gates of the animal pens," he told him. "Take any animals you want for yourself. If you don't want them, let them go free so that they won't starve to death."

"All of your animals have already been taken," the man told him.

"How is it possible they were taken?"

"Not just the animals. All your stored barley and wheat has been taken too. Everything you had has been stolen by the people of the region—especially by people you know."

No one was coming to save them. Qassem knew that now. He and his family members, in the dozens, scrambled up the mountain. He and other men and boys led the women, girls, and young children to a safer place a few hundred meters away from the shrine. They would be farther from the main road but now exposed to the heat of the day and the cold of the night. They would be safer there. Only his grandmother had stayed behind with the other elderly people. They had placed her in a building not far from the shrine, a small space built to hold supplies for digging graves. She was too weak to climb, and her rheumatism made even a few steps painful.

They decided they would descend every now and then to give her some of what little water they had.

Night was falling on their first day on the mountain. Qassem couldn't escape from the cold. He huddled beneath that same sky in which, as a boy, he had once tried to count the stars. He shivered in his summer clothes and sandals, unable to sleep.

Nearby, a man was speaking into his cell phone to his brother, safe in some far-off city, sobbing between his words. "Brother," he heard him say. "If I have done anything in my life to offend you, please forgive me now."

He opened his eyes as dawn rose on the second day, and he looked for his younger sisters. The one nearest to him in age, Lozin—the one who resembled him and who stayed so close beside him that they might have been twins—what would happen to her now? He had always watched over her, but in her own way she had taken care of him also. Feisty, swifter, and more agile than any of the boys at the game of five stones, she often refused to go to school but was always waiting for him when he returned, her voice full of tenderness, her laugh defiant. She possessed a certain radiance, with her red-tinted hair and her green-flecked eyes, and she knew that she was beautiful. Her affectionate rebelliousness made her the perfect match of wits for Qassem. He usually folded to anything she asked for at once.

Now he made sure to keep her in his line of vision. The women had heard what Osso had said about the men abducting his mother and sisters: there was no use trying to keep it from them. He huddled with his older brothers, his father, and his uncles, who were consulting one another on what to do next. His mother and aunts were approaching together, out of earshot from the younger ones.

His mother, strong of build and character to everyone who knew her, with broad shoulders and wide working hands, wearing the traditional white headscarf, spoke first. "If they come and find us, ISIS will kill the men," she said to them. "And that's fine for you; you'll be dead. But what about us? What they'll do to us women is far worse than death. And how will we live our lives without you? No, if they take us, we'll die every day."

Qassem waited. His mother, in his mother's voice—that mother who had held him and nursed him as a child—begged the men of the family: if the fighters of the Islamic State captured them on the mountain, the men of the family should shoot and kill the women first, before they could be taken hostage.

It was an impossible request. I never asked him, and Qassem never told me, if they agreed that they would.

25 | ADJUSTING TO THE DARKNESS

Qassem missed his grandfather, the family patriarch. Had he been there, he would have known what to do. He always had, until one day, when he was gone. Had he still been alive, he would have insisted that they stay together, whatever the costs. Family is family. They live together, and they die together.

As the only son of his parents, Qassem's grandfather had taken on the promise of his entire family line and therefore of transmitting history. Wearing the long white robe and head scarf of the oldest generations, with his wide white moustache and beard, he had been an imposing presence, and keeping the family together had been the primary goal of his life. Family was a treasure, that aspect worth saving in a world that had always been dangerous for the Yazidis. Family was a way of transmitting the past into the future; it was a book that had to be written and rewritten every generation so as not to disappear.

As head of the family, his grandfather had been the one to counsel them as children, scolding them every time they fought with one another. It was his grandfather who took him on his knee and reminded him, "Qassem, it doesn't matter if you have a million dollars. All that matters is family. Whoever has family is a wealthy man."

And it had been his grandfather who had moved the family to their village of Tel Qasab, years before Qassem was born, away from the heartache of the family's vast agricultural lands, where his grandfather had one day discovered his oldest son drowned in the well. Qassem's uncle had climbed in to fix the motor before getting trapped inside. After finding the body, Qassem's grandfather could no longer bear to work in that garden, suffused as it was with such loss. He had buried his oldest son's body in Mazar Amadin, rented the land out to other families to harvest, and started life over again in Tel Qasab, in the single house that in time became two. Here had been a place to plant a new garden, to grow the family, to heal from the past.

Qassem had known even when he was a boy that something about him was different than the others in his family. His brothers were smart, and yet he tried again and again in school but never seemed to move ahead. He compensated by his strength, his fierceness. Words seemed to go into his mind, only to fly away afterward. But his grandfather had understood him, had loved all of them without differentiating between them.

Life possessed a certain loneliness. It wasn't only school. It was the walking in his sleep. Qassem talked in his sleep at night too. Once, when a relative on his mother's side had died and the men had slept near a photo of the dead man laid out as remembrance, Qassem had talked so much in his sleep that his uncle thought the dead man's ghost had entered the room and was speaking to him. He had stayed awake all night, terrified. No, no ghosts. Only Qassem, hidden asleep in a corner, talking through his dreams all night long.

As a boy, he had often awakened in the middle of the night, sobbing. Why was he crying? What was he afraid of? He didn't know. After years of these terrors, his grandfather visited the kochek, the wise old Yazidi man who wrote words on a piece of cloth. Qassem's grandfather gave him the cloth to tie to his shirt while sleeping, and after that he could sleep through the night again.

His grandfather held the family intact until the day Qassem discovered him face down in the garden, felled by a stroke. That time he had survived, returning from the hospital weakened but still able to tend the plants in his garden. Qassem would crouch beside him, handing him what needed handing, holding what could be held, knowing that all of this would not last long.

When his grandfather fell again, Qassem's father had taken him to the hospital. His father had returned home, announcing solemnly, "Our father is dead."

For three days, they had set up the funeral tent, and the story-tellers had gathered beneath the funeral tent to tell the stories of what their ancestors had lived, the battles they had waged, the land they had fled. Tragedy was turned into story and song even as it happened so that one might learn to bear it and not to forget.

On the third day that they were trapped on the mountain, ISIS began firing on the shrine of Mazar Amadin, where they had been taking refuge. It was only a matter of time before they would have to flee to higher ground, toward the northern face of the mountain. They would need water for that journey, for the August heat meant that only a short time without drinking could result in death. Qassem's family was now fleeing two enemies: ISIS and the heat. It was no longer possible to gather water at Qiniyeh, and so Qassem and his cousin volunteered to fetch water in Zalaliya, an hour-and-a-half's walk from Mazar Amadin.

With its crags and passes, the mountain of Sinjar could be navigated from different paths—from the high places or the valleys. Mazar Amadin stood at the apex between two roads with no immediate access to water but with paths leading out from it to two different water sources. Many of those who had fled nearby villages had passed first through one water source or another, seeking supplies to help them survive the August heat. Those from the village of Tel Binat near Tel Qasab, at the base of Sinjar, had effectively split in two, depending on from which side of the village they had fled. Some had gone to Qiniyeh, as Qassem's family had done when they had fled their village; among them were the families who had been killed and kidnapped. Others had gone west, and they had hidden near Zilaliya so that they could gather sandy water from beneath the earth.

Qassem, like other Yazidis from his area, knew of Zalaliya because the earth of that region was different than that of other places on the mountain. The men of the villages had also traveled there to collect the special white clay that they used to coat their houses after the rainy season. He knew they would find water in Zalaliya—not clear springs or even a well but water that could be found beneath the earth if you dug for a time. It was water normally suited only for animals, but under the circumstances, it would have to do.

He and his cousin carried empty jerrycans over their shoulders to fill and walked. Zalaliya covered vast terrain, and as they began to approach, they saw families in the distance already scraping for water. Qassem suggested to his cousin that they take the risk to go in just a bit further, toward the main road, where water might be in greater supply. They walked for a time and then began to dig, and as water rose to the surface, he thought that under normal circumstances, he would not even allow his livestock to drink from it. They filled their containers, managing to collect two liters for thirty-six people.

But as the water seeped in, people began running toward them from the main road: *They're killing the men! They're taking the women and children away!*

Qassem and his cousin closed their water containers and ran back toward Mazar Amadin. On the way, his brothers and uncle intercepted them with terrifying news: Mazar Amadin had been taken while they were gone. The entire area was now under attack.

They climbed to higher ground, finding the others in the family who were waiting for them. Where was his grandmother? he asked. They told him what had happened.

With her rheumatism, she knew she would have been unable to climb the mountain, and that if she tried, she would endanger the rest of the family. And so, when her sons had come to fetch her in the small room, she had stopped them and ordered them to leave her behind. "I've lived my life," she told them. "Now go and live yours."

Darkness was falling. They could only walk at night to avoid the risk of snipers and also because they needed to save their water, and they would need less water in the cold. But then came the fear that they might be separated in the dark. They formed a line: two of the men walked in the front, two in the middle, and two at the end—each one tasked with counting the members of the family in their charge. They stumbled forward: men, women, children, among the hundreds escaping across the mountain, in the direction of the shrine called Pir Arwa. "Gradually, your eyes adjust to the darkness," Qassem told me. At around midnight, they stopped. Everyone was thirsty. The two liters of sandy water were already gone.

Out of the darkness, two goat herders, robed in white, approached them. They lived on the mountain and knew the footpaths to the shrine, having led their goats across the grooves and crevices of the sacred mountain. Now they offered to take a few of the men ahead so that they could gather water and bring it back to the women and children. Qassem and his cousin offered to go.

They set off, their feet finding landing points on the dark mountain. They were drawn ahead, barely able to see. Qassem concentrated on landmarks, turns, and shapes, anything that would help them find the way back to their family again, knowing that if they didn't, none of them would make it through the next day alive. That was the rule of the mountain: the first time you walked any path, you had to internalize its details so that it became a part of you, so that you would not get lost coming back.

They arrived at the end of a valley, where the outline of the shrine of Pir Arwa was visible between two sides of the mountain. A white conical building with its sunlike rays, pointing skyward, this shrine was much larger than Amadin. The goat herders motioned ahead: *Follow the valley to the shrine*. Then the two men, unnamed and unknown, disappeared, searching for others they could help. Qassem moved ahead, arriving finally at the well and the shrine he had only heard of in stories but had never witnessed with his own eyes.

Men from other families had already climbed down into the well and were lifting out water to desperate families huddled around. Qassem called out that they were coming from the south of Sinjar, where it was known there was no water. They made room for the two and offered them water before the others.

Qassem peered down into the well, at the water rising toward him. He and his cousin filled two jerricans, and with each of them balancing one on his shoulders, they headed back to their families.

By now, the sun was rising. Qassem had feared they would lose their way, but now he saw they could simply walk against the line of hundreds of families fleeing toward Pir Arwa. Chaos had taken over the mountain. There was no cap on his jerrycan, and by now water had become more precious than gold, so he removed his shirt and pressed it in as a lid to contain it.

Out of the corner of his eye, he spotted a small boy, holding a plastic bottle full of water, who had been separated from his family. Qassem called him over. *Come*. The boy followed the two boys for a time, weeping, before wandering off. They passed a large family, the women and elderly collapsed on the side of the road. He quietly poured them water and hurried on.

They paused to let their shoulders rest but not for long. There was no time. They made their way back to their family, waiting exhausted and thirsty. The children drank first, and then the women and elderly, the men, and last of all, the young men like Qassem, who could ration their strength. A small amount of water was enough to pull them forward. They banded together again—two men in the back, two in the middle, and two in the front—and the group walked together at a clip. They knew they needed to arrive back at the shrine where Qassem and his cousin had just been before the lethal sun rose too high, when they could be killed by both snipers and the heat.

He handed off the jerrycan to his older brother. Then he searched among the group for his beloved cousin Khalil, only a year old and weak of health, whom he had worried about on the mountain even more than his sister. He found him and folded the small boy's body against him in an embrace. Then he lifted the boy onto his shoulders. Water in one direction, the boy in the other, each time Qassem walking with the weight of life on his shoulders, carrying on.

26 | THE PHOTO ALBUM

The shrine of Pir Arwa came into view once more, by now busy with desperate families. Overnight, the once-remote shrine had transformed into a village for thousands. Displaced Yazidis, desperate for water, were organizing among themselves. Some of the men had volunteered to defend the group and were stationed around the camp to ward off attackers. Others had offered to draw and cart water out of the well.

The camp had become so swollen with people that the spaces near the well had all been taken. Qassem's family trekked farther and set up camp in the valley nearby, pushing four sticks into the earth and spreading a sheet above them to produce a small square of shade. Near them, a woman, nine months pregnant, huddled with her family.

Qassem wandered among them. Pir Arwa resembled a tent of collective grieving, the first time as a community they could process what had come to pass. News moved from family to family of what was happening in the villages below. The women known for lamenting gathered in a circle in the center of the camp, and as news came in of the dying, they pounded their chests and called out laments, naming the dead and weeping while family members gathered around them and sobbed.

She has been killed; now she will never bear children.

He has been killed; now he will never see his sons again.

Qassem watched as a man around fifty years old, who had just arrived at the entrance of the camp, collapsed to the ground. He took handfuls of dirt in his hands and covered his head with the earth and then began shouting and wailing. He had just received news that members of his family had been killed the night before at Zilaliya.

Zilaliya. Qassem remembered the families fleeing toward him from the main road as he had gathered dirty water from the earth. Once again, he had only just escaped. He could just as easily have been killed. Death and life, life and death.

The holy man in charge of the shrine delegated tasks for the community. Qassem's brother and cousin disappeared into the neighboring farms, isolated and scattered in the mountains, for several hours and then returned, carting dried bread and animal food they salvaged. They soaked dried bread in water and moistened it so people could swallow it. For the first time on the mountain, they drank fresh water and ate real food. Qassem looked up to see his brother's friend Osso standing among them, having survived his wanderings, and they all thanked God that he was still alive.

All the usual logic of their lives had collapsed. This was war, and the older men formed a council to prepare for the days ahead. Some of the men would have to search for food, which meant disappearing into the areas of the mountain that Daesh might still control. The decision of which of the men or boys would be able to sustain this—responsibilities that in the past would have been laid upon the older young men—were no longer so straightforward. One of Qassem's cousins was healthy of body, but he had just learned that much of the family on his mother's side—the side unrelated to Qassem—had been killed. This young man was now in shock, incapable of discerning his way through the mountain. A second older cousin was overweight, slow, and an easy target for snipers. A third cousin was his mother's only son: they wouldn't risk him getting killed and leaving his mother childless. One of his older brothers had recently been through surgery, and so he was deemed too weak to wander the mountain as well. Other cousins had broken down in fear, and in this context, fear became deadly, for a man afraid could easily lose his way in the mountains.

In the end, of a vast extended family, only a few could be asked to risk their lives to search for food. Qassem was one of them. He readied himself in his heart.

"Or you would live," he told me quietly. "Or you would die. There were things that were yours to do, and so you did them."

That first night at Pir Arwa, Qassem tried to sleep. His stomach hurt from the filthy water he had been drinking. In time, he heard wailing. The baby in the neighboring camp had been born.

The second morning in Pir Arwa, he awakened well before sunrise. His father and his uncles called him and three of his cousins over to speak to them. We have food and water now, his uncle said. Now you need to go back down the mountain for your grandmother.

He thought of his grandmother, who had ordered them to leave her behind, now left in a room at the foot of the mountain, at Mazar Amadin. She was surely dead by now. But what if she was still alive? It was as his grandfather had always told them: you don't abandon family.

They set out soon after that conversation. Qassem did not say much to me about the trip back down the mountain except that it took a long time. The facts of it are known from the telling up until now. They were approaching the very places from which they had fled, which ISIS had taken over. He recounted this part of his story with no pride or enthusiasm. "To be honest, I was terrified," he admitted. "Of course I was scared."

Qassem and his three cousins carried water and food. They knew that the chances of death were likely, and it seemed foolish for all of them to die at the same time when the family would be depending on them to help keep the rest of the women and children alive. As they finally approached their family shrine of Mazar Amadin, they separated into two groups. Two of his cousins would press ahead into the mountain and listen from the safety of a crevice. If they heard shooting, they would know that ISIS was trying to kill them and would run back and warn the others. If they were killed, the sound of bullets would provide ample warning for Qassem and his other cousin to flee.

When they approached Mazar Amadin, Qassem saw the cases of spent shells littering the earth. That's it, he thought; either they kidnapped the elderly and everyone else here, or all of them are already dead.

His two cousins went ahead. Later, they would tell him that his grandmother heard their voices, and she cried out, "I'm here."

In time, when his cousins didn't return, Qassem ignored his own advice and advanced with his other cousin to the room near the shrine. They were there together, his cousins and his grandmother. She was alive. She couldn't walk, and he knew they couldn't carry her, but they gave her the water and food they had brought. She told them that a man in the mountain had been sneaking down to give the elderly food and water. She urged them to go and not to come back again.

Qassem said goodbye. He gave me no more details than that. As they walked away, he turned back again to glance at the shrine he had known since he was a boy.

That was the last time Qassem would see Mazar Amadin.

They had given his grandmother the last of their water, and they knew they would not survive the walk back to Pir Arwa. They had no choice but to return to Zilaliya, where the members of that family had been massacred, to see if they might still salvage some sandy water from the earth. Either they would be killed gathering water, or they would die from the heat. It was a risk either way.

They separated into two pairs, splitting the little food they had. Qassem and one cousin headed toward the crossroads, where the road from Amadin met Zalaliya. The others stayed behind.

So much heat. So much death. So much of the familiar, now changed. On the side of the road, Qassem heard a whimpering. A baby goat cried out at the sight of them. "Please don't cry," Qassem whispered. "We don't want them to find us." He found himself overcome with a rush of compassion. He remembered all the animals he had left at home. He longed to take the baby goat with them as he knew that no one would return to rescue him.

He and his cousin moved ahead, and in time they commenced digging. They gathered liters of dirty water from the ground. He returned and gave some dirty water to the baby goat. "He kept following us, crying. There was nothing we could do but lead him back to the water and then sneak away while he drank."

As they were heading back, some abandoned farm equipment on the side of the path came into view. They went to see if there was any food inside. They found tea but no sugar. He glimpsed a red pair of pants that might fit a little girl. A blouse. A photo album had been left behind, near the seat of the farm implement. They opened it, and inside were photographs of families, unknowing of what was to come. Standing in rows, dressed up in their best clothes, their makeup and hair arranged for a wedding. His cousin recognized them as people from a neighboring village.

Qassem turned back a few pages to the first photos of the wedding, gazing at the faces. Then his cousin snapped him back to reality. "Are you crazy?" he said. "If there's no food, let's go!"

I noticed two diapers. I realized that Khalil, only a year old, must have been soiling himself for days. I took the two diapers, pants, and carried them, along with tea. We headed back. On the way, we saw figures in the distance. *That's it; we're dead,* I thought. But it was my brother and my uncle, meeting us on the way to help us carrying our burdens.

We stopped three times. We were exhausted. The heat was so strong that you could boil an egg in the sun. At four or five in the afternoon, we arrived again at Pir Arwa. The women were still lamenting the dead. Our family ran to us to give us water from the well. "Did you see your grandmother?" they asked. "How is she?"

"She's alive," I answered. "That is enough."

It was the sixth day on the mountain. Already babies and the elderly were starting to die. Somewhere on Sinjar, the mother of Khonaf, the neighbor girl he had played beside as a child, was succumbing to the heat, weak because of recent surgery. Some of the neighbors who had decided to stay behind in Tel Qasab had been killed outright.

His father disappeared for a time and returned with what should have amounted to a feast: a goat from one of the many flocks wandering across the mountain. But they lacked sufficient fire to cook it. Qassem found the meat impossible to swallow. The women added water to dried cheese and bread his brother had salvaged from farmsteads. Someone found the smallest bit of sugar, and they steeped a single cup of tea and passed it around from person to person. Each one took a sip to remember the taste of tea.

When they needed more water, Qassem took his place in the relay at the top of the communal well, along with his sister and cousin, lifting out the bucket of water filled by those who had climbed inside and distributing it to crowds gathered round, holding out their containers for water.

An elderly woman beside him pointed to a pigeon hovering above them. With its snow-white feathers, it seemed almost to resemble the Yazidis in their traditional robes. "Do you see that pigeon?" the woman exclaimed. "He's good luck. It means that we'll go back to our homes again."

But nothing made sense anymore, to him or to anyone else, and the words had barely left her mouth when Daesh began shooting at the shrine from a distance.

> I wanted to flee, but people kept coming for water. A woman. Then another woman. A second man saw me struggling and came to help me. We poured and lifted water from the well even as everyone around us ran. When we were done, I lifted the men out of the well so that we could flee. We were all about to run when a boy, crying, came to us, holding two small bottles.
>
> "Can you give me water?" he asked. We descended into the well.

We cannot know the full scope of history when we are living it. We have access only to the known. The Yazidis had thought they were escaping onto Mount Sinjar. But it is quite possible that Daesh had funneled and then trapped them there, in a four-pronged attack that left them with no other options. Later reports would describe those events on the mountain as genocide: a cold, calculated, careful, bureaucratic plan to wipe out a religious or ethnic group in its entirety.

As I listened to Qassem's story, I often found it to be repetitive. It seemed that frequently, when he arrived at a source of water, he was shot at. I could not grasp why he seemed to tell the same story in a different shape, over and over again—a new water source, a new attack. But he was telling the truth.

ISIS's Research and Fatwa Department had determined that the Yazidis were a "pagan" minority. The plan had been mercilessly simple: corral tens of thousands of Yazidis onto a mountain in the desert. Then cut off the exits and block all access to water. It was 110 degrees. As far as ISIS understood it, those Yazidis had set out on a death march, and it was a matter of days before everyone on that mountain, tens of thousands of people, would give out under the sun. The plan was not simply to take over Sinjar. The plan was to, as much as possible, wipe out the Yazidis.

But ISIS underestimated just how well the Yazidi people knew their sacred mountains, its water sources, its contours, its sacred wells. They didn't know how well their songs and stories had prepared them for the eventuality that they might need to take refuge there one day. Later, many of those who survived would say that the sacred mountain saved them.

The next morning, ISIS had retreated, but the well at Pir Arwa had nearly dried up. Qassem and his family had just enough water to survive one more journey. Many of the families were heading to Sharfadin, an eight-hundred-year-old shrine and the holiest place on Mount Sinjar, an entire day's walk. It was one of the places where Yazidis, should they die, might hope to be buried. Qassem's family decided that they would go as well, if for no other reason than to keep moving.

Qassem wondered if they were walking to their graves. "You reach a point where you think, 'There's nothing in life that can be harder than that,'" he said to me. "But no. There's something harder than that."

They set out walking against the line of the mountain at 4:00 a.m. Up ahead, he saw a dead man lying on the side of the path. The man's wife and daughter wailed beside him, trying to scrape the dried earth enough so as to bury him.

"My father took out the knives from the sides of our rifles, and he and my uncle began, together, to dig a shallow grave," Qassem said. "The woman would not stop crying. They put in the body and covered it with earth. 'Come with us,' we insisted. But she refused."

Night had fallen by the time they arrived. How strange, to arrive at the holiest shrine on the mountain—a shrine he had never visited—for the first time in his life like this. They had nowhere to sleep, and so he found a place on the hard, cold stones. He closed his eyes and drifted off.

His father went to search for food and returned with water and a goat. They set about cooking the goat on a fire they made. He had not eaten a solid meal in days, and the smell of food made him nauseous.

They were still preparing food when six cars became visible in the distance. ISIS had arrived, and he had known they would.

The rest of the details remain hazy in his memory: The shaking earth. A car that blew itself up.

The men with weapons headed out to fight, but Qassem remained with his family. They were still in hiding when, inconceivably, something began raining from the sky. Some of the cars exploded, and the earth trembled with a fierceness and fury he would never forget. Then Daesh was gone.

27 | A DRINK OF WATER

Qassem did not think to ask who had dropped those bombs that rained from the sky or how the cars had exploded. God had wanted it to happen, and so it did. If God wrote something, that is what became: even if it meant bombs suddenly raining from a previously empty sky. If God wanted something, no one could escape from it. That is what his grandfather had always said.

They slept on the cold stones, alive for now. They had been on the mountain for eight days. In the morning, word began passing through the families that a path had opened across the border and into Syria. None of them thought it was true. Qassem didn't believe anything anymore.

But the men convened once again and decided they had no choice but to try walking toward the border with Syria. It was only a matter of time before Daesh returned or supplies ran out. Either they would die walking, or they would die waiting.

All the families set out together, hundreds of people walking from the shrine of Sharfadin to the border. They stopped at another mazar, where they gathered water. The family voted. Half wanted to go ahead, and half wanted to stay behind. Qassem and his father and uncle and a few others decided to stay behind. His stomach ached from the filthy water that he had been drinking, and he was exhausted from carrying supplies and water.

He rested at the shrine. He wondered if he might live. An elderly couple maintained the shrine, each one wearing traditional clothes. The woman was gentle, kind. The man was mute. They seemed to be from another time. She cooked bulgur for Qassem, and he ate it, the warmth settling into him. As his body rested, it became aware of all its sicknesses.

At night, he and other family members who had stayed back slept among the graves of those buried around the shrine. The dead and the living were once again bound up in one another.

In the morning, they set out again. On the path, two men, dressed in military fatigues, approached them. *They have finally come to kill us*, Qassem thought, but he was too tired to resist. But the men were from Kurdish forces from across the Syrian border, and they were here to help. "The way to Syria is open," the men said. "Don't be afraid."

So they continued walking. On the way, a woman was holding a dead baby in one arm. In the other, she held her living son, who appeared to be two years old. She didn't seem to know what to do. Her eyes met his, blankly. "My son is dead," she told him. She seemed torn between the dead child and the child she needed to keep alive.

"My father and my uncle tried to make a small grave," he told me, "but the earth was too hard to penetrate."

This is some of what Qassem learned on the mountain. A car or a drink of water or the precise hour that you leave your home or your distance from a main road: all these details, never even contemplated, can mean the difference between life and death.

Later, he would learn that Khonaf's mother had died on the mountain. He would learn that his aunt Nada—the one he had accompanied every year to the shrine to pray that she would have a son, the one for whom he had asked *May God give her goodness*—had been kidnapped and sold as a slave. So had her daughter. Her husband was missing too. "She was like sugar," he told me. "Beautiful. And she was strong."

He would learn that Mazar Amadin, resting place of his ancestors and his last safe place, had been filled with explosives and blown up by ISIS. He would learn that it does not matter how many times you are told that a terrible thing is going to happen, through story or song. It does not prepare you for when it will happen, and the word *terrible* does not begin to describe it.

He would learn of the friends of his parents, in the villages neighboring Tel Binat, who were killed and of the neighbors of his cousins, on his mother's side, who were kidnapped. He would learn that people from the villages like his, closer to the mountain, had a fighting chance of making it but that those who lived closer to Mosul had not fared as well.

He would hear of what happened in Kocho, the Yazidi village of some 1,500 people closer inland than his village, where almost none of the men had escaped alive, where the elderly had been executed, the women kidnapped, and the children taken as slaves. One of those young women, Nadia Murad, would escape and tell the story around the world, advocating for the release of other women and winning the Nobel Peace Prize four years after she escaped.

He would memorize the names of slave markets, wondering if his beloved aunt had passed through them. He would find himself remembering his pigeons, again and again. Had they survived? Where did they go? Had someone taken care of them?

On the ninth day, Qassem and his family crossed the border into Syria, thirsty and tired. From there, they were transported across the border into northern Iraq, treated for their illnesses, and released. Once they were back in Iraqi Kurdistan, they slept in the street and then in a school. For the first four nights, he couldn't sleep, convinced that ISIS would find them. His stomach ached for weeks. Hundreds of thousands of displaced people had escaped north from the Nineveh Plains and cities like Qaraqosh and Mount Sinjar in a single week. "If anyone had a tree to rest under," Qassem said dryly, "that man was a king."

In time, camps for the internally displaced were built for the Yazidis, but his family moved into a concrete, unfinished building nearby, struggling to survive on limited rations. They didn't feel safe anywhere. Eventually, the family of thirty-six people fragmented as they escaped into Europe, one after another. They were one soul torn into many pieces.

His grandmother, who had survived Mount Sinjar, died the following year in exile.

Their father found a way to return to Tel Qasab in Sinjar for a single day, only to find their houses had been completely ransacked. Even the doors were gone.

When his father returned, he told the children, "I wish that I'd never returned to see what happened to our home." He had brought back one stone from the ground near their home, to remember.

28 | A STORY BENEATH A TREE

Over three nights, Qassem told me his story while we sat beneath the tree outside the convent in Germany. Nearly four years had passed since his family had escaped to Mount Sinjar. He was in his early twenties, but he seemed to me an old man held in the body of a young man or even a boy.

I had never met anyone who could focus for such a long time, who had such patience to pronounce a story in all its complexity. Raised in an oral culture, Qassem possessed a prodigious memory. To tell a story is not just to say it out loud; it is the only way to keep the past alive. He spoke every detail of his journey, often more than once: the pigeons, the white shrine, Khonaf. On the first night, he recounted to me the nine days on the mountain, moment by moment, three long hours of speaking without taking rest. The second night, he spoke of the three years in which he was stranded in Iraqi Kurdistan after the genocide, living in that unfinished building with his family. I listened.

In Iraqi Kurdistan, he had registered for school, but there was not enough room for all the students in the classrooms, and so he studied alone. On the mountain, he had discovered within himself a strength he did not know that he had. He wanted to offer that strength to others somehow.

Whenever kidnapped Yazidi women escaped from their ISIS captors, Qassem and his father would run to meet them at the border to Iraqi Kurdistan, begging for news of his missing aunt, uncle, and cousin. Had they seen them? Did they know where they might be?

Eventually, all three escaped after two long years. Qassem longed for the past, when he and his aunt had climbed to the shrine to pray together. "Even today, on the days I don't forget, I pray for all those I love," he told me. "That God will give them goodness, and then I pray for her specifically, that God will give her goodness."

As they languished in that unfinished building, thousands of Yazidis were spread in camps across the north of Iraq, freezing in winter and burning in summer, unable to return home again.

Many Yazidis began pooling money from family members to pay for smugglers to lead them to Europe. Children drowned on the sea passage, their names passing through the camps of northern Iraq as warnings to take the land route instead. Still, they crossed, by land and by sea. Once they arrived in Europe, they scattered.

As sentiments hardened against refugees in Europe, they were settled according to the Dublin laws of the European Union: in the first country where they had their fingerprints taken. Then as the world recognized the events of 2014 as a genocide, governments announced offers to help symbolic numbers of Yazidis. Handfuls were resettled in Canada, others in Australia and in France. The vast majority headed for Germany, where Yazidis had been settling for generations in the largest diaspora population of Yazidis in Europe and where therefore there remained a prospect of keeping the religion alive.

Yazidi tradition requires two Yazidi parents from the same caste to pass on the tradition to their children. Their life had been made possible by families who had lived together for centuries in small, isolated towns, with access to the pilgrimage shrines of their ancestors and proximity to their elders. Yazidism does not allow conversion. There are no holy books that would allow them to transmit the faith to those who don't regularly meet the storytellers.

The destruction of the religion and culture of the Yazidis began in Sinjar. But as they fled and families fragmented, it continued. The Yazidis might survive as individuals, but if something didn't change, they might not survive as a people.

A year after the genocide, when Germany opened its borders in the wake of the refugee crisis, two of Qassem's brothers and seven cousins escaped there. One of them, his brother Hassan, was only ten at the time. When they safely arrived, they applied for family reunification, hoping his parents and his siblings could join them by plane. But the courts ruled that only his parents could join them. As Qassem and his siblings were no longer minors, the courts considered them old enough to be self-sufficient. His father and mother and one younger sister boarded a plane to Germany a few months later, leaving Qassem and one of his other sisters, Lozin, with what they felt was no choice but to attempt the land route to Europe in order to reunite with them. Two of his brothers and one sister would stay behind in Iraq and hope to join them later. The family would be separated.

For Qassem, the journey to Europe brought back terrible memories of those nine days on Mount Sinjar. They traveled at night to evade detection. They attempted to cross impassable boundaries. Most of all, they simply tried not to get separated. The first time Qassem and his sister attempted the journey, they crossed with smugglers from Turkey to Bulgaria, but after two days in a cave, they were arrested. Qassem had his money and cell phone stolen. Then they were sent back to Turkey and returned, defeated, to Iraq. He told himself that he would never go through that experience again. But as the weeks passed, the reality—the bleakness of their surroundings and his separation from his parents—became more apparent.

Three months later, he set out again with his sister and members of his extended family. This time, the journey lasted twenty-nine days.

At one point, he phoned his parents in Germany to tell them that they were making progress. Soon after, however, they were arrested and had to turn back. His mother, who did not know, kept waiting for them. She cooked his favorite food, tashrib, every night to welcome him, and then when they did not show up, the next day she cooked it again.

When they finally arrived, weeks later, their application to remain in Germany was denied. Dublin laws meant they might be deported back to Romania, the first country where they had been fingerprinted—a fate that for Qassem seemed even worse than the camps in Iraq, where at least he had some of his siblings.

But they heard a story that carried some hope: a refugee who had been ordered to return to Bulgaria had instead found asylum in a church. And then they heard about a convent on the far end of the country of Germany from where they were, where nuns had created relationships with Yazidis settled nearby.

The phone at the convent rang one day in December 2017 with a request: A boy named Qassem, his sister Lozin, and their cousin Abid—all survivors of the genocide on Mount Sinjar—had arrived in Germany after traveling for weeks. Now they were in danger of being deported. Could they find refuge at the convent?

The community had a meeting to discuss the matter. Though they were accustomed to being in contact with the many refugees resettled nearby, giving asylum to them within the convent would be another matter entirely. The older nuns had grown up with the stories about Jews in World War II who had been turned away by ordinary Germans and then sent to their deaths. They were firm: those who had experienced a genocide must never, ever be turned away again. The nuns took a vote. All of them agreed to take them in.

Qassem, his sister, and his cousin boarded a train toward northern Germany. They arrived at seven at night, and the nuns were waiting at the train station to take them to their convent.

"We felt like family," Qassem tells me. "They treated us like their sons and daughters. If you were sick, they would take care of you. We could finally relax. And now we celebrate their feasts with them, and they celebrate ours with us."

And there—at that remote convent in the middle of the forest—is where I met him. Yes, that is where I met Qassem and where we sat together beneath the meeting tree, looking out onto a field where horses were standing in the dark, beneath the same sky of stars he had counted from the rooftop lying beside family so long ago and far away in Tel Qasab. That is where I heard the stories of the land that he had carried with him and saved on a mountain. That is where he taught me that story is a way of keeping community together, of remembering, of carrying the past into the present. Story is what keeps us whole. Qassem taught me all of that, beneath the tree, and I would not forget.

When Qassem's brothers had arrived in Germany in 2015, 97 percent of Yazidi asylum applications were approved by the government. By the time I met Qassem in 2018, that number had dropped to 60 percent. When Qassem and Lozin left the convent, they took their battle to court in Germany—and lost. They kept fighting in the courts and were allowed to stay with their parents and half of their siblings, at least temporarily. They entered school. They began to learn German. They tried to start over again.

Every now and then, Qassem sent me audio messages by phone, containing the small fragments of beauty he collected on his commute to school.

I saw a butterfly fly onto the train today.

I saw a house on the side of the road with animals like we used to raise in Iraq.

Today, I had an exam. I knew that the nuns have an important meeting. Before I began, I offered the exam to them in my heart.

The girls are learning to ride bicycles.

Today it's raining a bit, and everything is beautiful.

It was only months after I met him that Qassem told me a kernel at the center of his story: that he never should have been on Mount Sinjar that day when his family had to flee. He had considered trying to migrate to Europe in 2013, when ISIS was already growing in Syria and the political situation was deteriorating, so that he could earn money to send back to his family. That was a full year before the genocide. Yet in the end, they had not made the arrangements, and so he had not gone after all.

It would have been natural to think that he was unlucky—to expect that, looking back, he would regret he hadn't somehow left Iraq before the genocide. But Qassem understood his history differently. "I'm so glad I was on the mountain," he told me. "If my family was going to die, it would have been better for me to die with them."

I was quiet. "But they didn't die," I answered finally. "You helped to save their lives. You found water, and you searched for food, and that helped to keep them alive."

Qassem and I never spoke about what he saved. I listened, and he spoke to me about what he lost instead. But even in listening to his stories, I understood that he had saved so much among the devastation: His stories. His history. The memory of places now destroyed. But above all, he and his brothers and cousins and other family members had saved their family members on the mountain in those days. He was among the thousands of other Yazidis who selflessly tried to keep their families and communities alive in impossible circumstances.

He seemed to let my words sink in. "No, that's not really true," he answered in a low voice. "You must not think that I saved my family. I didn't save them. It was the women and children who kept us alive. If it wasn't for them, I would have let myself die on that mountain. But I stayed alive because they needed us to save them."

The birds still settle in trees, and the dead lie buried in Mazar Amadin, and the world moves forward. And there are the savers—those who give their lives once and twice and three times over. They are hidden in classrooms and walking on rainy streets, and they are carrying people, and we don't even know it. They are carrying their family members and strangers alike, off of mountains and across borders. They are carrying them through stories and small prayers breathed in the morning—carrying them so that they might also be carried, saving so as to be saved.

AFTERWORD

What you remember saves you.

—W. S. Merwin

As I finish this, six years have passed since Hana unfurled her dress for me in Jordan for the first time, showing me an entire world that she saved. Today, she lives in Australia with her husband, her children, and her grandchildren. She still sews shals for her daughters. Her mother and sister remain in Qaraqosh.

In a turn I could not have envisioned when I began writing this book, tens of thousands of Iraqi Christians have returned to their homes in Qaraqosh to try to start over, despite the precarious political situation. The churches and many homes have been restored. In Australia, new Syriac churches are also being built, and parents continue to speak Aramaic to their children. The story of Qaraqosh isn't finished just yet.

Ferhad lives with Mar and their son in England and continues his work preserving Kurdish music and heritage. Last year, Hozan also arrived in Europe just in time for them to record their first album together. As for Ferhad, it's time to buy books and notebooks, to sharpen pencils. This semester, ten years after he escaped from Homs, he is going back to music school to finish his studies.

After I met him, Munir attempted to move on from Lesvos to mainland Europe. He was sent back. And so he has stayed in Greece. Today, he remains, still seeking more permanent asylum, working. No longer forced to live in a camp, he also volunteers to

261

cook meals for refugees once a week, seeing in them his own past struggles to survive. "I try to help people," he tells me.

Ghadir, Adnan, and their children continue to live in the Netherlands. This year, they became Dutch citizens—finally, no longer refugees. The last time I saw them, we sat over a meal of Syrian breakfast, and I spread rose petal jam over flatbread. Their boys told me that they both want to become doctors when they grow up—to take care of people, just like their parents do. Adnan continues to work in his field. Ghadir received special training to help refugees who arrive in Amsterdam experiencing trauma. And when COVID-19 hit, she administered vaccines. They both agree, "We brought the pharmacy with us."

The war in Syria has entered its eleventh year, and over half of the country remains displaced: some 13.5 million people. Syrians are now dispersed in 128 countries around the world.

Qassem continues to live with part of his family in Germany, where he is learning German and working. He misses Mount Sinjar and dreams of the day when Yazidis will be able to live there in safety.

"Half of my family is still in Iraq," he recently told me. "My brothers were married there, and I was unable to attend the weddings. Can you imagine? My sister in Iraq hasn't seen her parents in years. And even this week, they discovered new mass graves in Sinjar, where hundreds of Yazidis are buried. Hundreds. And there are still mass graves that they haven't found."

We sat in silence, both of us, in different countries, connected only by our voices.

"I hope that people will hear our stories," he finally said. "I hope that people will begin to understand what happened to us."

At the time of writing, one in every seventy-eight people globally has been forced to flee from their homes.

ACKNOWLEDGMENTS

This story took six long years to bring to fruition and would not have been possible without the help of many people. Above all, I would like to thank all of those who trusted me to tell their stories in this book: Hana and Amer, Ferhad and Hozan and Mar, Munir, Adnan and Ghadir, Qassem, and so many others I met on my journeys. You opened your hearts and your homes to me, both during our initial meeting and for the years that followed—in many cases going over parts of the book line by line to help me be sure that I faithfully described your pigeons and stars and pharmacies, that I wrote the exact names of your grandfathers. I know you did so out of a hope that the world would understand, through your lives, the beautiful stories and cultures that you carried with you and the human stories of those displaced from their homes. It was the privilege of a lifetime, and I am forever changed by knowing you.

I would like to thank my family, who supported the idea of this book even though it meant I was often traveling and away from home. Thank you, Frederic, Sebastian, Carmel, and Joseph. I love you. I hope you know that I carry you with me wherever I go.

Thanks to my agent, Michael Palgon, who believed in the importance of this book and who never stopped supporting me even when I feared it would never find its way into the world. I'm also so grateful to my editor, Valerie Weaver-Zercher, whose sensitive eye made this a much better book, and to the team at Broadleaf Books, who were so dedicated to sharing these stories.

Thank you to my extended family and friends who have always been my support and sanity—you know who you are. Thanks in particular to Molly Mayfield Barbee and Eric Barbee for giving me a home away from home in Amman, and Susan Collin Marks for taking me in during my trips to Amsterdam, to Sr. Makrina, and to Laween and the community of Deir Mar Musa for welcoming me in Iraq. Thank you to Christian and Melinda Krokus, Brother Emile, Karen and Judy, Matti and Benjy, my siblings, and Fr. David Neuhaus, all of whom lent listening ears when I became discouraged and was tempted to abandon the work. Thank you to Sami, Matti, Sonia and Wassim, Nassir and Rania, and many others from Qaraqosh. As always, thank you to Bishop Ephrem and the Syriac Catholic Church in the Holy Land for being my spiritual home.

The memory of my father, Steven Saldaña, who worked tirelessly to welcome refugees and migrants as president of Catholic Charities in San Antonio, was never far from me during the years of writing. I am also grateful to my siblings, as well as to my mother, Roberta Cantu Saldaña, who taught me how much history can be passed down through a recipe and who kept my family's stories alive until I was ready to finally ask about them.

I am indebted to Widad Kawar—both for her vast scholarship on embroidery and for allowing me a glimpse into her magnificent collection of Palestinian dresses at the Tiraz museum in Amman. Without her books and decades of work on Palestinian dresses, it is unlikely I would understand how much historical knowledge is contained in a dress. It goes without saying that I am in debt to countless writers, musicians, journalists, mothers, and storytellers in the Middle East—those individuals who continue to be on the front lines of heritage preservation and who have so inspired me over the past decades.

A book like this one, which requires so much time and travel, would have been impossible without outside support. I'd like to recognize the Abraham Path Initiative and the Schmidt Family

Foundation for grants that allowed me to travel and to put aside time for writing. Particular thanks to Claire Kouatli for invaluable help in research, to William Ury for responding so positively to my initial idea, to Fr. Raymond Webb for his encouragement, and to John and Norma Davidson for their support.

The friends and kind people who shared with me all over the world are too long to list here, and there are some people I cannot name. But I recognize that this book has its origins in the day I walked into Damascus for the first time more than two decades ago. I would like to thank all of those Syrians who invited me into their homes and their lives so many years ago. You made me fall in love with your country, and it was your kindness, creativity, and love of beauty that laid the groundwork for this book. You are printed into my heart.

NOTES

PROLOGUE

More than half of Syria's population had been displaced: I began
my journey in October 2016. See Philip Connor and Jens Manuel Krogstad, "About Six in Ten Syrians Are Now Displaced from Their Homes,"
Pew Research Center, June 13, 2016.

A young musician from Homs, Syria: The story of Rami Basisah,
a Syrian refugee who carried his violin protected with cling film and
crossed eight countries in 2015, touched me deeply, and I found myself
returning to the image repeatedly. In 2017, as I was working on this
book, he released the album *My Journey* with The City of Prague Philharmonic Orchestra. See "Syria War: Refugee Who Fled Homs with
Violin Releases Album," BBC, May 5, 2017.

***Of Syrian mothers teaching their children recipes for eggplant
jam:*** Recipes are one of the most important instances of intangible
cultural heritage because they can be carried across borders. For stories
of recipes saved by Syrian refugees, see, among other books, Dina Mou-
sawi and Itab Azzam, *Our Syria: Recipes from Home* (New York: Running
Press, 2017).

Of an orchestra created from Syrian classical musicians in exile:
The Syrian Expat Philharmonic was founded in Germany in 2015 by
the Syrian musician Raed Jazbeh as a place for Syrian musicians who
had escaped to Europe to continue to perform. The orchestra remains
active at the time of writing. See https://www.sepo-philharmonic.com.

PART I: HANA'S DRESS

The town was like this—joyful and full of brides: From a poem
composed in the neo-Aramaic dialect of Qaraqosh by Talal Acam. See

Geoffrey Khan, *The Neo-Aramaic Dialect of Qaraqosh* (Leiden and Boston: Brill, 2002), 684.

CHAPTER 1: A TOWN NAMED BLACKBIRD

On August 6, 2014, ISIS had invaded the town of Qaraqosh: For a sense of how the media described the events of August 6, 2014, as they happened, see "Iraq Christians Flee as Islamic State Takes Qaraqosh," BBC, August 7, 2014.

In his poem "A Song on the End of the World": See Czeslaw Milosz, *New and Collected Poems, 1931–2001* (New York: Ecco Press, 2001), 56.

CHAPTER 2: HYMNALS

Nearly everyone was speaking a dialect of neo-Aramaic: The language of Qaraqosh is referred to in many different ways: as spoken Assyrian, as Sureth, as Syriac, or as Syriani. To simplify things, I have largely used the term *neo-Aramaic*.

I remembered that joint suicide bombers: Anthony Shadid, "Baghdad Church Attack Hits Iraq's Core," *New York Times*, November 1, 2010.

CHAPTER 3: THE MAP OF A WORLD

That 80 percent of the refugees in Jordan lived not in refugee camps: This remains true at the time of writing. For the most up-to-date figures on Syrian refugees in Jordan, see UNHCR Jordan, March 30, 2022, https://www.unhcr.org/jordan.html.

It took me a moment to understand that they were watching scenes of Qaraqosh: See "Mosul Battle: Iraq's Army Besieges Christian Town of Qaraqosh," BBC, October 18, 2016.

But we call it by its ancient name: Baghdeda: The name Bagdeda first appears in the seventh century, though scholars disagree on its origins. See Khan, *Neo-Aramaic Dialect*, 1.

She paused at two sheaves of wheat: The Nineveh Plains annually produced 20 percent of Iraq's wheat crops before ISIS invaded. "Minorities, Cultural Practices, and Destruction by the Islamic State—Tal Keif and

Hamdaniya," USAID, June 20, 2020, https://pdf.usaid.gov/pdf_docs/
PA00WR8N.pdf.

CHAPTER 4: THE ARCHIVIST OF PARIS

Palmyra, a Greco-Roman city: See Liam Stack, "ISIS Blows Up Ancient
Temple at Syria's Palmyra Ruins," *New York Times*, August 23, 2015.

Their blasting of the statues in the Mosul museum: See Graham
Bowley and Robert Mackey, "Destruction of Antiquities by ISIS Mili-
tants Is Denounced," *New York Times*, February 27, 2015.

Or the damage to the walls of Krak des Chevaliers: "Syria Crusader
Castle Krak des Chevaliers Has War Scars," BBC, March 22, 2014.

Aleppo soap was so famous: For more on how the soap was threatened during the war, see Golda Arthur, "Aleppo Soap: War Threatens
an Ancient Tradition," BBC, May 15, 2013.

The French constitution states that: See Sarah G. Thomason, *Endangered Languages: An Introduction* (Cambridge: Cambridge University Press,
2015), 24.

The linguist Ken Hale famously said: Quoted in his obituary, November 1, 2001, as referenced in Thomason, *Endangered Languages*, 73.

CHAPTER 5: A SEWING MACHINE

From our childhood, all of us spoke Syriani, a dialect of Aramaic:
For my understanding of the uniqueness and distinctiveness of Hana's
language in Qaraqosh and how it differs from even that of nearby villages, I am deeply indebted to the work of Geoffrey Khan as mentioned
above—both his book on Qaraqosh and his lectures about the regional
dialects. The examples of words in the Qaraqosh dialect, such as *narma*
and *ktawa*, are known to me from his work on Qaraqosh.

***His tomb had been an important site for Muslims, Christians,
and Jews:*** Eydar Peralta, "Video Shows Islamic State Blowing Up
Iraq's Tomb of Jonah," NPR, July 25, 2014.

Like many families in Qaraqosh, they had migrated from Tikrit:
The roots of the Christians of Qaraqosh in Tikrit is described from an
Iraqi Christian perspective in Suha Rassam, *Christianity in Iraq: Its Origins
and Development to the Present Day*, 3rd ed. (Leominster, UK: Gracewing

Publishing, 2016), 67, 75; and in Khan, *Neo-Aramaic Dialect*, 24. The history of Christianity in Tikrit is described in Amir Harrak, "Tagrit," in *Tagrit*, ed. Sebastian P. Brock et al., https://gedsh.bethmardutho.org/Tagrit.

According to tradition, Saints Behnam and Sara lived: There is no evidence that the saints actually lived in the fourth century as the first evidence we have for them in texts is from the twelfth century. Hana's description of the story differs significantly from older texts. For a description of the history of Mar Behnam and Sara, see *The History of Mar Behnam and Sara: Martyrdom and Monasticism in Medieval Iraq*, ed. and trans. Jeanne-Nicole Mellon Saint-Laurent and Kyle Smith (Piscataway, NJ: Gorgias Press, 2018).

At the beginning of May in 2010, hundreds of college-age students: Sam Daher, "Bomb Hits School Buses in North Iraq," *New York Times*, May 2, 2010.

Meanwhile, a group of extremists calling themselves ISIS: For an in-depth look at the development of ISIS, see Joby Warrick, *Black Flags: The Rise of ISIS* (New York: Anchor Books, 2016). For the developments of 2013 in Syria, see 286.

CHAPTER 6: A SONG AT THE END OF THE WORLD

There was Nasir: I first mentioned Nasir, including a video of him singing, in Stephanie Saldaña, "In Refugees' Bags, Memories of Home," *New York Times*, March 11, 2017.

In Amman, I also met Qaraqosh's artist Sami Lalu: I first wrote about Sami Lalu in Stephanie Saldaña, "The Artist of Memory," *Plough Quarterly*, November 29, 2019.

Even if a language does manage to survive: See Thomason, *Endangered Languages*, 83.

CHAPTER 7: RED BULGUR

Only a few days earlier, ISIS had swept in from Mosul: See Part V of this book for more information on the events of Mount Sinjar.

Just over a month before, believing that ISIS was attacking Baghdeda: On June 25, 2014, almost the entire town of Qaraqosh left, only to return a few days later. This may explain why so many people brought so little with them when they escaped again in August. See the timeline on Amnesty International's 2014 report: *Ethnic Cleansing on a Historic Scale: Islamic State's Systematic Targeting of Minorities in Northern Iraq.*

CHAPTER 8: THE ROAD TO QARAQOSH

I traveled to Lalish, where Yazidis believe that the world first became covered with vegetation: See Eszter Spät, *The Yezidis* (London: Saqi Books, 2005), 50.

I asked them for directions to the tomb of the prophet Nahum: I gathered details on the Jewish feast at Shavuot at the tomb from interviews with Mordechai Yona, who was born in Zakho and went on this pilgrimage as a boy before immigrating. He now lives in Jerusalem and works to preserve the memory of the Jewish presence in the city as well as its Aramaic. For more on the Jews of Zakho, including scenes describing their leaving, see also Ariel Sabar's book about the life of his father, who immigrated from Zakho and became a linguist in the United States: Ariel Sabar, *My Father's Paradise: A Son's Search for His Family's Past* (Chapel Hill, NC: Algonquin Books, 2009).

PART II: FERHAD'S SONG

Take hold of me, my friend, as one we shall: This epigraph comes from a newly discovered section of Tablet V of Gilgamesh, which was looted by thieves and then acquired by the Sulaymaniyah museum in the Kurdistan region of Iraq from a smuggler in 2011 to prevent it from leaving the country. The lines are spoken by Gilgamesh to Enkidu when he is afraid, confronting Humbaba. F. N. H. Al-Rawi and A. R. George, "Back to the Cedar Forest: The Beginnings and End of Tablet V of the Standard Babylonian Epic of Gilgameš," *Journal of Cuneiform Studies* 66 (2014): 66–90.

CHAPTER 9: LOOKING FOR A BUZUQ

A suspension bridge once straddled the Euphrates: "Syria's Suffering Revealed in Satellite Images," BBC, March 18, 2015.

I had traveled to the area with a friend to visit the archaeological remains of Dura Europos: See Yale University Art Gallery's online tour of the excavations: *Dura-Europos: Excavating Antiquity*, https://artgallery.yale.edu/online-feature/dura-europos-excavating-antiquity.

At a conference on endangered Syrian music organized by UNESCO, Gani Merzo: See Alexandra Di Stefano Pironti, "With Syria's Kurdish Music in Danger of Dying, UNESCO Steps In to Help," Rudaw, May 18, 2016.

People had taken to calling the neighborhood of Aksaray "Little Syria" because many of the 500,000 Syrian refugees: See "Integrating Syrian Refugees in Istanbul's 'District of Victimhood,'" International Crisis Group Report 248, January 29, 2018.

That was Salloura, a sweet shop: See Lauren Bohn, "Salloura, An Epic of Sweets," Culinary Backstreets, https://culinarybackstreets.com/cities-category/istanbul/2016/salloura-an-epic-of-sweets-chap-1-out-of-syria/.

CHAPTER 10: A FIELD OF ASHES

A famous Kurdish legend called Derwêshe 'Evdî: Interestingly, I was able to confirm this story through the Yazidi oral tradition, which retains many of the same details in their telling of the story. "I went to the waters of the Khabur / I washed the cloak from Basra, which belonged to Derwêsh Sheykh Evdî . . ." See Christine Allison, *The Yezidi Oral Tradition in Iraqi Kurdistan* (Richmond: Curzon Press, 2001).

Through the streets they carried the Bride of Rain—the Bûka Baranê: At the time of writing, Kurds in Syria are continuing the ritual in the face of record droughts. See "Syria Kurds Revive an Ancient Rain Ritual as Drought Bites," Agence France-Presse, November 19, 2021.

CHAPTER 11: MICROTONES

There was a generousness about the old markets: I was able to acquire this view of Homs's Old City due to the writing of the Syrian architect Marwa al-Sabouni, who convincingly argues that the roots of the conflict in Homs can be recognized in the architectural shifts in the city. See Marwa al-Sabouni, *The Battle for Home: The Vision of a Young Architect in Syria* (London: Thames & Hudson, 2017).

On April 19, 2011, the BBC reported that security forces had fired on protestors: "Scores Die in Protests around the Country," BBC, April 19, 2011.

By May, the news service was reporting that government tanks had entered the city: "Syria Tanks Shell Protest City of Homs," BBC, May 11, 2011.

CHAPTER 12: THE SPANISH PHRASE BOOK

The Mahmoud Darwish collection with his favorite poem: Mahmoud Darwish, *Mural*, trans. Rena Hemmami and John Berger (London: Verso Press, 2009).

ISIS targeted the Kurdish Feast of Nowruz in al-Hasakeh: See "Twin Bombings Kill Many in Northeastern Syria," Al-Jazeera, March 21, 2015.

So much had been contained in their music: For more on Kurdish music and dance, see Nezan Kendal, "Kurdish Music and Dance," *World of Music* 21, no. 1 (1979): 19–32.

CHAPTER 13: A DROP OF WATER

Lo Hevalo: Music and lyrics by Ferhad. Printed with permission from the author. All rights belong to him.

PART III: MUNIR'S LIGHT

See the beautiful patience of the candle: I was unable to find the original of this quote. It is known to me in Arabic from the calligraphy of the French-Iraqi calligraphy artist Hassan Massoudy.

CHAPTER 14: A HAIRCUT

From the plane, I could see only water: I first wrote about my time in Lesvos in Stephanie Saldaña, "Where Jesus Would Spend Christmas," *New York Times*, December 22, 2017.

The country was in the middle of a violent civil war: For reports of the conditions in Yemen during my time in Lesvos, see UNHCR,

"UNHCR Alarmed at Deteriorating Conditions in Yemen," November 14, 2017, https://www.unhcr.org/en-us/news/latest/2017/11/5a0afc624/unhcr-alarmed-deteriorating-conditions-yemen.html.

Now it was December, the last month of a year in which more than 171,635 migrants: Numbers given by the United Nations International Organization for Migration for 2017, https://www.iom.int/news/mediterranean-migrant-arrivals-reached-171635-2017-deaths-reach-3116.

The city of Deir Ezor in Syria had been under ISIS rule: See "UNFPA Aid Reaches Deir Ez-Zor City for the First Time in Three Years," United Nations Population Fund, September 15, 2017.

CHAPTER 15: A CANDLE

A few people from the Bedoon class in Kuwait: For insight into the continued repression of the Bidoon (or Bidūn) people, see "Kuwait: Mandate of Abusive Government Body in Charge of Stateless Bedun People Extended," Amnesty International, November 24, 2020.

The problems started after 2003, when the extremists started kidnapping people: See Dominic Nutt, "Child Kidnapping on the Rise in Iraq," *Guardian*, October 15, 2003.

In June 2014, ISIS took over Mosul: ISIS took over Mosul decisively on June 10, and Abu Bakr al-Baghdadi announced the Caliphate later that month.

Twelve hundred Iraqi soldiers died, and six thousand were wounded: See James Verini, *They Will Have to Die Now: Mosul and the Fall of the Caliphate* (New York: W. W. Norton, 2017), 268.

That year, the Associated Press would estimate: See Susannah George, Qassim Abdul-Zahra, Maggie Michael, and Lori Hinnant, "Mosul Is a Graveyard: Final IS Battle Kills 9,000 Civilians," Associated Press, December 21, 2017.

US and Iraqi forces used white phosphorus: Alison Meuse, "US-Led Forces Have Used White Phosphorous in Fight for Mosul, General Says," NPR, June 13, 2017.

It was not only that they might get caught in the crossfire: United Nations (press release), "Mosul: UN Receives Reports of Mass Killings of Fleeing Civilians by ISIS," June 8, 2017.

Do you promise me that you'll take us to Greece?: The refugees were worried that the Greek officials would push them back to Turkish waters.

This process, referred to as "pushback," has been documented repeatedly by human rights organizations and has resulted in the deaths of migrants and refugees.

CHAPTER 16: THE SMALL KINDNESS

The inhabitants of the Old City even spoke their own dialect: When the Old City of Mosul was devastated by fighting and the inhabitants were killed or escaped, the specific dialect of the Old City became one more aspect of the heritage that was endangered. See Sam Kimball, "Iraqis amid Silent Ruins Fear for Loss of Dialect," Associated Press, January 28, 2019.

During their three years in Mosul, ISIS would destroy: My writing on the destruction in the Old City of Mosul and the confirmation of Munir's story would not have been possible without the work of the Monuments of Mosul in Danger project website, which provided in-depth maps and aerial photographs of cultural sites, and later their book: Karel Nováček, Miroslav Melčák, Ondřej Beránek, Lenka Starková, *Mosul after the Islamic State: The Quest for Lost Architectural Heritage* (New York: Palgrave MacMillan, 2021).

But many instead found themselves in a kind of moral danger: See Anthony Feinstein and Hannah Storm, "The Emotional Toll on Journalists Covering the Refugee Crisis," Reuters Institute for the Study of Journalism, July 2017, 3. "Among the most common reactions that emerged during a series of conversations with journalists and news managers were feelings of guilt at not having done enough personally to help the refugees, and shame at the observed behavior of others."

The EU paid and trained Libyan coast guards to intercept those migrant boats: See *Italy-Libya Agreement: Five Years of EU-Sponsored Abuse in Libya and the Central Mediterranean*, Medicins Sans Frontieres, February 2, 2022. For an in-depth look at the European Union's destructive policies on the Central Mediterranean Route, see Sally Hayden, *My Fourth Time, We Drowned: Seeking Refuge on the World's Deadliest Migration Route* (London: Melville House, 2022).

The EU signed the "Joint Way Forward" pact: See "Afghanistan Is Not Safe: The Joint Way Forward Means Two Steps Back," September 17, 2017 (https://www.amnesty.eu/wp-content/uploads/2020/09/NGO-joint-Statement-on-Afghanistan-September-2020-converted.pdf).

At the time of writing, policies are shifting due to the increase in Afghan refugees following the US withdrawal from Afghanistan and the subsequent return of the Taliban to power. For an in-depth exploration of the refugee route from Afghanistan, see Matthieu Aikins, *The Naked Don't Fear the Water: An Underground Journey with Afghan Refugees* (New York: Harper Collins, 2022).

Against the principle of non-refoulement: Article 33 of the 1951 UN Convention Relating to the Status of Refugees states that "no Contracting State shall expel or return ('refouler') a refugee in any manner whatsoever to the frontiers of territories where his life or freedom would be threatened on account of his race, religion, nationality, membership of a particular social group, or political opinion."

The year I visited Lesvos, the number of refugees resettled in the United States decreased: Phillip Connor and Jens Manuel Krogstad, "For the First Time, U.S. Resettles Fewer Refugees than the Rest of the World," Pew Research Center, July 5, 2018.

Families regularly risked their lives crossing the southern border of the United States: As I finish this manuscript, fifty-three migrants have been recently found dead in a truck in my own hometown of San Antonio, Texas, after being left in the heat. See Andrés Martínez and Daniel Victor, "What We Know about the Migrant Deaths in San Antonio," *New York Times*, June 29, 2022.

Yet 78 percent of the refugees Australia accepted: See A. Odysseus Patrick, "Australia's Immoral Preference for Christian Refugees," *New York Times*, May 3, 2017.

The Iranian Kurdish poet Behrouz Boochani composed a book about the horrors: Boochani was imprisoned on Manus island as a refugee for six years. In an astonishing act, he composed his autobiography via text message while still imprisoned, which went on to win several literary awards. See Behrouz Boochani, *No Friends but the Mountains: Writing from Manus Prison*, trans. Omid Tofighian (Toronto, ON: House of Anansi Press, 2019).

PART IV: GHADIR AND ADNAN'S PHARMACY

The coffee of Aleppo is omnipresent: From my own interview with the artist in Paris, France, about his life in Aleppo.

CHAPTER 17: THE SHADOW WALL

By 1944, more than 100,000 Jews: The Dutch Holocaust Memorial of Names in Amsterdam lists 102,163 known Dutch victims of the Holocaust.

Or the muwashahat music: Arabic sung poetry developed in medieval Spain. Aleppo was the capital of Syria's traditional music scene. A group of Syrian refugee musicians from Aleppo developed a project to save *muwashahat* and other endangered music in Gaziantep, Turkey. See *Nawa: Ancient Sufi Invocations and Forgotten Songs from Aleppo*, Lost Origin Productions, 2014.

CHAPTER 20: THE GARAGE

2012. That was the year that a fire: See Anne Barnard and Hwaida Saad, "In Syria's Largest City, Fire Ravages Ancient Market," *New York Times*, September 29, 2012.

That was the year the stunning eleventh-century minaret of Aleppo's Great Mosque: "Syria Clashes Destroy Ancient Aleppo Minaret," BBC, April 24, 2013.

By June, the UN estimated that ninety-three thousand people: "Updated Study Shows That at Least 93,000 People Have Died in the Conflict," UN High Commissioner for Human Rights, June 13, 2013.

During that month, the UN would announce that at least 100,000 people: "UN: More than 100,000 Killed in Syria's Civil War," Associated Press, July 23, 2013.

2014. More than half of the healthcare facilities: "Aleppo City Profile: Multi Sector Assessment," UN Habitat, May 2014.

And hospitals were being bombed: "Death Everywhere: War Crimes and Human Rights Abuses in Aleppo, Syria," Amnesty International, May 5, 2015.

CHAPTER 22: HOLDING THE KEYS

That was the year Russia officially intervened: "Russia Joins the War in Syria: Five Key Points," BBC, October 1, 2015.

That was the year Alan Kurdi: Robert Mackey, "Brutal Images of Syrian Boy Drowned off the Coast of Turkey Must Be Seen, Activists Say," *New York Times*, September 2, 2015.

That was the year a truck full of the dead bodies: Seventy-one Iraqi, Syrian, and Afghani refugees and migrants were found dead in the back of a truck on the way to Austria. Alison Smale and Melissa Eddy, "Grisly Discovery in Migrant Crisis Shocks Europe," *New York Times*, August 27, 2015.

That was the year more than eight hundred migrants: The UN estimated that eight hundred people died in the accident. See Allesandra Bonomolo and Stephanie Kirchgaessner, "The UN Says 800 Migrants Dead as Italy Launches Rescues of Two More Vessels," *Guardian*, April 20, 2015.

That was the year nearly a million refugees: William Spindler, "2015. The Year of Europe's Refugee Crisis," UNHCR, December 8, 2015.

PART V: QASSEM'S FAMILY

CHAPTER 24: A HOUSE OF CLAY

There, they became Yazidis who spoke a language that Qassem and his family call "Yazidia": Most scholars refer to the language that the Yazidis of Mount Sinjar spoke as a dialect of Kurdish. Yet some Yazidis, like Qassem, don't agree with having their language or ethnicity defined by a dominant group, particularly as their tradition in the region is ancient, and so insist on using their own community as the point of departure. As the question of refugee status for Yazidis in Europe has become more urgent, these arguments have taken on even deeper symbolic importance. Some Yazidis felt that if they were defined on their papers as ethnically and linguistically Kurdish, then this would mean they believed that their homeland was Iraqi Kurdistan and that they could be returned to Iraq without the violation of the principle of non-refoulement, as that geographic area remained safe. For the Yazidis of Mount Sinjar, their homeland could only be the region of Mount Sinjar, with its own distinct history—and that homeland remained unsafe for return. I have chosen to respect Qassem's terms in describing his language and ethnicity here, while providing the necessary context for why he uses those terms and recognition that scholars generally refer to his language as a dialect of Kurdish.

Some had gone to Qiniyeh: The massacre at Qiniyeh has been well documented. It was also part of a larger strategy by ISIS to cut off all sources of water near the base of the mountain so that people would die of thirst on the mountain. See "Ethnic Cleansing on a Historic Scale: Islamic State's Systematic Targeting of Minorities in Northern Iraq," Amnesty International, 2014.

But why would they start murdering Yazidis?: When ISIS took over Mosul, they allowed Christians to either convert or flee. Many Yazidis expected that as minorities, they would receive similar treatment. However, ISIS had decided that the Yazidis were in fact pagans and not People of the Book, using this fact to justify the genocide and slavery that they would then pursue. For details on the theological justification by ISIS and the ongoing actions as genocide, see the Office for the United Nations High Commissioner for Human Rights, Human Rights Council 32nd session, *They Came to Destroy: ISIS Crimes against the Yezidis*, June 15, 2016.

CHAPTER 26: THE PHOTO ALBUM

That was the last time Qassem would see Mazar Amadin: I was able to confirm the destruction of Mazar Amadin due to the work of the Forensic Architecture program, in collaboration with the Yazda organization. Using drones, they were able to create aerial photographs of the destroyed Mazar Amadin and create a 3D model of what it looked like. These images greatly helped me in understanding this section of Qassem's story. See their investigation: *The Destruction of Yazidi Heritage*, September 20, 2018.

Then Daesh was gone: What Qassem was experiencing was in fact US airstrikes. For the story behind the US strikes on the shrine of Sharfaddin, see Jenna Krajeski, "The Daring Plan to Save a Religious Minority from ISIS," *New Yorker*, February 19, 2018.

CHAPTER 27: A DRINK OF WATER

He would hear of what happened in Kocho: Kocho was farther away from Mount Sinjar than other villages, and as a result, the residents did not make it to the mountain. Despite the US military having knowledge of the village's predicament, no one intervened. ISIS rounded up and killed men, boys, and older women and kidnapped the rest of the women and girls and sold them into slavery. For an insider's account of what happened in Kocho and its aftermath, see Nobel Prize winner Nadia Mourad's memoir, *The Last Girl: My Story of Captivity and My Fight against the Islamic State* (New York: Crown, 2017).

AFTERWORD

In a turn I could not have envisioned, tens of thousands of Iraqi Christians have returned: Jason Horowitz and Jane Arraf, "Amid the Rubble of Mosul, Francis Offers a Salve for Iraq's Wounds," *New York Times*, March 7, 2021.

The war in Syria has entered its eleventh year: "11 Years On, Mounting Challenges Push Many Syrians to the Brink," UNHCR, March 15, 2022.

And even this week, they discovered new mass graves in Sinjar: See "Exhumation Ceremony in Qani Village, Sinjar," Nadia's Initiative, June 12, 2022, https://www.nadiasinitiative.org/news/qani-village -exhumation-ceremony.

One in seventy-eight people: UN announcement as of May 23, 2022, https://www.unhcr.org/refugee-statistics/insights/explainers/100-mil lion-forcibly-displaced.html.